W9-AQN-420

Lanzarote
Pages 82–97

0 kilometres 50

0 miles 50

ISLA DE ALEGRANZA

ISLA DE MONTAÑA CLARA

LA GRACIOSA

LANZAROTE

Arrecife

Atlantic Ocean

ISLA DE LOS LOBOS

Puerto del Rosario

FUERTEVENTURA

Gáldar

Arucas

Las Palmas de Gran Canaria

GRAN CANARIA

Maspalomas

Gran Canaria
Pages 42–67

Fuerteventura
Pages 68–81

EYEWITNESS TRAVEL

CANARY ISLANDS

EYEWITNESS TRAVEL

CANARY ISLANDS

Main Contributors **Piotr Paszkiewicz, Hanna Faryna-Paszkiewicz, Gabriele Rupp**

Penguin Random House

Produced by Hachette Livre Polska Sp. z o.o., Warsaw

Senior Graphic Designer Paweł Pasternak
Contributors Piotr Paszkiewicz, Hanna Faryna-Paszkiewicz, Małgorzata Wiśniewska,
Barbara Sudnik, Eligiusz Nowakowski, Gabriele Rupp
Consultant Carlos Rubio Palomera
Graphic Designers Paweł Kamiński, Paweł Pasternak,
Piotr Kiedrowski
Editor Robert G. Pasieczny
Typesetting and Layout Ewa Roguska, Piotr Kiedrowski

Cartographers
Magdalena Polak, Dariusz Romanowski, Olaf Rodowald

Photographers
Paweł Wójcik, Bartłomiej Zaranek

Illustrators
Monika Sopińska, Bohdan Wróblewski

Dorling Kindersley
Translator Magda Hannay
Editors Irene Lyford, Michelle de Larrabeiti, Matthew Tanner
Senior DTP Designer Jason Little
Production Controller Melanie Dowland

Printed and bound in Malaysia

First American Edition, 2003

16 17 18 19 10 9 8 7 6 5 4 3 2 1

Published in the United States by Dorling Kindersley Limited,
345 Hudson Street, New York, New York 10014

Reprinted with revisions 2006, 2008, 2010, 2013, 2017

Copyright © 2003, 2017 Dorling Kindersley, London
A Penguin Random House Company

Published in the UK by Dorling Kindersley Limited.
A catalog record for this book is available from the Library of Congress

ISSN 1542-1554

ISBN 978-1-4654-5738-7

Floors are referred to throughout in accordance with European
usage; ie the "first floor" is the floor above ground level.

MIX
Paper from
responsible sources
FSC™ C018179

**The information in this
DK Eyewitness Travel Guide is checked regularly.**
Every effort has been made to ensure that this book is as up-to-date as possible
at the time of going to press. Some details, however, such as telephone numbers,
opening hours, prices, gallery hanging arrangements and travel information, are
liable to change. The publishers cannot accept responsibility for any consequences
arising from the use of this book, nor for any material on third-party websites, and
cannot guarantee that any website address in this book will be a suitable source of
travel information. We value the views and suggestions of our readers very highly.
Please write to: Publisher, DK Eyewitness Travel Guides, Dorling Kindersley,
80 Strand, London, WC2R 0RL, UK, or email: travelguides@dk.com.

Front cover main image: Playa Blanca beach in Puerto del Carmen, Lanzarote

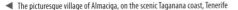 The picturesque village of Almaciga, on the scenic Taganana coast, Tenerife

Contents

Madonna from a church façade
at Santiago del Teide

How to Use this Guide **6**

Introducing the
Canary Islands

Children at the carnival in Las Palmas de
Gran Canaria

Rocky coastline and blue waters near Cofete, Fuerteventura

Façade of the parish church in Vega del Río de Palmas

Traditionally decorated pot from La Orotava

Map of Ferry Routes *inside back cover*

Aquatic life of the Canary Islands *(see pp20–21)*

HOW TO USE THIS GUIDE

This guide will help you to get the most out of your visit to the Canary Islands. It provides recommendations on places to visit, as well as detailed practical information. The section *Introducing the Canary Islands* gives an overview of the geographical position of the islands, their natural environment, their culture and their history. Individual sections describe the main historic sites and star attractions on each of the archipelago's seven inhabited islands. Information on accommodation, restaurants, shopping, entertainment and recreational activities can be found in the *Travellers' Needs* section, while the *Survival Guide* provides useful practical information and advice for visitors.

The Canary Islands Area by Area

Each of the seven inhabited islands has a section devoted to it. Towns and sights of interest on each of the islands are shown on the relevant map.

TENERIFE

1 Introduction

This section provides a brief overview of each island, describing its history, geographical features and cultural characteristics as well as main tourist attractions.

Colour-coded thumb tabs identify pages devoted to individual islands.

Exploring Fuerteventura

2 Island Map

This shows the main roads and topography of the island. It also locates all the places that are later described in detail.

A locator map indicates the position of the island within the archipelago.

3 Detailed Information

All the major towns and places of interest are described, listed and numbered to correspond with the island's map. Each entry provides information on the star sights and local attractions.

Boxes contain information about events and people associated with an area.

4 Major Towns
At least two pages are devoted to each major town, with detailed descriptions of historic remains and local curiosities that are worth seeing.

A **Visitors' Checklist** provides tourist and transport information, including opening hours of tourist attractions, admission charges and details of local festivals and market days.

A **Town Map** shows the location of all the main sights within the town centre and provides tourist information on post offices and car parks.

5 The Canary Islands' Star Sights
Two pages are devoted to each major sight. They include an area map and, in the case of larger towns, a street map of the town centre.

An Area Map indicates the main sights, which are numbered for easy reference.

6 National Parks
Separate pages in the guide are devoted to the national parks on the islands. Topographic maps in these sections indicate the star sights and any other special features of the park.

Photographs illustrate the most interesting areas and the most scenic spots within the park.

Maps show the area's main roads, walking trails and topography, as well as useful tourist information.

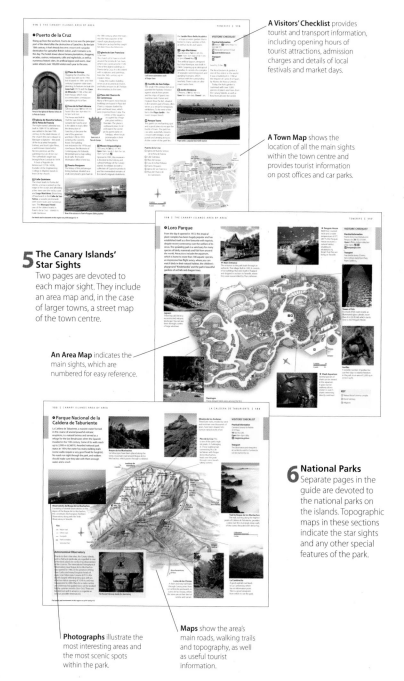

INTRODUCING THE CANARY ISLANDS

DISCOVERING THE CANARY ISLANDS

The Canarian archipelago includes seven main islands – Gran Canaria, Tenerife, Lanzarote, Fuerteventura, La Gomera, La Palma and El Hierro. Each island has a unique personality, from the golden sands of Fuerteventura to the lush greenery of La Palma; the black volcanic beaches of El Hierro to the red hues of Lanzarote. The following tours have been designed to take in as many of the islands' highlights as possible, while the itineraries on pages 10–11 are themed. Follow and combine these tours or simply dip in for inspiration.

Gran Canaria

- Pine-clad mountains
- Historical Las Palmas
- Exciting theme parks
- Buzzing nightlife

Visitors in their thousands arrive at the Canaries' third-largest island every year. Some come for the incredibly healthy climate and invigorating mountain walks on trails such as those found in the area around **Roque Nublo** (see p64). Others delve into the history, mirroring the footsteps of Christopher Columbus in Vegueta, the old quarter of **Las Palmas** (see pp46–51). But most seek little more than that sacred trinity of sun, sand and sea. This can be interspersed with daytime strolls in pretty villages such as **Puerto de Mogán** (see pp60–61), or an action-packed visit to one of the many theme parks such as **Aqualand** (see p62) in **Maspalomas** (see pp62–3). At night, the scores of bars and clubs of the southern resorts offer lively entertainment.

White sands and clear azure sea at Papagayo beach in Lanzarote

The picturesque harbour at Puerto de Mogán, Gran Canaria

◀ A scenic trail in Caldera de Taburiente National Park, La Palma

Fuerteventura

- Glorious beaches
- World-class water sports
- Los Lobos nature reserve

Like a vast playground for sand lovers old and young, Fuerteventura's coast has more beaches than any other Canary Island. The two main resorts – **Corralejo** (see pp72–3) in the north, and **Morro Jable** (see p78) in the south – are where most visitors sunbathe. Here you'll also find great windsurfing as well as snorkelling opportunities. Lying a few kilometres from Corralejo is the small volcanic island of **Los Lobos** (see p73). The island is a nature reserve and makes for a peaceful day's excursion.

Lanzarote

- Dramatic volcanic scenery
- Underground grottoes
- Secluded coves

Lanzarote is a varied island of dramatic volcanic scenery, pristine white villages and beautiful, broad beaches.

Lava plays a big role in the island's attractions, which include the volcano-fuelled barbecue in **Timanfaya National Park** (see pp94–5). The island differs from the other Canaries largely due to César Manrique's environmental and conservational efforts, chronicled at the **Fundación César Manrique** (see p87). At **Jameos del Agua** (see p88) there are underground grottoes illuminated and furnished by the artist and architect. Lanzarote's resorts are contained and few in number, but amenities are still abundant. Hidden coves like those found around **Papagayo** (see p96) are a magnet for holidaymakers.

Tenerife

- Spain's highest peak
- Museum Masterpieces
- Pretty mountain towns

The most celebrated of the islands, Tenerife is beautiful and offers all the highs and lows of a sub-tropical paradise. Ride a cable-car up the world's third-largest island-volcano, towering above the lunar landscape of **Parque Nacional del Teide** *(see pp120–21)*. Take a boat trip to watch whales and dolphins dance through the waters, or visit the **Loro Parque** *(see pp116–17)*. In the capital, **Santa Cruz** *(see pp102–4)*, visit the **Museo Municipal de Bellas Artes** *(see p103)* and bag some bargains in the shopping zone. Drive to the pretty town of **La Orotava** *(see pp110–13)*, which offers the Tenerife of old, with Canarian mansions and cobbled streets. Alternatively there's charming **Masca** *(see p118)*, where whitewashed houses cling to the mountainside.

Whitewashed houses perched on the mountain top in Masca, Tenerife

La Gomera

- **Breathtaking hikes**
- **Ancient forests**
- **Tiny fishing villages**
- **Intriguing customs and traditions**

Certainly not an island for the neon-loving dance set, Tenerife's nearest neighbour is a green, hilly outcrop scarred with deep ravines and fertile valleys. A walker's paradise, La Gomera is etched with hiking trails. In the ancient laurel forests of the **Parque Nacional de Garajonay** *(see pp132–3)* you might hear the distant whistling of El Silbo, La Gomera's unique whistling language. On an island of tiny fishing villages and clusters of mountainside cottages, **Valle Gran Rey** *(see p130)* bears the closest resemblance

to a holiday resort, but only just. Here you'll find a beach and several bars catering for the mainly Spanish visitors. For culture-seekers, the pretty harbour town and capital of **San Sebastián** *(see p128)* has a museum and visitor centre showcasing legacies of Christopher Columbus's time on the island.

El Hierro

- **Fragrant pine forests**
- **Dramatic coastline**
- **Giant lizards**

Known locally as "La Isla Chiquita" (the Small Island), El Hierro is by far the least commercialized (and the least visited) of the Canary Islands. Its appeal lies mostly with nature lovers keen to enjoy the varied and peaceful landscape of flower-speckled meadows, aromatic pine forests and junipers of **El Sabinar** *(see p139)*. Moreover, there's wild

coastline hammered by crashing waves, such as that of **Roques de Salmor**, home to colonies of birds *(see p138)*. The solitude also suits a shy reptile indigenous to El Hierro. Efforts to conserve these giant lizards can be seen at **Lagartario** *(see p139)*.

Colourful balconies overhang the streets of Santa Cruz de La Palma

La Palma

- **Lush mountain trails**
- **Unrivalled stargazing**
- **Fine Canarian architecture**

This lush green gem is the most verdant of all the Canary Islands, and a major draw for hikers and botanists. The vast **Caldera de Taburiente** *(see pp152–3)* is one of the largest volcanic craters on earth, and the view from its rim is spectacular. The vista overhead is also out of this world; the skies above La Palma are among the clearest anywhere, so the stargazing opportunities are unbeatable. The capital, **Santa Cruz de La Palma** *(see pp146–7)*, offers fine Canarian architecture at every turn.

Waves crashing onto rocks on the northern shore of El Hierro

Guanche Culture

- Admire the painted caves at Parque Arqueológico Cueva Pintada
- Discover Guanche artifacts at Museo Canario
- Imagine Guanche life at Mundo Aborigen
- Marvel at the exhibits in the Museo Arqueológico del Puerto de la Cruz

Day 1: Gran Canaria

Morning: Start the day in **Gáldar** *(see p59)*, the ancient centre of the Guanche natives *(see pp32–3)*, where many roads still bear Guanche names. First stop by the **Parque Arqueológico Cueva Pintada** *(see p59)* to see the Cueva Pintada, a cave painted by the Guanches, featuring beautiful geometric patterns. There is also a museum, which displays cult figures, ceramics and knives.

Drive on to **Túmulo de la Guancha** *(see p59)*, located about 2 km (1 mile) north of Gáldar. This 11th-century cemetery was the burial place of high-ranking Guanches and has tombs carved out of vast lava blocks. Around the graveyard are the ruins of former Guanche settlements.

Next, head to the nearby bar La Bodeguita Ca Juancri (Calle Tagoror, 1) for a sumptuous lunch of authentic Canarian tapas.

Afternoon: After a refreshment, take the road to the **Museo Canario** *(see p49)*, in Las Palmas. Many archaeological finds from the Guanche era, such as statuettes of gods, vessels, jewellery and tools, as well as skeletons and mummies from all over the island, are displayed in this musuem.

Proceed to **Cueva de Cuatro Puertas** *(see p66)*, an archaeological site named after the four entrances to an artificial cave. On the hill above the cave, there is an *almagorén* (place of worship) with channels cut into stone in typical Guanche style. There is also a collection of old Canarian cave dwellings on the southern slope of the mountain.

Continue on to **Maspalomas** *(see p62–3)* and visit **Mundo Aborigen** *(see p63)*, 5 km (3 miles) to the north. This open-air museum depicts the life of the Guanches, including a reconstructed village. A marked path leads through a lively scene with more than 100 life-size figures of butchers, farmers and doctors, and takes a close look at the daily life of the Guanches in their native environment.

Statue of a Guanche chief

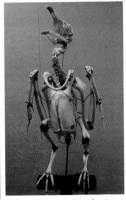

Skeleton of a bird in the Museo Canario, Las Palmas de Gran Canaria

End a long day of sightseeing in one of the bars or restaurants in Maspalomas.

Day 2: Tenerife

Morning: Start the day early to catch the morning ferry to Tenerife, the largest Canary Island. Here, rent a car and head to the **Museo de la Naturaleza y el Hombre** *(see p102)* in Santa Cruz de Tenerife. The museum houses mummies and skulls of the Guanches. It also displays the Zanata Stone, a small rock with inscriptions thought to be of Guanche origin. Its characters appear to be in Tifinagh, an alphabetic script used to write Berber languages. The stone is thought to have been used by the Guanches in ritualistic ceremonies. After taking in the museum's exhibits, walk to **La Rambla de Santa Cruz** *(see p104)* for lunch at one of the restaurants here.

Afternoon: After a hearty lunch, drive for about 40 km (25 miles) to the **Museo Arqueológico** in **Puerto de la Cruz** *(see p114)*. This museum is small but has over 2,600 fascinating specimens from the Guanche culture, including aboriginal pottery and the mummified remains of the island's first inhabitants. Conclude your afternoon with a drink in one of the many restaurants and bars on the lovely waterfront.

The Neo-Classical façade of the Museo de la Naturaleza y el Hombre, Tenerife

The Natural World

- **Gaze at the skies from the Teide Observatory**
- **Hike through the ancient laurel forest of the Parque Nacional de Garajonay**
- **Picnic in the great outdoors around Vallehermoso**

Day 1: Tenerife

Begin your day with a visit to Tenerife's main landmark – Teide, a dormant volcano and the highest point in Spain, found at the heart of **Parque Nacional del Teide** *(see pp120–21)*. On the edge of the national park, on Izaña mountain, the **Teide Observatory** *(see p121)* is located 2,400 m (7,874 ft) above sea level. The world's largest solar observatory is joined by three other solar telescopes – GREGOR, VTT and THEMIS – plus a number of smaller telescopes for night-time observation. The observatory, on the slopes of the Teide, forms part of the Instituto de Astrofísica de Canarias (IAC) and, together with the **Observatorio del Roque de los Muchachos** *(see p152)* in La Palma, comprises the European Northern Observatory. The Teide Observatory has an open day just once a year, but visitors can book a guided tour online (www.iac.es) in advance. There are a number of villages surrounding the park, where you can stop for sustenance.

Day 2: La Gomera

Rise early, pack a picnic, and board a ferry to La Gomera.

On arrival, hire a vehicle (consider something with four-wheel drive, which is best reserved in advance) and head for La Gomera's main attraction – **Parque Nacional de Garajonay** *(see pp132–3)*. Declared a UNESCO World Heritage Site in 1986, the dense woodland here has many hiking trails offering magnificent views. The lush forest is criss-crossed with ravines. Don't miss the views of the **Los Roques** *(see p133)*, volcanic formations that are best seen from the Mirador El Bailadero, and be sure to visit the Roque Cano, formed from a volcanic peak, which is just off the GM-1, near **Vallehermoso** *(see p129)*. There are four picnic zones where you can enjoy your lunch in the great outdoors: Ermita de Lourdes, Laguna Grande, Las Creces and Epina.

Food and Drink

- **Sample local *majorera* cheese in Fuerteventura**
- **Try the fine local wines in Gran Canaria**

Day 1: Fuerteventura

The special climate of Fuerteventura has enabled the development of its own breed of goat, the Majorera goat. From its milk, the island's herders produce *majorero*. Depending on the degree of maturation, the cheese is available as a fresh cheese *(majorero tierno)*, as semi-ripe *(majorero semicurado)* and as ripe *(majorero curado)*. The more mature the cheese, the spicier it is. In cheese dairies

Volcanic Los Roques in Parque Nacional de Garajonay, La Gomera

across Fuerteventura, such as in La Oliva, Puerto del Rosario, Antigua, Betancuria, Tuineje and Pájara, you can not only purchase this local produce in specialty shops, but also, on prior request, see how it is produced. At Finca Pepe (Granja la Acaravaneras, Betancuria; www.fincapepe.com/en), you can visit a working farm and taste the cheese produced in their dairy. There is also a museum and a souvenir shop.

About 11 km (7 miles) east in **Antigua** *(see p75)*, you can visit the sales outlets of local cheese producers on the *Ruta del Queso* (Cheese Route). There are signs and information panels in Spanish, German and English all along the circuit. You can book a guided tour online (www.ruta delqueso.com) in advance.

Day 2: Gran Canaria

Catch a ferry to **Las Palmas de Gran Canaria** *(see pp46–51)* and eat breakfast on board. On arrival, rent a car and drive about 15 km (9 miles) to Destilerías Arehucas *(see p168)*. Among other types of rum, the sweet Ron Miel is also produced at this distillery. You can take a free tour of the factory, and purchase rum in their gift shop. Make sure the designated driver avoids the free samples! Drive onto Casa Museo del Vino in **Santa Brígida** *(see p54)* to taste delicious local wines and learn more about their production. Conclude the day back in Las Palmas de Gran Canaria, heading to Pastelería & Gourmet Di Nardi (C/León y Castillo, 14) for a bite to eat.

Barrels of rum at the Arehucas Rum distillery in Arucas, Gran Canaria

Putting the Canary Islands on the Map

Dotted in a gentle curve, the archipelago of the Canary Islands lies in the Atlantic Ocean to the west of Morocco in Saharan Africa. The seven main islands are inhabited with a total population of more than 2 million – the majority living on the larger islands of Gran Canaria and Tenerife. The total area of these volcanic islands is 7,447 sq km (2,875 sq miles) and encompasses a surprisingly rich variety of landscapes, from beaches and desert-like areas to dramatic mountain ranges and green woods. Hot winds from the Sahara ensure that the islands enjoy a warm climate all year round with temperatures averaging 18° C (64° F) in winter and 24° C (75° F) in summer.

Pico del Teide, Tenerife
At 3,718 m (12,198 ft), Tenerife's Pico del Teide is the third highest island volcano in the world and the highest mountain in Spain. The area around it has been designated a national park (see pp120–21).

Key

━━━ Motorway/Highway
━━━ Major road
---- Ferry route

La Palma From Outer Space
This satellite photograph shows the heart-shaped island of La Palma from outer space. In the centre rises the Roque de los Muchachos at 2,426 m (7,959 ft).

Port of La Palma
Large vessels, including cruise ships, dock at the port of the island's capital, Santa Cruz de La Palma (see pp146–7), on the east coast of the island.

For keys to symbols see back flap

↑ *Cádiz, Huelva*

Playa de Amadores in Gran Canaria
"Lovers' beach" is located on the southwest coast of Gran Canaria in a sheltered bay. The beach of golden sand is about 800 m (2,625 ft) long, and the water is crystal clear.

ISLA DE ALEGRANZA

ISLA DE MONTAÑA CLARA

LA GRACIOSA

Tinajo

San Bartolomé

LZ10

LZ1

LANZAROTE

LZ30

Arrecife

LZ2

Juguete del Viento
This wind chime by César Manrique *(see p87)* in Arrieta in Lanzarote is almost always in motion due to the harsh trade winds.

Playa Blanca

ISLA DE LOS LOBOS

Corralejo

FV10

FV1

FUERTEVENTURA

Puerto del Rosario

Betancuria

FV20

Tuineje

FV2

FV2

Morro Jable

Gáldar

Las Palmas de Gran Canaria

GC2

GC30

Arucas

Agaete

GC15

Telde

GC100

GC200

Santa Lucía

GC60

GC1

GRAN CANARIA

Maspalomas

| 0 kilometres | 40 |
| 0 miles | 40 |

Location of the Islands
Although just 100 km (62 miles) from Africa, the Canary Islands belong to Spain – a country over 1,100 km (690 miles) away. The islands' population of over 2 million is swollen each year by more than 7.5 million tourists.

Western Europe and North Africa

IRELAND

UNITED KINGDOM

Atlantic Ocean

FRANCE

PORTUGAL

SPAIN

Azores

Balearics

Madeira

MOROCCO

Canary Islands

ALGERIA

WESTERN SAHARA

MAURITANIA

The Formation of the Canary Islands

Along with other Atlantic islands, such as Madeira, the Azores and the Cape Verde Islands, the Canaries are of volcanic origin. They emerged from the sea millions of years ago: Lanzarote and Fuerteventura are believed to be the oldest at between 16 and 20 million years old, with Gran Canaria, Tenerife and La Gomera appearing around 8–13 million years ago. The remaining islands are much younger. Most of the islands lie in the shadow of a central volcanic cone surrounded by smaller cones and areas of solidified lava.

Near El Golfo *(see p93)* on Lanzarote is a crater filled with seawater. A black sand beach separates the ocean from the grey-green waters of the lake.

La Geria's vineyards on Lanzarote *(see pp96–7)* flourish in the fertile volcanic soil. Semicircles of stones protect the vines from the prevailing winds, and the resulting grapes are used to produce the amber-coloured Malvasía wine.

The origin of the islands

The Canary Islands are the tips of volcanoes pushed up from the floor of the Atlantic Ocean by the movement of the Earth's crust. As the crust buckled along fault lines, hot liquid rock (magma) bursts up through the cracks.

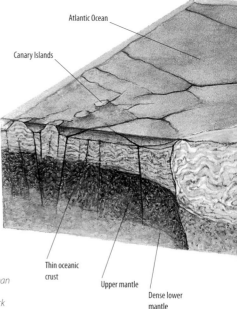

Atlantic Ocean

Canary Islands

Thin oceanic crust

Upper mantle

Dense lower mantle

Los Azulejos on Gran Canaria show the beauty of the multicoloured volcanic rocks. Their varied chemical compositions, including copper salts and iron hydrites, create a stunning palette of colours from grey and brown, through ochre and red, to blue and green.

Malpaís means "badlands" and refers to this almost completely barren landscape on Fuerteventura *(see pp80–81)*. Only the most desert-hardened flora and fauna survive here.

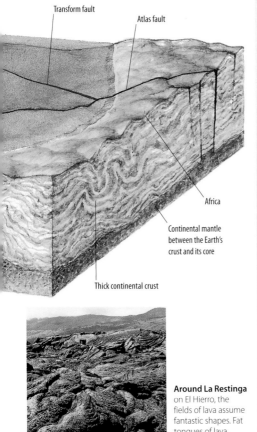

Transform fault

Atlas fault

Africa

Continental mantle between the Earth's crust and its core

Thick continental crust

Around La Restinga on El Hierro, the fields of lava assume fantastic shapes. Fat tongues of lava, which resemble solidified tar, are created by under-water volcanic eruptions. As the flowing lava rapidly cools, it forms large areas of magma nodules.

Evolution of Volcanic Islands

The islands in this archipelago are at various stages in their geological evolution. Tenerife, El Hierro, Lanzarote and La Palma are still volcanically active, with the last experiencing its most recent eruption in 1971.

Fissures

Feeder dyke

Mantle

Magma chamber

Crust

Basalt lava flow

1 **The islands of** La Gomera, El Hierro and La Palma are really the tops of volcanoes that rise from the ocean's bed. They consist of basalt rock produced by solidified lava. Below, the Earth's crust bends under the weight of the islands.

Caldera

Shallow magma chamber

2 **When the magma** chamber empties during an eruption, the top of the cone collapses downwards. This creates a crater, known as a caldera – such as the Caldera de Taburiente on La Palma. This stage of an island's evolution is marked by abundant flows of lava.

Sea level

Exposed solidified magma chamber

3 **When the eruption** has ended, the volcano begins to erode. The mountains of Gran Canaria are in the early stages of erosion, while Fuerteventura's volcanic chambers, with their solidified lava, are typical of a more advanced stage of evolution.

Flora of the Canary Islands

The flora of the Canary Islands is unique. La Gomera, for example, is home to a rare ancient forest that is now a UNESCO World Heritage Site. More than half of the islands' 1,800 species are indigenous, and botanists have long been attracted to the unusual character of these exceptional plants. They are the relics of the old Mediterranean flora, which became extinct throughout the region because of changes in climate. The local flora that remains has survived thanks to the fairly stable and relatively humid climate of the Canary Islands, along with a variety of colourful, exotic imported plants.

Canary Island pine is one of the native species, growing at altitudes of over 1,000 m (3,280 ft). Its needles reach up to 30 cm (12 in) in length.

Viper's bugloss
(*Echium vulgare*)

Canary Island juniper

Canary Island date palm (*Phoenix canariensis*) is endemic – it grows in bushland and semi-deserts. Although its fruits are edible, it is used solely as an ornamental plant.

The basalt slopes of volcanoes are not conducive to plant growth. The few species found here are often indigenous plants, which have evolved to be able to retain water.

This type of spurge olive has silvery leaves

Balsamic spurge grows in semi-desert areas. Its juice is sometimes made into chewing gum, but it is also valued as an ornamental plant.

Plant Zones

Coastal zones, mostly rocky, are home to plants that can tolerate salt and temperature variations.

Semi-desert plants, found above 400 m (1,310 ft), store water within their fleshy leaves and stalks.

Low shrubs are found above 500 m (1,650 ft), particularly in areas with a low annual rainfall.

Erysimum scoparium, a woody, native shrub with lilac-pink flowers, grows in the highest regions of the Canary Islands.

The Dragon Tree

One of the most unusual plants in the Canaries, the dragon tree *(Dracaena draco)* erupts into swollen branches that end in tufts of spiky leaves. Its red sap (known as dragon's blood) and its fruit were used in Roman times to make a medicinal powder, and it was used in pigments, paints and varnishes. One specimen at Icod de los Vinos, on Tenerife, known as *Drago Milenario*, is said to be 1,000 years old.

Typical island

The mountains of the Canary Islands provide a home for a diverse array of flora, with different plants growing at each level. As the ground rises, the salt-tolerant and semi-desert vegetation gives way to humid rainforests, pine forests and, in the highest regions, to hard-leaf shrubs and rock plants.

Canary Island holly is an evergreen shrub, and one of the most common inhabitants of the laurel forests. Its bark has medicinal properties.

Canary Island spurge
(Euphorbia canariensis)

Canary samphire *(Astydamia latifolia)* is found on the coastal basalt rocks of the Canary Islands. This native genus, with its distinctive fleshy, green leaves flowers from December until April.

Canary Island strawflower
(Helichrysum gossypium)

Limonium papillatum

Laurel forests cover the northern slopes of the islands, where humidity is constantly high.

Pine forests occur at up to 2,000 m (6,560 ft). Their undergrowth consists mainly of shade-loving shrubs.

Areas above 2,000 m (6,560 ft) feature cushion-like shrubs. Rock grass covers the highest slopes.

The Underwater World

Despite the Canary Islands' favourable position on the edge of the tropics, the waters around the islands are relatively cold. This explains the lack of coral reefs, which would normally occur at such latitudes. Nevertheless, the sea conditions are congenial to many species of fish, mammal and seaweed. Divers in coastal and offshore waters will find a rich variety of marine life, including several species of whales and dolphins, shoals of small cardinal fish, huge crabs, colourful parrotfish and tiny seahorses.

Long-finned pilot whales (blackfish) belong to the dolphin family. The coastal waters of Tenerife are home to the world's second-largest colony of these mammals.

Sea Life

The ocean floor around the Canary Islands is mainly composed of rock with occasional patches of sand. This environment, illustrated here, is one reason for the richness of the local fauna, which includes some 600 species of seaweed.

Seahorses appear in great numbers among clumps of seagrass, clinging to the shoots by their tails. The young hatch out of spawn that is laid by the female in the male's brood pouch.

The blue-spotted puffer fish is so-called due to its habit, when threatened, of inflating its alimentary canal with air, to scare off the enemy.

Bandtail puffer

Worm shell

Pearly razorfish

Starfish

Coral

The parrotfish is among the most colourful inhabitants of the Canary Islands' waters. Its distinctive, beak-like mouth is formed by large teeth fused together.

Sea urchin

Spider crabs hide in the nooks of the seabed. Their red shells, which can be as much as 20 cm (8 in) in length, are densely covered with spikes.

The brown scorpionfish's markings and colour make it difficult to spot against the rocky sea floor, despite its large size. The hard spikes of its dorsal fin deliver venom to its prey during night hunts. The fish remains still by day.

The Moroccan octopus is a common sight in the areas of rocky seabed that lie around the Canary Islands. It catches its prey with its tentacles, which are armed with suckers.

This small mollusc is the Murex trunculus, and has been used for 2,000 years to make purple dye. It hides inside its thick, striped shell, and eats putrefied matter, including other, dead molluscs.

Limpet

Chiton

Diving and Snorkelling in the Canaries

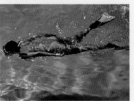

The Canary Islands provide very attractive diving grounds. Here, beginners can gain experience, while more advanced divers can explore the underwater caves off Gran Canaria, La Palma and El Hierro and the coral reefs near Lanzarote. The water is at its clearest between November and February. The water temperature of 15–20° C (59–68° F) is also conducive to diving and snorkelling. However, strong currents, particularly at greater depths, can present difficulties for divers.

The conger eel has a blackish body, with a pale belly, large head and wide mouth. It is active at night, while hiding in caves and cracks during the day.

The moray eel, with its elongated, snake-like body and sharp teeth, is one of the fiercest predators of the coastal waters. This marine creature, which can be up to 3 m (10 ft) long, inhabits caves and cracks in the rocks.

Cardinalfish with their scarlet bodies are small, fast-moving fish that may be seen mostly at the entrances to underwater caves. The male carries the spawn in his mouth.

Crafts of the Canary Islands

The inhabitants of the Canaries are enthusiastic about keeping alive their strongly rooted tradition of local handicrafts. These include embroidery, lace-making, basket-weaving, ceramics and woodcarving. Different islands specialize in particular crafts: La Gomera is known for its basketware and for pottery made without using a wheel; Tenerife is a centre for traditional, Guanche-style pots; El Hierro produces beautifully woven rugs and bags; and the town of Ingenio (see p66), Gran Canaria, produces some of the best embroidery in the islands.

Potter at work in La Orotava workshop, Tenerife

Pottery

Thanks to archaeological discoveries, we now know that pottery was one of the best-developed crafts of the Guanches – the indigenous people of the Canary Islands. Using local clay, they made vessels of various shapes and sizes, which they used for cooking, storing food and carrying water. The Guaches also wore bead necklaces made out of baked clay.

Although locally made pottery can be found on all the islands, there are a few centres that pride themselves on their ceramic workshops. La Gomera, Tenerife and La Palma are particularly well known for traditional pottery. Produced from dark clay, without the use of a potter's wheel, this is the most popular style of pottery, and it is regarded as a classic reinterpretation of Guanche work. Other islands also make pieces that are based on original Guanche designs copied from archaeological finds and produced by traditional methods.

As on the Spanish mainland, there are tiles, plates and vases in the multicoloured style of the Moorish-inspired *azulejos*, for sale in pottery shops.

Colourful displays of pottery adorn many local village shops, and most markets will have at least one stall selling ceramics. Workshops where you can view the pots being made also offer an array of wares and this can make choosing difficult.

Ornamental water vessel

Embroidery

Practised mainly by the women, the skills and styles of Canarian embroidery are passed down from mother to daughter. The craft of embroidery is a source of great pride in the areas that specialize in it. Gran Canaria is famous for embroidery, particularly the towns of Ingenio (see p66) and Agaete (see p59), as is La Orotava (see pp 110–13) on Tenerife. Original patterns, hand-embroidered onto silk or linen, are among the most exquisite souvenirs that visitors can take home. Richly embroidered bed linen, tablecloths and napkins are among the most popular items. The only drawback is their often very high price, which is a reflection of the skill and time taken by the embroiderer.

Clothing, especially the islands' national costumes, is often decorated with embroidery. White shirts, blouses and aprons are all adorned with openwork frills that are threaded with ribbons. Modern, somewhat garish copies of these clothes are on sale in craft markets.

Traditional embroidery in Betancuria Museum, Fuerteventura

Lace-making

Lacework is among the most beautiful and most striking of Canarian handicrafts. The subtlety of the designs and colours reflects the continuation of European and Mediterranean traditions.

There are several small, specialized co-operatives producing lace tablecloths and curtains on the islands. These are very popular among the locals as well as the tourists. Unlike embroidered items, lacework is not too expensive.

The beautiful openwork tablecloths and placemats are always produced in white and beige. Their designs usually consist of symmetrical patterns with abstract or floral motifs, featuring circles and suns linked together to create uniform compositions.

Experts regard the lace produced in Vilaflor, on Tenerife, as being the most beautiful. In fact, Tenerife lace was thought to be the inspiration for mid-19th-century lace made from agave leaves.

Lace tablecloth from San Bartolomé on Lanzarote

Weaving

This is another traditional handicraft that continues to thrive in the Canary Islands, and there are many established weavers' shops still working in the islands today. As in past centuries, simple hand-looms are still used to produce carpets, which are based on traditional designs. Long and narrow, often with randomly mixed colours, these carpets are very popular with the local population. You will also find

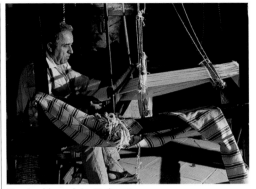

Weaver's workshop, producing striped carpets

carpets with regular stripes or with more sophisticated designs, based on traditional local patterns. Hand-woven cloth is still used to make rugs, tapestries and bags, and, until recently, some elements of the local national costumes were also hand-woven.

The islands of La Palma and La Gomera are known for their woven products.

Long, multi-coloured striped carpet

Other Handicrafts

Always very popular with tourists are items woven from palm leaves or willow. These include baskets and bowls, which are not designed to last forever, but are nevertheless very reasonably priced. Also for sale are the wide-brimmed hats that are indispensable parts of farm workers' clothing.

On religious feast days, the women of the islands wear small hats with an upturned brim. This particular fashion has helped to further a demand for these locally produced, plaited straw hats, which are light and airy to wear.

Highly regarded for their artistic merit are local carpentry and woodwork products. The tradition of adorning the surfaces of wooden gates, doors and shutters with carved

motifs goes back many centuries. Old gates and shutters, as well as church ornaments, are often masterpieces of woodcarving. The distinctive wooden balconies and oriels, with their carved brackets and balustrades, are based on historic designs. Local trees, including pine, chestnut and beech, provide timber for many household items such as bowls, spoons and ladles. The Canary Tea pine, in particular, does not require additional treatment for external use and is often used for outdoor fittings, such as carved window frames.

The *timple* – a small, wooden, five-stringed instrument resembling a ukulele – is a popular souvenir from the Canary Islands. The town of Teguise on Lanzarote *(see pp90–91)* is renowned for producing these instruments.

Timple-maker at work

Canary Islands Carnivals

Often compared to the extravaganzas in Rio de Janeiro and New Orleans, the Santa Cruz carnival in Tenerife takes place each year in the 10–14 days before Ash Wednesday. It is one of the largest carnivals in Europe, with a spectacular display of costumes and Latin American music. In Gran Canaria, festivities start when the Tenerife carnival ends. The Carnival Fiesta in Lanzarote takes place at the beginning of March, with one in Fuerteventura two weeks later. Although street parties were banned under the Franco regime, the tradition of holding carnivals – renamed "winter festivals" – survived on the islands, re-emerging in their full glory after Spain's return to democracy in 1975.

A candidate for the coveted title of "Carnival Queen"

The Carnival Queen

The carnival begins with the election of its queen. Accompanied by colourful carnival crowds, the hopeful candidates arrive in front of the jury on their lavishly decorated floats.

The contestants are usually local beauties, but any girl may take part in the competition. The beauty and grace of the prospective queens are emphasized by their magnificent costumes. The queen's dress must be unique and command general admiration.

The newly elected queen, accompanied by her equally beautiful ladies-in-waiting, reigns over all the carnival festivities. Her float takes the place of honour in all the parades, and the happy "sovereign" looks down from her throne, greeting her cheering carnival subjects as she passes by.

Flamboyant procession in the streets of Santa Cruz de Tenerife

Street Parades

Since 1987, each carnival has had a different theme, which dictates the character of the street parades, the costumes worn by revellers and the choice of decorations. Street processions, in particular, are a popular element of the carnivals.

Organized marchers are accompanied by floats with tableaux of historical or allegorical scenes, plus music and performances. A considerable amount of care goes into creating the music and costumes for them.

The Stage

Another essential element of each carnival is the stage, which is usually built in the town centre. A main venue for night-time revels, this is where the spectacular carnival shows are held each evening,

with bands and acrobatic displays attracting huge crowds. Keenly fought competitions are held here, such as one for the best formation dancing team. Comedy shows also attract large audiences. The same stage provides a venue for classical concerts, including programmes of choral works.

Drag show on stage in Las Palmas de Gran Canaria

Children

Carnival means fun and games for everyone, not just the adults – children also enjoy the festivities with many events just for them. They march in separate "small" parades and participate in their own stage shows and competitions. Little girls compete for the title of "Carnival Princess".

Children's costumes, made for the occasion, are often masterpieces of dressmaking. They include traditional Spanish folk dresses, Brazilian samba costumes and fairytale and circus figures. Pint-sized participants, thrilled with the excitement and their roles, quickly enter into the spirit of carnival.

Children's dancing display, with exotic costumes

Dazzling carnival costume with sparkling head-dress

Carnival Costumes and Make-Up

It often takes months to make the extravagant costumes and masks and to design and con-struct the floats. As the theme of the carnival changes every year, the Canarios begin planning the next carnival as soon as one ends.

The general aim is always originality, and the ideas for carnival costumes are often unique. The shapes and forms of the outfits are inspired by many cultures, but one indispensable element is an unusual hairstyle – the more extravagant the better.

Another important factor is the make-up, which often sets the theme and is an integral component of the costume. Carnival events often include exhibitions of the most unusual or spectacular body paintings.

Drag Queens

Another notable feature of the Canarian carnivals is the drag queen. Mixing with the masquerading crowds they are conspicuously tall as they walk on their high-heeled, platform shoes. At night-time, drag queens flaunt their costumes and demonstrate their dancing skills. The one judged most striking and beautiful becomes queen.

Masqueraders

In contrast with the carnival in Rio de Janeiro, where the main procession consists only of organized groups, in the Canary Islands almost everybody wears a mask and costume. Since the masquerade fever also affects tourists, the parade inevitably turns into a huge fancy dress ball, with druids, pirates, samurai warriors and other iconic figures, such as Charlie Chaplin or Disney cartoon characters, packing the streets and squares. The ever-popular game of pretending to be someone else creates a great sense of euphoria and encourages masqueraders to let their hair down and party.

The Burial of the Sardine

The Santa Cruz carnival ends with a grand funeral procession, called *El Entierro de la Sardina* (The Burial of the Sardine). This ritual is rooted in the past when carnival was the one occasion when people could deride such powerful institutions as the church. Today, crowds still dress up as clerical figures.

Carried at the head of the procession is an enormous papier-mâché sardine. The "mourners" wail and laugh, as they escort the fish to the sea. Here it is set alight, and hundreds of fireworks inside it create an explosive display.

Carnival reveller, dressed as a pirate

THE CANARY ISLANDS THROUGH THE YEAR

The inhabitants of the Canary Islands are deeply devoted to tradition – a fact that is reflected in the numerous religious feast days, or fiestas, that they celebrate. Some of these traditions go back to the time of the Guanches *(see pp32–3)*. Fiestas are normally associated with the cult of saints, and in particular with various patron saints. In agricultural areas, fiestas mark the end of the harvest. During the fiesta, people abandon their work to pray, dance and join colourful parades. Canarian fiestas tend to last for several days, some for as long as two or three weeks. In the Islands' larger cities such fiestas are often accompanied by music, theatre and cinema festivals, and some have an international flavour. Of the other events on the islands, sporting events, particularly *lucha canaria* (Canarian wrestling) and football, attract enormous crowds.

Flowering apple trees at the foot of Roque Nublo, Gran Canaria

Spring

Although the year-round mild climate of the Canary Islands gives the impression of perpetual spring, true spring weather is most noticeable between March and May, when the landscape is at its greenest. This is also the season of intense rainfall, particularly on Tenerife.

March

Fiesta del Almendro en Flor *(early Mar)*, all islands. The almond blossom fiesta is celebrated on a grand scale in the towns of Tejeda and Valsequillo, Gran Canaria. There are displays of classic folk dancing, and almonds, wines and sweets are distributed by each village.
Rally El Corte Inglés *(Mar/Apr)*, Gran Canaria. Car rally attracting international competitors.

Semana Santa *(Mar/Apr)*, all islands. Holy Week, with a Good Friday procession.

April

Fiesta de los Pastores *(25 Apr)*, La Dehesa, El Hierro. The annual feast of this western island's shepherds.
Fiesta de Ansite *(29 Apr)*, Gran Canaria. Music and dancing mark the final uprising of the Guanches against the Spanish and Spain's victory over the island.

May

Festival de Música y Danza *(May)*, Las Palmas de Gran Canaria. Concerts and dance performances.
Fiesta del Queso del Flor *(30 Apr–7 May)*, Santa María de Guía, Gran Canaria. Much eating of cheese in this small town famed for its production.

Feria del Caballo *(1 May)*, Valsequillo. An annual horse market.
Transvulcania (early May), La Palma. Mountain runs with three track lengths – ultra-marathon, marathon and half-marathon.
Romería de San Isidro *(15 May)* in Uga, Lanzarote. Elaborate procession.
Ironman Lanzarote Canarias (mid-May), Lanzarote. This triathlon has taken place in Lanzarote since 1992.
Maspalomas Gay Pride (mid-May), Maspalomas, Gran Canaria. Week-long celebrations, culminating in the iconic parade.
Festival Internacional de Cine (late May–early Jun), Las Palmas. International Film Festival. Visitors can walk along the "Walk of Fame," where famous festival attendees have left handprints next to their stars.

Bunch of ripe bananas

Traditional fiesta procession on El Hierro

Average Daily Hours of Sunshine

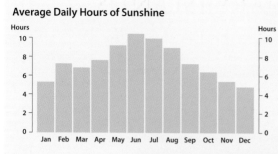

Hours

Jan	Feb	Mar	Apr	May	Jun	Jul	Aug	Sep	Oct	Nov	Dec

Hours of Sunshine
The islands differ considerably in their daily hours of sunshine: Lanzarote and Fuerteventura enjoy about 12 hours of sunshine per day in August; northern parts of Tenerife and Gran Canaria can sometimes be cloudy, while the southern regions of the islands bask in sunshine.

Summer

In summer, temperatures in the islands can reach 40° C (104° F). During July and August, there is very little rainfall, except in the region of Las Palmas de Gran Canaria. In August, the crowds of foreign tourists are swollen by holidaymakers from the Spanish mainland. This is when most fiestas take place.

Crowded beaches of Puerto del Carmen, Lanzarote

Gathering cochineal insects on a prickly pear plantation

June

Corpus Christi *(Jun)*, all islands. Celebrations include processions, and are at their most colourful in Arucas, Gran Canaria, and La Laguna and La Orotava, both in Tenerife.
Día de San Juan *(24 Jun)*, Las Palmas de Gran Canaria. Commemorates the city's foundation with a big party.
Bajada de Nuestra Señora de las Nieves *(every 5 years, Jun–Aug)*, Santa Cruz de la Palma, La Palma. Amazing costumes and a lavish procession at this important festival.

Día de San Pedro y San Pablo *(29 Jun)*, all islands. The feast of St Peter and St Paul.

July

Fiesta de San Marcial del Rubicon *(early Jul)*, Femés and Yaiza, Lanzarote. Celebrates the island's patron saint.
Fiesta del Carmen *(16 Jul)*, Gáldar, Gran Canaria. Fiesta honouring the patron saint of fishermen and sailors. There are boat processions in Arguineguín and Puerto de Mogán.
Bajada de la Virgen de los Reyes *(early Jul, every 4 years: 2017, 2021)*, El Hierro. Festival celebrating the patron saint, with procession.
Festival Internacional Canarias Jazz *(mid-Jul)*, all islands. Jazz concerts by international musicians.
Día de San Buenaventura *(14 Jul)*, Betancuria, Fuerteventura. On this day, effigies of the town's patron saint processes through the streets.
Día de Santiago Apóstol *(25 Jul)*, Santa Cruz, Tenerife. Celebrates Spain's patron saint and the town's defeat of the English and Horatio Nelson.

August

Bajada de la Rama *(4 Aug)*, Agaete, Gran Canaria. Colourful fiesta with roots in the Guanches' rain dance.
Romería de San Roque *(16 Aug)*, Garachico, Tenerife. Traditional festival to honour San Roque.
Fiesta de San Ginés *(mid- to late Aug)*, Arrecife, Lanzarote. Feast of St Ginés, the patron saint of the capital of Arrecife.
Día de San Bartolomé *(24 Aug)*, San Bartolomé, Lanzarote. Processions, music and dancing honour the saint.
Fiesta de la Cuevita *(24 Aug)*, Artenara, Gran Canaria. Festival honouring the Virgin Mary.

Bajada de Nuestra Señora de las Nieves, La Palma

Average Monthly Rainfall

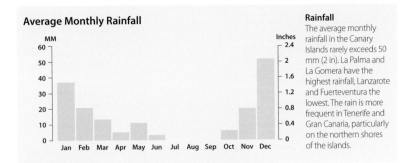

Rainfall
The average monthly rainfall in the Canary Islands rarely exceeds 50 mm (2 in). La Palma and La Gomera have the highest rainfall, Lanzarote and Fuerteventura the lowest. The rain is more frequent in Tenerife and Gran Canaria, particularly on the northern shores of the islands.

Kite festival on Corralejo beach, Fuerteventura

Autumn

Autumn does not differ much from summer, except that high daytime temperatures give way to somewhat cooler nights. Large temperature differences may be felt at higher altitudes on Tenerife or Gran Canaria, where you can find yourself suddenly enveloped in fog, with a rapid drop in temperature.

September

Semana Colombina (*1–6 Sep*), San Sebastián, La Gomera. Shows and processions celebrate Christopher Columbus.
Fiesta de la Virgen del Pino (*6–8 Sep*), Teror, Gran Canaria. The island's most important celebration includes an evening procession with offerings of produce to the patron saint of Gran Canaria.
Fiesta del Charco (*7–11 Sep*), La Aldea de San Nicolás, Gran Canaria. Participants jump into a pool of salt water to catch fish.
Romería de Nuestra Señora de Los Dolores (*mid-Sep*), Lanzarote. A pilgrimage to

the sanctuary of Los Dolores, in Mancha Blanca.
Fiesta de la Virgen de la Peña (*3rd Sat in Sep*), Celebration of the patron saint of Fuerteventura.
Fiestas de San Mateo (*21 Sep*), San Mateo, Gran Canaria. Pilgrimage paying homage to the municipality's patron saint.
Tenerife Opera Festival (Mid-Sep–late Oct), Santa Cruz de Tenerife.

Fishing, an all-year-round occupation in the Canary Islands

October

Travesía a Nado "El Río" (early Oct), Lanzarote. In this long-distance swimming event, competitors cross the strait between Lanzarote and La Graciosa.
Bajada de la Virgen de Guadalupe (*early Oct, every five years*), La Gomera. Fishermen carry a statue of the Virgin Mary from Puntallana to San Sebastián by sea.
Fiesta de la Naval (*6 Oct*), Las Palmas, Gran Canaria. Festival to celebrate victory over Sir Francis Drake.
Romería de Nuestra Señora de la Luz (*mid-Oct*), Las Palmas, Gran Canaria. Procession of boats at sea celebrate the Virgin.
Festival Internacional de Cine de Las Palmas (Oct–Nov), Gran Canaria. Film festival attracting many international movie stars.
MASDANZA (late Oct), Maspalomas, Gran Canaria. International dance festival.

November

Festival Internacional de Cometas (early Nov), Parque Natural Dunas de Corralejo. Kiteflyers' festival.
Fiestas en Honor a San Gregorio Patronales Taumaturgo (early–mid-Dec), Telde, Gran Canaria. Festival in honour of the saint who protects against floods and earthquakes.
Fiestas de San Andrés (late Nov), Guía de Isora, Tenerife. This celebration coincides with the wine cellars releasing their latest vintages.
Atlantic Rally for Cruisers (last Sun in Nov), Gran Canaria. A transatlantic rally for yachts from Las Palmas to the Caribbean.

Average Monthly Temperature

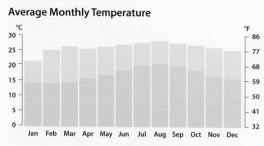

Temperature
The chart shows the average minimum and maximum monthly temperature. The mild climate of the Canary Islands produces average temperatures of between 18° C (64° F) in the winter and 24° C (75° F) in the summer months.

Winter

Many people decide to spend the winter months on the Canary Islands, not least because of the mild climate at this time of the year. For this reason, the height of the tourist season on the Canary Islands is from December to February. Although the peak of the Teide volcano is sometimes covered with snow, the coastal areas remain warm.

December

Día de Santa Lucia *(13 Dec)*, Gran Canaria. Churches and villages are illuminated for this celebration honouring Saint Lucy.
Carrera Atlética de San Silvestre *(mid-Dec)*, Maspalomas, Gran Canaria. An annual 10-km (6-mile) run.
Santos Inocentes *(28 Dec)*, all islands. This is the Spanish equivalent of April Fools' Day, when tricks are played.
Noche Vieja *(31 Dec)*, is the New Year's Eve celebration.

Animal purification at the Festividad de San Sebastián, Tenerife

January

Festival de Música de Canarias *(Jan/Feb)*, most islands. Classical music concerts.
Noche de los Reyes *(5 Jan)*, all islands. The three kings throw sweets to the children at this pre-Epiphany celebration.
Festividad de San Sebastián *(20 Jan)*, Adeje, Tenerife. Farmers drive their animals into the sea for a symbolic purification.

February

Carnival *(Feb/Mar)*, all islands. Several weeks of partying and masquerades start with the election of the carnival queen and build up to a climax on Shrove Tuesday.
Romería de la Virgen de Candelaria *(1–2 Feb)*, Candelaria, Tenerife. Candlemas. The Feast of the Virgin Mary, the patron saint of the islands, is celebrated with a candlelit procession.
Fiestas del Almendro en Flor *(early Feb)*, Valsequillo, Gran Canaria. Celebration of the blossoming of the area's 2,000-plus almond trees.

Public Holidays

Año Nuevo New Year's Day (1 Jan)
Día de los Reyes Epiphany (6 Jan)
Jueves Santo Maundy Thursday (Mar/Apr)
Viernes Santo Good Friday (Mar/Apr)
Día de Pascua Easter Sunday (Mar/Apr)
Fiesta de Trabajo Labour Day (1 May)
Día de las Islas Canarias Canary Islands Day (30 May)
Corpus Christi (early Jun)
Asunción Assumption of the Virgin Mary (15 Aug)
Día de la Hispanidad Columbus Day (12 Oct)
Día de Todos los Santos All Saints' Day (1 Nov)
Día de la Constitución Constitution Day (6 Dec)
Día de la Inmaculada Concepción Day of the Immaculate Conception (8 Dec)
Día de Navidad Christmas Day (25 Dec)

Drag queen in procession during carnival

THE HISTORY OF THE CANARY ISLANDS

The early history of the Canaries is shrouded in myth and legend. Some believed the islands to be the lost land of Atlantis, which, according to Plato, was destroyed by an earthquake. To others they were known as the Fortunate Islands, poised at the edge of the world, and whose inhabitants knew no sorrow.

It is believed that the first inhabitants of the Canary Islands came from North Africa, and probably arrived here around 3,000 BC. Although scholars disagree about the origins of the islands' early dwellers, one prominent theory is that they were Neolithic people from the Cro-Magnon era. Typically they were tall and well built with narrow skulls.

Around the second century BC, the islands became populated by the next wave of arrivals – the Guanches. Their origins have also not been clearly established. Linguistic and genetic testing suggests that they were most likely linked to the Berbers. It is believed that prior to the conquest of the islands by Spain in the 15th century, the Guanche population of the islands consisted of some 30,000 in Gran Canaria and Tenerife, over 4,000 in La Palma, over 1,000 in El Hierro and a few hundred in Fuerteventura and Lanzarote.

There is evidence that the ancients knew about the islands. Sailors used to visit the Canaries, and information about the archipelago can be found in the writings of Roman historians. In AD 24, King Juba II, who was once the king of today's western Morocco, sent a naval force and discovered the Canary Islands for the Western world. In AD 150, a fairly accurate map by the Egyptian geographer, Ptolemy, represented the islands as the edge of the world. Following the fall of the Roman Empire, Europe forgot the Canaries for over 1,000 years.

Conquest of the Canary Islands

The Canary Islands were rediscovered by Mediterranean sailors. In 1312, Captain Lanzarotto (or Lancelotto) Malocello, a native of Genoa, reached the furthest northeast island, where he encountered the native population, the Guanches. The island was subsequently named after him – Lanzarote.

Throughout the 14th century, Italians, Portuguese and Catalans sent their ships to the islands to bring back slaves and furs. The rapid process of the islands' conquest began in 1402, when the Norman knight, Jean de Béthencourt, arrived in Lanzarote. Two years later, he returned with the backing of the Castilian crown. Encountering little resistance, the conquistadors took over the sparsely populated islands of El Hierro, La Gomera and Fuerteventura.

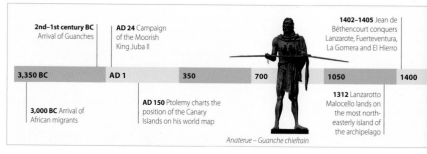

2nd–1st century BC Arrival of Guanches

AD 24 Campaign of the Moorish King Juba II

1402–1405 Jean de Béthencourt conquers Lanzarote, Fuerteventura, La Gomera and El Hierro

3,350 BC   AD 1   350   700   1050   1400

3,000 BC Arrival of African migrants

AD 150 Ptolemy charts the position of the Canary Islands on his world map

1312 Lanzarotto Malocello lands on the most north-easterly island of the archipelago

Anaterue – Guanche chieftain

◀ Christopher Columbus, discoverer of the Americas

The Guanches

The ancient inhabitants of the Canary Islands were known as the Guanches from the words "guan" (meaning "man") and "che" (meaning "white mountain"), referring to the snow-capped Teide volcano on Tenerife. According to Spanish historical records, the Guanches were tall, strongly built and blue-eyed. Their origins and date of arrival on the islands are still unknown, as is the language they spoke. Their society was based on a tribal structure, with a king or chieftain at its head. They worshipped Abor – a powerful god who could bring rain and stop the flow of lava. Their tools and weapons were produced from roughly cut wood, stone and bone.

Rock Carvings
These rock carvings, many of which have been preserved, once adorned caves inhabited by the Guanches.

Guanche family
in their cave

Rock Paintings
Cave paintings bear testimony to the artistic skill of the Guanches. Gáldar's Cueva Pintada, on Gran Canaria, is decorated with striking red, white and black geometric patterns.

Quern
The Guanches used querns (mills) made from lava to grind barley, to make their staple, a cornmeal called *gofio*.

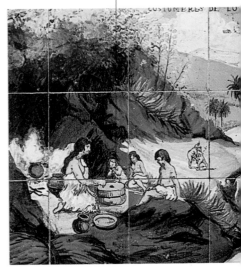

Daily Life of the Guanches
One of three small mosaics in the main park in Santa Cruz de Tenerife illustrates the life of the Guanche tribe during peacetime. In a landscape and climate similar to that of the present day, the Guanches cultivated land and raised animals.

Cave Dwellings
The Guanches lived in natural caves, such as La Palma's Cueva de Belmaco, or in grottos carved into the rocks. Caves also served as granaries and places of worship, and were used to bury the dead.

Domestic Animals
Goats and sheep are the only animals that can find food in the hard mountainous terrain of the Canary Islands. The Guanches depended on these animals to supply them with skins, milk and meat.

Shepherds fought daily battles for better grazing grounds for their flocks of sheep and goats. In the face of external dangers, they would unite and become warriors.

Guanche Chief
Guanches were led into battles by their tribal kings, known as "guanarteme" in Gran Canaria and as "menceyes" in Tenerife and La Palma.

ICHES Y VALLE DE OROTAVA

Long, strong poles or spears were used as weapons in battles and were also useful when traversing the difficult mountainous terrain.

Remains of the Guanche Culture

Apart from the caves, the early indigenous population lived in somewhat primitive low huts built of stone, such as those that have been partially reconstructed in the ethnographic park Mundo Aborigen, in Gran Canaria. The bodies of the tribal elders were mummified, and you can see them today in Canarian museums, along with stone and bone ornaments, clay pots and woven bags.

Circular Guanche tombs in Mundo Aborigen, Gran Canaria

The mummified skull of a Guanche is one of many such items housed in the Museo de la Naturaleza y el Hombre, located in Tenerife.

Founding of Santa Cruz de Tenerife

The 15th Century

The Portuguese followed in the footsteps of the Spanish conquistadors in the mid-15th century. The rivalry between the two seafaring powers lasted until 1479, when the Alcáçovas Treaty gave the Canary Islands to Spain, who, in return, let Portugal annex the Azores, the Cape Verde Islands and Madeira.

Mosaic depicting the ship of Christopher Columbus

The following years brought a new wave of bloody conquests: 1483 saw the fall of Gran Canaria, followed five years later by La Gomera and, in 1496, La Palma. In 1495, following three years of intense battles, Tenerife, which had put up the fiercest resistance, fell into the hands of the Spanish. The Guanches, deprived of their land and forced into slavery, were soon dying out. Those who survived were forcibly converted to Christianity and became assimilated.

In 1541, Italian historian Girolamo Benzoni, on visiting the islands, noted that the Guanches were "nearly extinct" and that their language had not survived the century following their subjugation by Spain.

The Sugar Era

The 16th century brought about a rapid growth in the numbers of European settlers on the islands, particularly in Gran Canaria and Tenerife. Sugar cane, imported from Madeira, was used to produce sugar, which quickly became the main export from each island. Large sugar-cane plantations sprang up, employing European workers and African slaves, despite the ban on the slave trade introduced by Spain in 1537. This industry resulted in the transformation of the local ecosystem. Stripped of their trees, forests gave way to sugar-cane fields, and bare slopes became prone to erosion.

The growth of the sugar industry was halted by the colonization of America and the Caribbean, where sugar could be produced more cheaply.

Castillo San Miguel, guarding Garachico against pirates

1478–83 The Spanish, led by Juan Rejón and Pedro de Vera, occupy Gran Canaria

1494–6 Occupation of Tenerife by Alonso Fernández de Lugo completes the conquest of the archipelago

1537 The Spanish introduce a ban on the slave trade, which is not observed in the Canary Islands

| 1450 | 1500 | 1550 | 1600 |

1479 The Alcáçovas Treaty gives the Canary Islands to Spain

Christopher Columbus stopped in the Canary Islands to provision his ships

1588 *Descripción de las Islas Canarias*, by Leonardo Torriani

The Wine Trade

The Canary Islands' economy was saved by the growing export demand for wine, which was produced mainly in Tenerife and Gran Canaria. So popular was the local Malvasia that it was praised by the character Falstaff in Shakespeare's play *Henry IV, Part II*. The Canary Islands' Company was founded in 1665 in London, and came to monopolize the Canarian wine trade in Great Britain.

Map from around 1600 showing the Canary Islands situated off the west coast of Africa

At the turn of the 18th century, however, income from wine production fell drastically. One of the reasons was a plague of locusts from 1685 to 1687 that destroyed the vineyards. In addition, the emergence of competition from new brands of wine from Madeira and Málaga, and the War of the Spanish Succession, which Spain fought with England and Portugal, reduced the demand.

The closing years of the 18th century witnessed a further reduction in wine production and export. This led to the near total collapse of the economy on the islands. It was at this time that carmine – a natural dye obtained from cochineal insects – became a major export. To this day the islands are major exporters of cochineal, used to produce dye for the food industry.

The Islands Under Attack

Spanish rule of the Canary Islands was threatened almost from the start. Throughout the 16th and 17th centuries, pirates and slave traders, from Europe and the northwest coast of Africa, harassed the islands. Several castles were built during this period to defend port entries from French, Dutch and British fleets; they also provided shelter for the local population when under attack. The last attempt at conquering the Canary Islands was made in 1797 by Admiral Horatio Nelson, who launched an attack on Santa Cruz de Tenerife. He not only failed to take the town, but lost his arm in the battle. The Governor of Santa Cruz, in a truly magnanimous gesture, presented the vanquished enemy with some local wine.

Ornate Baroque altar from the Iglesia de Nuestra Señora de la Regla, in Pájara, Fuerteventura

1665 Establishment of the Canary Islands' Company, in London

British fleet attacking San Sebastián de La Gomera

1797 British fleet, commanded by Admiral Horatio Nelson, attacks Santa Cruz de Tenerife

1650   **1700**   **1750**   **1800**

1666 Peasants destroy English *bodegas* in Garachico, Tenerife

1706 Garachico destroyed by the eruption of Volcán Negra

1744 Benedict XIV permits Augustine monks to establish a university in La Laguna

El Tigre gun from Santa Cruz de Tenerife

19th-Century Island Rivalries

In 1821, the Canary Islands became a province of Spain, with their capital in Santa Cruz de Tenerife. This situation served to intensify the rivalry between the two most populated islands – Tenerife and Gran Canaria. In 1852, Queen Isabella II granted duty-free status to the Canary Islands.

In view of the growing domination of Tenerife in 1911, local rule was re-established on individual islands, thus weakening the control that Santa Cruz de Tenerife exercised over the whole archipelago. In 1927, the rivalry between Santa Cruz de Tenerife and Las Palmas de Gran Canaria led to the division of the archipelago into two provinces: the western province including the islands of Tenerife, La Gomera, La Palma and El Hierro, and the eastern province

Coat of arms of the
Canary Islands

including Gran Canaria, Fuerteventura and Lanzarote. This division remains in force to this day.

The Banana Trade

The collapse of cochineal production in the 1870s led to a period of mass emigration of Canarios to Latin America. The archipelago's economy was saved by bananas, which at that time became the main export product. Their cultivation on an industrial scale was introduced by the French Consul, S. Berthelot, in 1855. Production peaked in 1913, when more than 3 million bunches of bananas were exported from Tenerife, Gran Canaria and La Palma.

The outbreak of World War I and the Allied blockade of the European continent ruined international trade, however, and banana exports dropped by more than 80 per cent. The ensuing harsh economic conditions resulted in a second wave of emigration.

The Franco Era

The proclamation of the Second Spanish Republic in Madrid, in 1931, led to increased tension. In 1936, fearing a coup d'état, the Republican government "exiled" General Francisco Franco, a hero of the Moroccan wars, to the Canaries. In July 1936, Franco seized control of the islands, marking the beginning of the Spanish Civil War, which lasted until 1939. Franco's Spain was ostracized by the international community. This hampered economic development in the Canary Islands, and resulted in yet more inhabitants emigrating during the 1950s.

Elected representatives of the first provincial government of Tenerife, in 1912

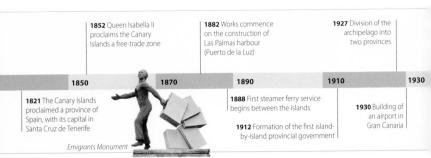

1852 Queen Isabella II proclaims the Canary Islands a free-trade zone

1882 Works commence on the construction of Las Palmas harbour (Puerto de la Luz)

1927 Division of the archipelago into two provinces

1850　　　　**1870**　　　　**1890**　　　　**1910**　　　　**1930**

1821 The Canary Islands proclaimed a province of Spain, with its capital in Santa Cruz de Tenerife

1888 First steamer ferry service begins between the islands

1930 Building of an airport in Gran Canaria

1912 Formation of the first island-by-island provincial government

Emigrants Monument

Opening the borders to sun-seeking European tourists in the 1960s failed to improve the situation. Growing resistance to Franco fed on the fertile ground of revived Canary nationalism. The Canary Islands Independence Movement (MPAIC), founded in 1963, became the vehicle of the islands' drive for independence. In the late 1970s, companies and military establishments on the Spanish mainland became targets for terrorist attacks by the nationalists.

The Canary Islands Today

Changes following Franco's death in 1975 brought about the devolution of power in Spain, and, in August 1982, the Canary Islands were granted autonomy. Local authorities are now in control of education, health services and transport, leaving matters of defence, foreign policy and finances in the hands of the central government. In 1986, Spain became a member of the European Union (EU).

Today, tourism and related services account for some 70 per cent of the islands' revenue. However, the economy of some

Sculpture at the entrance to the César Manrique Foundation in Tahiche, Lanzarote

of the islands still relies on agriculture and fishing. High unemployment and low wages continue to create problems. These, along with the need to protect the environment, present the greatest challenges to today's provincial authorities.

Several environmental programmes have been initiated to protect the vast geological wealth of the islands. El Hierro, the smallest of the Canary Islands, has become the first isolated territory in the world to meet all its energy needs using renewable wind-hydro power. This major accomplishment, together with the island's natural heritage, led to El Hierro being recognised as a UNESCO Geopark in 2014.

The Auditorio de Tenerife "Adán Martín" in Santa Cruz de Tenerife

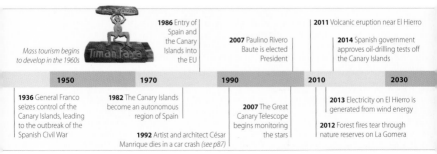

Mass tourism begins to develop in the 1960s

1986 Entry of Spain and the Canary Islands into the EU

2007 Paulino Rivero Baute is elected President

2011 Volcanic eruption near El Hierro

2014 Spanish government approves oil-drilling tests off the Canary Islands

1950	1970	1990	2010	2030

1936 General Franco seizes control of the Canary Islands, leading to the outbreak of the Spanish Civil War

1982 The Canary Islands become an autonomous region of Spain

1992 Artist and architect César Manrique dies in a car crash (see p87)

2007 The Great Canary Telescope begins monitoring the stars

2013 Electricity on El Hierro is generated from wind energy

2012 Forest fires tear through nature reserves on La Gomera

THE CANARY ISLANDS AREA BY AREA

The Canary Islands at a Glance

The Canary Islands are diverse enough to cater to all tastes, from the individual traveller to groups on package holidays. Those who shy away from the noisy modern resorts of Tenerife and Gran Canaria can find repose in the islands' interior. Fuerteventura can be recommended to admirers of beautiful windswept beaches, while Lanzarote offers a lunar landscape, spotted with craters and featuring curious architectural edifices built by the most famous Canarian artist – César Manrique. The wild, lush island of La Gomera and the perpetually green La Palma provide a paradise for hikers. El Hierro attracts lovers of nature, regional cuisine and handicrafts.

Pico del Teide *(see pp120–21)*, the highest mountain in Spain and an active volcano, is one of few places on the Canary Islands where snow can sometimes be seen.

In Santa Cruz de la Palma *(see pp146–7)* stands a replica of the *Santa María*, the ship in which Christopher Columbus "discovered" the Americas.

Santa Cruz de la Palma

LA PALMA
(See 142–153)

Atlantic Ocean

LA GOMERA
(See 124–33)

San Sebastián de La Gomera

Puerto de la Cruz · Santa Cruz de Tenerife

TENERIFE
(See 98–123)

Valverde

EL HIERRO
(See 134–41)

Hermigua *(see pp128–9)* nestles in a beautiful ravine, with steep slopes covered by the picturesque terraces of a banana plantation.

El Sabinar *(see p139)*, a remote point on El Hierro, is named after the ancient juniper trees that grow here, twisted into strange shapes by ceaseless winds.

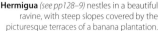

0 kilometres 30
0 miles 30

◀ Colourful houses in the beautiful town of Teror, Gran Canaria

Haría *(see p90)*, a small town lying in a valley, is reminiscent of a Saharan oasis with its low, whitewashed houses shaded by palm trees, acacias and rubber plants.

Goats are the most frequently encountered animals in Fuerteventura. Unsurprisingly, they are a symbol of the island.

LANZAROTE
(See 82–97)

Arrecife

Orchids, in a host of fabulous colours, along with numerous species of exotic birds and butterflies from all over the world, attract tourists to Palmitos Park *(see p63)*.

Puerto del Rosario

FUERTEVENTURA
(See 68–81)

Las Palmas de Gran Canaria

Atlantic Ocean

GRAN CANARIA
(See 42–67)

Maspalomas

Ibis, a wading bird with a long, sabre-like beak, is one of the main attractions of Guinate Tropical Park *(see p90)*, one of the many theme parks found throughout the larger islands.

Puerto Rico *(see p62)* is a modern resort on the south coast of Gran Canaria, offering facilities for all kinds of water sports and fishing and diving trips.

GRAN CANARIA

Lying at the heart of the archipelago and occupying an area of 1,560 sq km (602 sq miles), Gran Canaria is the third largest of the Canary Islands. It is one of the most densely populated islands, with 830,000 inhabitants – a third of the entire population of the archipelago. It is also one of the most popular islands, attracting some 3.3 million visitors each year.

The centre of Gran Canaria is occupied by the rocky volcano summit of Pico de las Nieves (see pp64–5). The mountain sides, sloping towards the ocean, are criss-crossed by deep canyons.

The island is divided by a mountain range into two climatic zones. The northern part is more humid and fertile, with long stretches of banana plantations running along the coast, while the southern part is dry and hot.

Gran Canaria's landscape displays similar diversity, with the northern and western coasts steep and rocky, and the eastern and southern slopes falling gently towards the sea. This diversity has given the island the nickname of a "miniature continent".

Gran Canaria enjoys a mild climate throughout the year, with an average air temperature of 21° C (70° F). Water temperature, however, is somewhat lower than average for these latitudes, due to a cool current flowing from the Gulf of Mexico.

The island was conquered between 1478 and 1483 by the Spanish, led by Pedro de Vera, and fully colonized during the 1520s. Today it offers a multitude of tourist attractions. Las Palmas has museums and historic buildings alongside its own beach, the Playa de las Canteras, with its nightclubs, cafés and shops. In contrast, in the rugged environs of Pico de las Nieves, hikers can follow in the footsteps of the Guanches.

Large sand dunes surrounding Maspalomas

◄ A picturesque street in the town of Puerto de Mogan

Exploring Gran Canaria

Gran Canaria is the second most frequently visited island of the archipelago (after Tenerife). Each year it receives over 3.3 million visitors, who are attracted by its fine scenery, consistently mild climate and numerous tourist attractions. The island's capital, Las Palmas, is situated in the northeast; it has a fascinating history *(see pp31–7)*, and its colonial past is reflected in its delightful old town and many museums. Sun-seekers favour the warmer, southern parts of the island, where sunshine is guaranteed all year round. Maspalomas is one of the largest, purpose-built tourist developments in Spain. At its heart is Playa del Inglés with its vast hotels, restaurants, bars, nightclubs and, above all, golden sandy beaches.

Getting There

Gran Canaria has scheduled flight connections with all the islands in the archipelago and with mainland Spain, as well as charter flights from many European cities. There are regular ferries to Tenerife, Lanzarote and Fuerteventura. Gran Canaria has a good network of bus routes, but to reach some of the villages, particularly those at the centre of the island, you will need to hire a car. Most of the island's roads, major and minor, are well surfaced.

Atlantic Ocean

Santa Cruz de Tenerife

Las Palmas de Gran Canaria

Locator Map

Faro de Sardina
Túmulo de la Guancha
Sardina
GALDAR 11
Cenobio Valer
GC2
10
SANTA MARÍA DE GUÍA DE GRAN CANARIA
Puerto de las Nieves
12 **AGAETE**
GC70
San Pedro
Fagajesto
El Risco
Tamadaba 1444 m
Pinos de Gáldar 1377 m
GC200
Parque Natural de Tamadaba
Mirador del Balcón
Acusa
Artenara
Tejeda
Puerto de la Aldea
LA ALDEA DE SAN NICOLÁS 13
GC210
Roque Bentaiga 1412 m
GC60
Roque Nublo 1760 m
GC200
Montaña de Sándara 1570 m
El Juncal
Ayaca
Tasartico
Tasarte
Parque Rural del Nublo
Embalse de Soria
Embalse de Chira
Las Casas de Veneguera
Mogán
Parque Natural de Pilancón
Playa de Tasarte
Lomo Central
Playa de Veneguera
Las Burrillas
El Sao
Palmitos Park
PUERTO DE MOGÁN 14
Taurito
Playa de Amadores
Monataña de la Data
PUERTO RICO 15
GC500
GC1
GC200
Arguineguín

Walking trail in the mountainous region of Presa de los Hornos, near Pico de las Nieves

For keys to symbols *see back flap*

Sardina del Norte, on the coast near Gáldar

Key

- ▬ Motorway
- ▬ Major road
- ▬ Minor road
- ▬ Scenic route
- ▲ Summit

Sights at a Glance

- ❶ Las Palmas de Gran Canaria *pp46–51*
- ❷ Tafira Alta
- ❸ Caldera de Bandama
- ❹ Santa Brígida
- ❺ Vega de San Mateo
- ❻ Teror
- ❼ Arucas
- ❽ Firgas
- ❾ Moya
- ❿ Santa María de Guía de Gran Canaria
- ⓫ Gáldar
- ⓬ Agaete
- ⓭ La Aldea de San Nicolás
- ⓮ Puerto de Mogán
- ⓯ Puerto Rico
- ⓰ Maspalomas
- ⓱ San Bartolomé de Tirajana
- ⓳ Santa Lucía
- ⓴ Agüimes
- ㉑ Ingenio
- ㉒ Barranco de Guayadeque
- ㉓ Telde

Tours

- ⓲ Around Pico de las Nieves *pp64–65*

Orchids in Palmitos Park, near Maspalomas

Map labels

Las Coloradas
La Isleta
Bañaderos
El Roque
Cambalud
MOYA ❾
❽ FIRGAS
GC2
❼ ARUCAS
Tamaraceite
LAS PALMAS DE GRAN CANARIA ❶
GC21
San Lorenzo
GC3
San Cristobal
Jardín Botánico Viera y Clavijo
GC30
GC75
❻ TEROR
Vallseco
TAFIRA ALTA ❷
Marzagan
SANTA BRÍGIDA ❹
CALDERA DE BANDAMA ❸
GC15
La Estrella
VEGA DE SAN MATEO ❺
GC15
Tenteniguada
Valsequillo
GC41
TELDE ❷❸
Melenara
GC130
GC100
Pico de las Nieves 1949 m
Las Breñas
El Goro
Cuevas de Cuatro Puertas
BARRANCO DE GUAYADEQUE ㉒
Aguatona
SAN BARTOLOMÉ DE TIRAJANA ⓱
INGENIO ㉑
Punta de Gando
SANTA LUCÍA ⓳
Temisas
AGÜIMES ⓴
Carrizal
La Sorrueda
Vargas
GC100
ataga
GC1
Cruce de Arinaga
GC65
Sardina
Arinaga
Aldea Blanca
Vecindario
GC60
Hoya de Toledo
Sioux City Park
Punta de Corral
Mundo Aborigen
Juan Grande
Castillo del Romeral
GC500
San Agustín
Playa del Inglés
MASPALOMAS ⓰
Dunas de Maspalomas

0 kilometres   5
0 miles   5

❶ Las Palmas de Gran Canaria

The largest city of the archipelago, Las Palmas was founded on 24 June 1478 by the Spanish conquistadors. It soon became an important port for ships sailing around the African continent and heading for America. In the late 19th century, Sir Alfred Lewis Jones founded the Gran Canaria Coal Company here, and the town began to flourish. The port became the main stopping point on the transatlantic route and a new town sprang up around it. In 1927, Las Palmas became the capital of the eastern province of the Canary Islands, encompassing Gran Canaria, Fuerteventura and Lanzarote.

Sights at a Glance

① Castillo de la Luz
② Harbour
③ Playa de las Canteras
④ Parque Santa Catalina
⑤ Museo Elder
⑥ Muelle de Santa Catalina
⑦ Playa de las Alcaravaneras
⑧ Parque Doramas
⑨ Hotel Santa Catalina
⑩ Museo Néstor
⑪ Parque San Telmo
⑫ Casa-Museo Pérez Galdós
⑬ Teatro Pérez Galdós
⑭ Casa de Colón
⑮ Catedral de Santa Ana
⑯ CAAM
⑰ Museo Canario

| 0 metres | 500 |
| 0 yards | 500 |

The pretty marina in Las Palmas harbour

Exploring La Isleta and Playa de las Canteras

Situated on a small, round peninsula, La Isleta is a residential quarter built on steep terrain, featuring narrow streets and small local shops, bars and street vendors offering dried fish. The peninsula is separated from the modern part of Las Palmas by a narrow inlet.

Playa de las Canteras is a mixed district of hotels and offices. Scores of hotels, shops, bars and restaurants line the seaside promenade – Paseo de las Canteras. This district has one of the town's biggest shopping centres – Las Arenas.

🏰 Castillo de la Luz

C/Juan Rejón, s/n. **Tel** 928 461 372.
Open 11am–7pm Mon–Sat; 11am–2pm Sun (by appt.). **Closed** between exhibitions. 🎨

On the south shore of La Isleta, near the harbour, stands Castillo de la Luz – the Castle of Light. This well-preserved fortress dates from the 16th century and was built to guard the town of Las Palmas against pirates. It was restored in 1990, and is now used as a venue for art exhibitions.

🚢 Harbour

Las Palmas harbour boasts a long and glorious history and is an important factor in the prosperity of Gran Canaria. Around 1,000 ships use the harbour each month. The traffic here was even heavier when the Canary Islands enjoyed duty-free status and the harbour was one of the most important in the world.

The harbour area includes a marina, which is the starting point for the annual boat race from the Canary Islands to Santa Lucia. It is held between November and December.

🏖 Playa de las Canteras

This stretch of yellowish-brown sand is 2.8 km (1.7 miles) long and in places 100 metres (328 ft) wide. This is the best beach in Las Palmas. It is well served by cafés and restaurants. La Barra, a natural rock barrier protecting the beach against strong surf, makes bathing possible, even in rough conditions.

At the southern end of the beach is the Auditorio Alfredo Kraus, the home of the

The long and sandy Playa de las Canteras

For hotels and restaurants in this region see p158 and pp170–71

Colourful fun at the Las Palmas carnival

Philharmonic Orchestra of Las Palmas. The building, named after the Canarian tenor Alfredo Kraus (1927–99), has ten concert halls that are also used as meeting venues.

Exploring Santa Catalina
The narrow streets of this district are filled with Indian shops, offering electronic goods, alcohol, tobacco products, jewellery and clothes. Shopping here is not quite as profitable these days, but it is still acceptable to haggle in order to pick up some bargains. Santa Catalina has many hotels, most of which seem to face north, towards the long, golden sands of the popular Las Canteras beach.

🅲 Parque Santa Catalina
At the heart of the district is Santa Catalina Park, which has long been established as one of the city's major squares. Thanks to its proximity to the port, it is traditionally one of the first places visited by those

VISITORS' CHECKLIST

Practical Information
🗺 383,000. 🈷 Parque de San Telmo. **Tel** 928 446 824.
📅 Sun. 🎭 Carnival (Feb/Mar); Festival Internacional de Cine de Las Palmas (Mar/Apr); Día de San Juan (24 Jun).
🌐 laspalmasgc.es
🌐 grancanaria.com

Transport
✈ 18 km (11 miles) south.
🚌 Estación de Guaguas.

who arrive by boat, and as a result, there are a great many bars and restaurants to choose from. Be on the lookout for the shoeshiners, who provide a link to the city's past. There is also a tourist information office here.

🏛 Museo Elder
Parque Santa Catalina, s/n. **Tel** 828 011 828. **Open** 10am–8pm Tue–Sun. 🈂
🌐 museoelder.org
The wonders of technology and science are explained in this interactive museum. Exhibits explain everything from gravity and supersonic speeds to intelligent robots.

🚢 Muelle de Santa Catalina
On the south side of Avenida Marítima del Norte is the ferry terminal, which provides ferry and hydrofoil services to Tenerife and the other islands. This modern building is visible from a considerable distance away.

Sunbathers at Playa de las Alcaravaneras

The exclusive Hotel Santa Catalina, in Ciudad Jardín

(*see below*). Views of the park can be enjoyed by non-resident visitors from the bar.

🏛 Museo Néstor

Pueblo Canario. **Tel** 928 245 135. **Open** 10am–7pm Tue–Sat; 10:30am–2:30pm Sun, public holidays.

w laspalmasgc.es/mnestor

Opened in 1958, the museum exhibits works by Néstor, including sketches and symbolic paintings. One of the museum's highlights is the dome of the rotunda, which is decorated with eight murals illustrating Torre's *Poema del Mar* (Sea Poem).

🚇 Playa de Alcaravaneras

South of the ferry terminal, within the district of Alcaravaneras, is Alcaravaneras beach,1-km (0.6-mile) of golden sand. This is the second longest of the Las Palmas beaches, after Las Canteras. The modern yacht marina of the **Real Club Náutico**, south of the beach, is packed with glamorous boats.

Exploring Ciudad Jardín

Ciudad Jardín is an oasis of peace in the bustling city of Las Palmas. This leafy residential district was created in the early 20th century by British residents, who dominated the economic life of the town at that time.

This "Garden City", with its regular layout, has many embassies and beautiful houses that display a variety of architectural styles. The district's main feature is Parque Doramas with its interesting statues.

🌳 Parque Doramas

This beautifully landscaped park, featuring water cascades and a municipal swimming pool, is named after the Guanche chieftain Doramas, who, in the late 15th century, put up a fierce resistance against the Spanish invaders. His struggles are symbolized by the monument depicting Guanches tumbling over a precipice to escape capture.

🏨 Hotel Santa Catalina

C/Leon y Castillo, 227. **Tel** 928 243 040. **w** hotelsantacatalina.com

Set among the sub-tropical greenery of the Parque Doramas stands the Hotel Santa Catalina. Originally built in 1890 for the British employees of the Canary Island's Company (*see p35*), the building was redesigned between 1947 and 1952 to blue-prints left by the late Canary artist Néstor Martin Fernandez de la Torre

Tiled café in the Modernist kiosk in Parque San Telmo

Exploring in Triana

To the north of the motorway that borders the area of Vegueta lies Triana, the commercial district of the town, marked to the north by **Calle Bravo Murillo**, along which runs the old city wall. This street leads up to an old castle – **Castillo de Mata**. The centre of this regularly shaped area is cut across by **Calle Mayor de Triana**. The ground floors of this boulevard's Modernist houses are occupied by shops. A bust of Christopher Columbus, unveiled in 1892, is one of many landmarks symbolizing the town's links with great geographic discoveries.

🌳 Parque San Telmo

San Telmo is reached via **Calle Mayor Triana**. At the edge of the park stands the small, 17th-century **San Telmo Chapel**, devoted to this patron saint of fishermen. On the opposite side is a Modernist

---

Néstor Martín Fernández da la Torre

Painting by Néstor in Museo Néstor (*see above*)

Néstor Martín Fernández de la Torre (1887–1938), known simply as 'Néstor,' was one of the most original artists to come from the Canary Islands. Born in Las Palmas, he studied in Paris, where he became familiar with the work of Pre-Raphaelite, Symbolist and Secessionist artists. In 1910, he represented Spain in the World's Fair in Brussels. He produced paintings, stage designs, theatre and opera costumes and interior designs, but was known principally for his murals. In 1934, he settled in Gran Canaria and devoted the last years of his life to developing and publicizing Canarian art forms.

kiosk, built in 1923 and decorated with ceramic tiles. On the side of the park is the **Gobierno Militar** building, where, on 18 July 1936, General Franco declared his opposition to the Republican government, signalling the start of the Spanish Civil War.

🏛 Casa-Museo Pérez Galdós

C/Cano, 2 & 6. **Tel** 928 366 976.
Open 10am–6pm Tue–Sun. 📷📷
🌐 casamuseoperezgaldos.com

The Museum of Benito Pérez Galdós, the most distinguished writer from the Canary Islands, occupies the house in which he was born and where he lived until 1862. This five-storey building has a small patio adorned with a statue of the writer. The museum, which opened in 1964, still has the original interior decor. It contains objects associated with the writer's life, as well as photographs of many actors who appeared in his plays.

🎭 Teatro Pérez Galdós

Pl. Stagno, 1. **Tel** 928 433 334.
🌐 teatroperezgaldos.es

In the south of Triana, almost opposite Mercado Municipal de Vegueta, stands a theatre named after the writer Benito Pérez Galdós (1843–1920).

Built in 1919, this structure is the work of architect Miguel Martín Fernández de la Torre. The opulent interior and the auditorium for 1,400 spectators were designed by his brother, Néstor Martín Fernández de la Torre. Today this is the best theatre

Patio of Casa-Museo Pérez Galdós in Triana, with the writer's statue

in Las Palmas and one of the most famous in the Canary Islands.

Exploring Vegueta

Vegueta, the oldest district of Las Palmas, consists of a labyrinth of narrow streets, lined with historic houses and beautiful patios. Equally charming are the old town squares, including **Plaza de Santo Domingo**.

Right at the edge of the district is an indoor market selling a variety of goods, including fruit, fish, meat, cheeses and local handicrafts.

🏛 Catedral de Santa Ana

Plaza Santa Ana.

The building of the cathedral began in 1497 and took 400 years to complete. The lengthy gestation affected both its architectural form and interior furnishings.

The Neo-Classical façade hides Gothic vaults resting on slender columns, altar retables, Baroque pulpits and sculptures by José Luján Pérez. The crypt contains

the tomb of José de Viera y Clavijo, Canarian traveller and the author of *History of the Canary Islands*. Another chapel is the resting place of diplomat Fernando de León y Castillo (*see p67*). A lift in the south tower whisks visitors to the viewing terrace, which offers outstanding views.

🏛 Centro Atlántico de Arte Moderno (CAAM)

Los Balcones, 11. **Tel** 928 311 800.
Open 10am–9pm Tue–Sat;
10am–2pm Sun. 📷 🌐 caam.net

CAAM organizes exhibitions, mainly of avant-garde art. It also has its own collection of works by artists influential in shaping 20th-century Canarian art and provides a venue for academic symposia on the subject of modern art. In contrast to the 18th-century façade of this former hotel, the modern interior, designed by Francisco Sainz de Oiza and Martín Chirino, is light and airy.

🏛 Museo Canario

C/Dr Verneau, 2. **Tel** 928 336 800.
Open 10am–8pm Mon–Fri; 10am–2pm Sat–Sun. 📷 🌐 elmuseocanario.com

The Canary Island Museum opened in 1879 and was refurbished in the mid-1980s. The collection includes such archaeological finds as statuettes of gods, pottery, jewellery and tools of the Guanches, as well as skulls, skeletons and mummies. Among the star attractions are copies of the paintings discovered in Gáldar's Cueva Pintada, as well as *pintaderas* – terracotta stamps used for printing geometric patterns on clothes.

The Neo-Classical Catedral de Santa Ana

Casa de Colón

In the oldest district of Las Palmas stands the palace of the first governors of the island. According to tradition, Christopher Columbus stayed here in 1492 during a break in his voyage while one of his ships was repaired, hence the name Casa de Colón, or Columbus House. This charming building, with its beautiful wooden balconies, was rebuilt in 1777. Since 1952 it has housed a museum that includes models and artifacts relating to voyages made by the famous navigator.

Ship's Interior
A reconstructed, full-size fragment of the interior of *La Niña*, one of the ships that sailed with Columbus's expedition, demonstrates the living conditions that sailors endured while crossing the oceans.

Ground floor

Main entrance

Santa María
Models of the three ships from Columbus's fleet (Santa María, La Niña, La Pinta) and navigation instruments illustrate the equipment available to mariners in the early 16th century.

Key

- Ecuadorian art
- Mexican culture
- Yanomami culture
- Cartography and nautical instruments
- Columbus and his voyages
- Canary Islands and discovery of the New World
- Las Palmas de Gran Canaria
- Gran Canaria
- 16th- to 20th-century paintings

Astrolabe
One of the early navigational instruments, the astrolabe was developed in the 2nd century BC. It was used to measure the height of heavenly bodies above the horizon. The collection here includes a bronze astrolabe from the first half of the 16th century.

★ St Lucia

This painting by Guamart de Amberes is part of the museum's vast collection of works by 16th-century Dutch and Italian painters. Some of these collections belong to the Museo del Prado. They include paintings by Guido Reni, the Carracci brothers and Guercino.

VISITORS' CHECKLIST

Practical Information
Colón 1. **Tel** 928 312 373.
Open 10am– 6pm Mon–Sat,
10am–3pm Sun. **Closed** 1 Jan,
24, 25 & 31 Dec. 🖂
ⓦ casadecolon.com

Transport
🚌 Alameda de Colón,
Estación Teatro Pérez Galdós,
Mercado de Vegueta.

First floor

★ External Portal

Casa de Colón features a magnificent portal crowned by a Tudor arch. This exquisite ornament combines plant and animal motifs, with two lions supporting the town's crests.

Courtyard

At the centre of the inner courtyard stands an old well. Centuries-old galleries and arcades, in typical Canary style, keep the rooms cool and shady.

Basement vaults

★ Pre-Columbian Art

An extensive collection of pre-Columbian artifacts of gold and other metals includes original items and replicas associated with the Spanish conquests in Central and South America.

Gallery Guide

The exhibits are arranged on three levels, in 12 rooms surrounding two inner courtyards and in underground chambers, which contain treasures of pre-Columbian art. The ground floor is given to Columbus's expeditions, the development of cartography and the history of the Canary Islands as the gateway to the New World. The first-floor rooms present an overview of Las Palmas history, from the 15th until the 19th century. There are also separate rooms displaying items on loan from Madrid's Museo del Prado.

Fishing boats moored at the marina in Puerto de Mogán ▶

Jardín Botánico Viera y Clavijo, near Tarifa Alta

plants from all the islands in the archipelago. They include species of the native Canary palm, Canary pine and heathers. Also featured are plants from other regions including the Azores, Madeira and the Cape Verde Islands, as well as two thousand cacti, from all corners of the world.

🏠 Jardín Botánico Viera y Clavijo
Tel 928 219 580.
Open 9am–7:30pm daily (to 6pm in winter).
🌐 jardincanario.org

❷ Tafira Alta

🏔 2,760. 🚻 Jardín Canario. **Tel** 928 219 580. 🎉 San Francisco (Oct).

Set among the hills is the small town of Tafira Alta, famous for its beautiful residences surrounded by gardens. These colourful villas, featuring a variety of architectural forms and details, have maintained the original colonial atmosphere of the place. Many houses show the influence of Moorish or Bauhaus style. No wonder then, that Tarifa Alta is a favourite with Las Palmas' financial elite and with wealthy foreigners.

At the beginning of the 20th century, the British built several elegant hotels here, including **Los Frailes**. This was used as a meeting place by General Franco's supporters as they plotted to overthrow Spain's Republican government in 1936.

Environs
The Botanical Gardens, Jardín Botánico Viera y Clavijo, situated on the outskirts of town, are named after José de Viera y Clavijo (1731–1813), the author of the *Canary Islands Dictionary of Plants*. The gardens were created in 1952 by a Swede, Eric Sventenius (1910–73), who remained their director until his death. Set on terraces and growing in their natural environment are

❸ Caldera de Bandama

It is worth travelling the 5-km (3-mile) distance from Tafira, half of which is over a narrow mountain road, in order to reach the peak of the volcano Pico de Bandama. This relatively low mountain (570 m/1,870 ft) provides one of the best viewpoints on Gran Canaria. The Mirador de Bandama offers a magnificent view over the whole of Las Palmas and the mountainous centre of the island. Below is the vast volcanic caldera of Bandama, 1,000 m (3,280 ft) in diameter and 200 m (650 ft) deep. It is named after a Flemish merchant, Daniel von Damme. In the 16th century, von Damme, together with his wife Juana Vera, who was born in Gran Canaria, grew vines

inside the crater. Today the area is overgrown with orange and fig trees and palms. Eucalyptus and agaves grow on the slopes, among shrubs and bushes.

A golf course, just south of Pico de Bandama, was set up by English residents of the island in 1891. It is the oldest golf course in Spain.

❹ Santa Brígida

🏔 19,000. **Tel** 928 648 181. 🚌 🏪 Sat–Sun. 🎉 Corpus Christi (Jun).

The prosperous old town of Santa Brígida lies on the slopes of a gully covered with cypress and tall palms. Its picturesque narrow streets are lined with eucalyptus trees and flower-filled balconies. As a result of its proximity to Las Palmas, Santa Brígida is often visited by the capital's inhabitants.

The slopes of the neighbouring mountain are clothed with vineyards producing Vino del Monte – the best red wine on the island. The terrace in front of **Santa Brígida Parish Church** provides a good view over the surrounding palm groves. This triple-nave, Neo-Gothic basilica was built in 1904 on the site of a chapel constructed in 1520 by Isabel Guerra, the grand-daughter of Pedro Guerra – a conquistador and one of the conquerors of Gran Canaria. The chapel was subsequently replaced by a church built in 1580. This, in turn, was almost destroyed by fire in the late 19th century. The only part that escaped destruction was the tower, built in 1756.

Caldera de Bandama, rich in vegetation

Annual Fiesta de la Virgen del Pino, Teror

❺ Vega de San Mateo

🏠 7,800. **Tel** 928 661 350. 🚌 Sat, Sun. 🎉 San Mateo (21 Sep).

This small town is situated in a fertile, green valley 26 km (16 miles) from Las Palmas. It is known for its large agricultural market, which is held every weekend. As well as fruits, vegetables and numerous types of cheese, the local farmers also bring goats, pigs and cows for sale. San Mateo is equally known for its wickerwork baskets and for producing Canary Island knives, leather goods and woodwork. These and other local arts and crafts are often available at the weekend market.

On Calle Principal stands the church of San Mateo, a fine example of neo-Canary architecture. Above this two-nave building hangs a bell sent from Cuba by local emigrants. The church also houses a 17th-century statue of St Matthew – the town's patron saint.

❻ Teror

🏠 12,700. 🚌 ℹ️ C/Padre Cueto, 2. **Tel** 928 613 808. 🚌 Sun. 🎉 Fiesta del Agua (last Sun in Jul), Virgen del Pino (6–8 Sep). 🌐 **teror.es**

Since her first appearance atop a pine tree in 1481, Nuestra Señora del Pino (Our Lady of the Pines) has played an important role in the history and everyday life of Gran Canaria. In 1914, Pope Pius XII proclaimed her the patron saint of the island. Teror, with its sanctuary, became the religious capital of the island. Every year, in early September, the town is visited by many pilgrims, who travel here from all over Gran Canaria.

Large historic houses line the town's main square, **Plaza de Nuestra Señora del Pino**. Some of these mansions date from the 16th century and have lavishly carved wooden and stone balconies.

The basilica of **Nuestra Señora del Pino**, completed in 1767, was the third church to be built on this site. Only the tower remains from the earlier church; it dates from 1708. The octagonal shape and striking mix of Moorish and Baroque elements make the tower a distinctive landmark.

The main feature of the large, triple-nave interior is the vast, Baroque altar with its 15th-century carved figure of the Virgin. The Virgen (known both as of the pine and of the snow) is the patron saint of the island and the reason for one of the biggest fiestas in the Canary Islands (see p27). Other attractions include the Treasure Room, which contains precious gifts, donated at past festivals, to celebrate the saint.

Not far from the church is **Plaza Doña María Teresa de Bolívar**, named after María Teresa, the wife of Simón Bolívar – a hero of South America's fight for independence. Her family came from Teror, and the family crest adorns the square. The **Casa Museo de los Patrones de la Virgen**, built on the site of Bolívar's former home, is a museum displaying old photographs, plus weapons and furniture, including the bed slept in by King Alfonso XIII during a 1906 visit.

Central part of the church façade in Teror

🏛️ **Casa Museo de los Patrones de la Virgen**
Plaza Nuestra Señora del Pino, 8. **Tel** 928 630 239. **Open** 11am–4pm Mon–Fri, 10am–2pm Sun. 🎟️

Drawing room in Casa Museo de los Patrones de la Virgen in Teror

● Arucas

🏘 36,800. 🚌 *i* C/León y Castillo, 10.
Tel 928 623 136. 🛒 Mon–Sat.
🎭 Corpus Christi (Jun).

When approaching Arucas, the first sight you see is the towers of the Neo-Gothic parish church of **San Juan**. The church, mistakenly called a "cathedral", was designed by Manual Vega March and built in 1909. As well as the fine stained-glass windows and retable, the interior features the sculpture of Cristo Yacente (the Recumbent Christ), which is the work of a local sculptor, Manuel Ramos.

The old **town hall** in Plaza de la Constitución, designed by José A. López de Echegarret, was built in 1875 and then rebuilt in 1932. On the opposite side of the square is the leafy **town park**, which boasts many species of rare tropical trees, including the soapbark tree (*Quillaja saponaria*).

Encircling the park, **Calle de la Heredad** features one of the town's most beautiful buildings, **Heredad de Aguas de Arucas y Firgas**, which was built in 1908 and now houses the Water Board. In the second half of the 19th century, and the early years of the 20th century,

Ceramic ornaments in Paseo de Gran Canaria, Firgas

the Board initiated the construction of an irrigation system and the town itself acquired its present shape. The Canary Islands' largest **rum factory** was built in Arucas in 1884. The factory has a good museum devoted to the history and distillation method of the spirit. Near the factory entrance stands an early 18th-century chapel – **La Ermita de San Pedro**.

Environs

About 2 km (1 mile) north of Arucas stands the **Montaña de Arucas**. At the highest point of the town is a restaurant that offers panoramic views of the town and the entire island.

● Firgas

🏘 7,600. **Tel** 928 616 747. 🚌
🎭 San Luis (21 Jun).

Firgas is famous for its production of sparkling mineral water. The water is drawn from a spring some 6 km (4 miles) away, in Barranco de la Virgen, and 200,000 bottles a day are produced. Firgas water is very popular throughout the islands, where there is a shortage of fresh water.

A feature of Firgas, which celebrated its 500th anniversary in 1988, is the Paseo de Gran Canaria, where cascades of water flow along passages that were laid out in 1995. On either side of the passage, by the walls of surrounding houses, are benches with back-rests decorated with landscapes or historic symbols of Gran Canaria. The white walls of the houses feature colourful town crests. Above **Plaza de San Roque**, the passage is filled with giant slabs with ceramic maps and views of the individual islands. These provide an unusual lesson in the geography of the Canary Islands. Still further along the passage there is a fine display of the flags of all the Canary Islands fluttering in the breeze.

The historic 15th-century **Molino de Gofio** and the 19th-century fountain were restored in 1988. The whole town is decorated with modern sculptures, including an amusing statue of a peasant with a pink cow.

Neo-Gothic Parish Church of San Juan, Arucas

❾ Moya

🏔 8,000. 🛈 C/Juan Delgado, (Parque Pico Lomito) 6, 928 612 348. 🚍 🎪 Sun. 🎭 Virgen de la Candelaria (2 Feb), San Antonio (13 Jun).

Tucked away from the main tourist attractions, the road to this small town meanders through volcanic valleys, with countless turns and bends. The village is worth visiting for its vast Neo-Romanesque church, dating from the first half of the 20th century. The church is imposing with two towers and a position at the edge of the **Barranco de Moya** precipice – a gully criss-crossed with wild crevasses.

Moya is the birthplace of Tomás Morales – a Modernist Canarian poet. The house in which he was born and lived was converted into a museum, **Casa-Museo Tomás Morales**, in 1976. There is a permanent exhibition dedicated to the poet, which includes photographs, manuscripts and first editions of his works, displayed in rooms decorated in period style. The museum also organizes exhibitions of contemporary art.

By the entrance to the nearby catacomb cemetery, typical of the Canary Islands, stands a large stone cross – a monument to the victims of the Spanish Civil War.

🏛 Casa-Museo Tomás Morales
Plaza de Tomás Morales. **Tel** 928 620 217. **Open** 10am–6pm Tue–Sun (Jul–Sep: to 7pm). 🌐 **tomasmorales.com**

Tomás Morales (1884–1921)

Morales is hailed as one of the Canary Islands' most outstanding poets. Although he completed medical studies at the university in 1909 and practised in Agaete and Las Palmas, his true passion was poetry. He started writing poems at the age of 15 and had his first works published in 1902. In 1908 his first book, *Poems of Glory, Love and Sea* appeared, and two years later Las Palmas Theatre Group staged his *Dinner at Simon's House* – a dramatic prose poem. His strong identification with his homeland is reflected in his work – a complex brew of feelings that combine a love of the sea, loneliness, warmth and eclecticism. His great poem *Ode to Atlantic* celebrates man, ship and ocean.

Bust of Morales in front of the museum in Moya

❿ Santa María de Guía de Gran Canaria

🏔 14,000. 🛈 C/San José, 9, 928 553 043. 🚍 🎭 Fiesta del Queso de Flor (Apr & May), Nuestra Señora de Guía (15 Aug), La Rama de las Marías (3rd Sun in Sep).

The only noteworthy historic building in this town is the church of **Santa María de Guía**, built on the site of a chapel erected between 1483 and 1509. Some parts of this triple-nave church date back to the 17th century; the façade was completed only in the middle of the following century.

Guía is the birthplace of José Luján Pérez (1756–1815), who was the most popular of the Canary Islands' sculptors during his lifetime. His works, such as the statue of Nuestra Señora de las Mercedes or St Sebastián, adorn the interior of the local church. However, Guía is best known for its cheese – *queso de flor* – made of cows' and goats' milk, with the flower of the blue thistle added. This gives the cheese its distinctive flavour and allows it to remain moist even when stored for a long time.

Environs

Some 5 km (3 miles) east of Guía is **Cenobio de Valerón**, a group of about 300 caves set into a cliff at various levels. The caves were used for grain storage and for religious services. Guanche individuals were chosen to spend years in solitude here, giving themselves to the service of the god Acoran. Their prayers were to ensure the god's protection for the island's people.

🏛 Cenobio de Valerón
Open 10am–6pm Tue–Sun (Oct–Mar: to 5pm). **Closed** 1, 5 & 6 Jan, 1 May, 24, 25 & 31 Dec.

Cenobio de Valerón, the largest pre-Hispanic granary in Santa María de Guía de Gran Canaria

How Rum is Made

Rum, a by-product of sugar production, is a drink normally associated with the Caribbean, where its most famous producers are Jamaica, Cuba, Barbados and Venezuela. However, the legacy of the Canary Islands' sugar plantations *(see p34)* is a respected and thriving rum industry. The local rum is generally valued for its outstanding flavour and its warming and even medicinal properties. Its alcohol content can vary from 40 to 80 per cent. It is the main ingredient of another famous beverage, grog, which is 50 per cent rum, as well as of cocktails such as Daiquiri and Cuba Libre, which use rum. One of the Canary Islands' specialities is *ron miel* – a honey rum. Rum is also used in confectionery.

1 Rum is made from sugar cane, which is processed in order to obtain sugar syrup and molasses – both are used in the later stages of production. As there are no big sugar-cane plantations on the islands, local rum is produced mainly from imported semi-finished products.

2 Inside these large vessels, sugar juices or molasses undergo a fermentation process. Strong rums are produced by combining molasses with the foam collected from the boiling juices and the brew known as "dunder". The alcohol obtained by fermentation subsequently undergoes a distillation process.

3 To ensure a refined flavour, the rum is left to mature in traditional oak barrels – a process that can last anywhere between three and ten years. The room in which the barrels are stored must be maintained at a constant temperature and humidity.

5 The Canary Islands' rums are well known even outside of the archipelago. Particularly highly regarded is the rum from La Palma – the best brand is believed to be Ron de la Aldea. Also popular are mead rums, whose ingredients include palm juice. The resulting orange coloured beverage is weaker than rum, and its unique flavour resembles neither rum nor mead.

4 Bottling and labelling are the final stages of rum production. This is a fully automatic process, which takes place in perfectly sterile conditions, with no people present. The bottles are appropriately labelled, showing the brand and provenance of the product.

Vast banana plantations around Gáldar

⓫ Gáldar

🏘 24,200. 🚌 ℹ C/Plaza de Santiago, 1, 928 895 855. 🎭 San Isidro (15 May), La Rama (20 Aug).

At the foot of Pico de Gáldar volcano stands Gáldar, a sizeable town that was once the centre of Guanche civilization. There are no traces left of the ancient court of their ruler *(Guanarteme)*, since, along with a small Spanish fort, it was destroyed to make way for the construction of the church of **Santiago de los Caballeros**. This vast Neo-Classic church has three naves and was designed by Antonio José Eduardo. The construction works started in 1778 and were not completed until the mid-19th century.

Inside the church is the *pila verde* – a baptismal font brought from Andalusia in the late 15th century and, since the island's conquest, used for baptising the local population. Other noteworthy features are the statues of Christ and the Virgin Mary – both the work of Luján Pérez.

On the square, opposite the town hall, grows the oldest dragon tree *(see p19)* in Gran Canaria, planted in 1719.

The star attraction of Gáldar is the **Cueva Pintada**. Discovered in 1873, the cave is decorated with rock paintings consisting of geometric patterns. Following conservation works, carried out between 1970 and 1974, the cave was closed to prevent the paintings from being destroyed by the increased humidity. The archaeological park features a museum. A replica of the cave can be seen at the Museo Canario in Las Palmas *(see p49)*.

Environs

Just 2 km (1 mile) or so north of Gáldar is **Túmulo de la Guancha**. Discovered in 1936 during agricultural works, this Guanche cemetery dates from the late 11th century and consists of 30 round tombs, built of vast lava blocks. These were the burial places of members of the Andamanas royal family, who ruled this part of the island.

At 6 km (4 miles) west, Sardina del Norte is a bustling fishing village and diving centre. Nestled between high cliffs and a sandy beach, it tempts swimmers with its crystal-clear water and golden sands, as well as its excellent seafood.

🏛 Parque Arqueológico Cueva Pintada

C/Audiencia, 2. Museum: **Open** Oct–May: 10am–6pm Tue–Sat, 11am–6pm Sun; Jun–Sep: 10:30am–7:30pm, Tue–Sat 11am–7pm Sun.
🌐 cuevapintada.org

⓬ Agaete

🏘 5,800. 🚌 ℹ C/Nuestra Señora de las Nieves. **Tel** 928 554 382.
🎭 Fiesta de la Rama (4 Aug).
🌐 agaete.es

Agaete lies on the northwest coast of the island, at the end of a steep ravine – **Barranco de Agaete**. Plantations of banana, papaya, avocado and mango flourish on the steep slopes. The small town of Agaete, with its narrow streets and whitewashed houses surrounded by lush greenery, has become popular

with artists and art-lovers, who have converted local houses and garages into art galleries. Despite being an old town, which celebrated its 500-year anniversary in 1981, Agaete has few historic sites. The oldest is the parish church, which was built in the second half of the 19th century. There is also a charming, small botanical garden, **Huerto de las Flores**, which features over 100 species of Canary and subtropical flora.

Punta Sardina lighthouse

Environs

About 2 km (1 mile) to the west is a small harbour, **Puerto de las Nieves**, with a terminal for ferries to Santa Cruz de Tenerife. This picturesque fishing village, nestling against tall cliffs, has become popular with tourists, drawn by its craft shops, galleries and seafood restaurants. Puerto de las Nieves' rich history can be seen in the opulent furnishings of the Ermita de las Nieves, a chapel built in the 16th century. It contains a display of model sailing ships and a triptych devoted to the Virgen de las Nieves (Virgin of the Snows), painted by the Flemish artist Joos van Cleve (1485–1540). During the Fiesta de la Rama (Branch Festival) in August, the chapel's altar is carried in a procession to the nearby parish church in Agaete.

🌿 Huerto de las Flores

C/Huertes. **Tel** 928 554 382. **Open** 10am–4pm Tue–Sat.

The whitewashed exterior of the Ermita de las Nieves

Cactualdea – a cactus park in La Aldea de San Nicolás

⑬ La Aldea de San Nicolás

🗺 8,200. 🚌 ℹ C/Doctor Fleming, s/n, 928 890 378. 🎉 Bajada de la Rama (10 Sep), El Charco (11 Sep).

A fertile, green valley, crisscrossed with ravines, is the setting for this small town. It is surrounded by plantations of banana, orange, avocado, papaya and mango, and the slopes are overgrown with cacti and bamboo. The main building worth visiting is the church of **San Nicolás**, built in 1972, featuring sculptures by Luján Pérez. It was built on the site of an old chapel dating from the early 18th century.

A popular tourist attraction is **Cactualdea** – a park with thousands of cacti imported from Madagascar, Mexico, Bolivia and Guatemala; other plants include palms, dragon trees *(see p19)* and aloe. Other features of interest include an amphitheatre, used for wrestling matches, and a Guanche Cave.

Environs
Some 9 km (6 miles) to the north is the **Mirador del Balcón** – a viewpoint poised on the edge of rugged cliffs, 500 m (1,640 ft) above the sea. It offers views over northeastern Gran Canaria.

🌵 **Cactualdea**
Tel 928 891 228. **Open** 10am–6pm daily. 🅿 🇼 grancanarialocal.com/cactualdea-park

⑭ Puerto de Mogán

🗺 1,300. 🚌 ℹ C/General Franco, 928 158 804. 🚢 Fri. 🎉 Virgen del Carmen (16 Jul).

Easily accessible by car, via an extension of the motorway GC1, this picturesque town and yachting marina lie at the end of the green Mogán Valley, at the foot of a rocky plateau. Canals and bridges linking the marina to the

Gran Canaria Beaches

With its 236-km (147-mile) coastline, Gran Canaria has around 80 beaches, small and large. Unlike the northern ones, which are rocky, the southern beaches are sandy. In some places, such as the Playa del Inglés or Maspalomas (popular with naturists, *see p181*), they stretch for miles and are lined with hotels, restaurants and clubs.

② **Taurito** can boast the attractive beach around Mogán, on a par with Playa de Cura and Arguineguín.

① **Puerto de Mogán**
Hidden among high cliffs, the sandy beach of this popular resort can barely accommodate all its guests.

0 kilometres   5
0 miles   5

③ **Playa de los Amadores**
This popular wide beach near Puerto Rico is fringed with beautiful palm trees and a wide, elegant promenade.

fishing harbour have earned the town the nickname "Little Venice".

The old fishing port lies adjacent to and behind the attractive, purpose-built marina and resort. The resort consists of a village-like complex of colourful, flower-decked apartments, prettily designed in Mediterranean style, lining narrow pedestrianized streets. The waterfront is home to various bars, shops and restaurants.

Swimmers will enjoy the man-made rocky beach that shelters between the cliffs. It is filled with several layers of sand imported from Africa.

There is a range of tourist trips available from here. A little yellow submarine offers tourists the opportunity to glimpse the rich underwater life of the Atlantic. Small replicas of old sailing ships ferry passengers to the beaches of Puerto Rico and Maspalomas several times a day. There are also deep-sea

Yellow submarine in Puerto de Mogán harbour

fishing trips to catch tuna and marlin. The renowned "Blue Marlin" angling competition is held here every July.

Environs
Around 8 km (5 miles) north of Puerto de Mogán, in a fertile valley planted with such

exotic crops as papaya and avocado, lies **Mogán**. This picturesque town is the capital of the district. There is a choice of good bars and restaurants here, including Acaymo, on the edge of town, and one of the best on the island.

⑦ **Maspalomas**
Long, golden beaches backed by vast, wind-sculpted dunes, set against the blue ocean, create an impression of an African desert in this often crowded resort in the south.

④ **Playa del Cura**
Near Playa del Cura, with its small beach, is one of the few camp sites on Gran Canaria.

⑧ **San Agustín**, together with Maspalomas and Playa del Inglés, forms a region known as "Costa Canaria". The beach of San Agustín has the darkest sand.

GC1 GC1

⑥ **Arguineguín** is a busy resort built up around an old fishing village. The village is well served by restaurants serving freshly caught fish and shellfish.

Key

━━ Motorway

━━ Major road

━━ Minor road

⑤ **Puerto Rico**
This golden beach attracts countless sunbathers and swimmers and provides excellent facilities for all kinds of water sports.

Puerto Rico, one of Gran Canaria's most popular resorts

⑮ Puerto Rico

🏙 4,400. ⓘ Avda. de Mogán.
Tel 928 158 804. 🎭 María de
Auxiliadora (May).

Puerto Rico lies on the coast, at the mouth of a large valley. This former fishing port has developed into a popular resort, thanks to its reputation as the sunniest place in Spain. Scores, if not hundreds, of hotels and apartments have been built on the terraces of the steeply descending slopes as a result.

One of the best features of this town, which is swamped in greenery, is its small but picturesque beach, covered with sand imported from the Sahara. Other attractions include golf courses and a water park, featuring all kinds of amusements. Puerto Rico's numerous attractions range from water sports including water-skiing, sailing, diving and windsurfing to leisure excursions such as glass-bottomed boats and open sea cruises for dolphin-watching. This helps to compensate for the fact that this is a rather over-built resort with remarkably limited beach space for the numbers of visitors it receives.

Another very popular activity is sport-fishing for marlin, shark, eel and ray. Puerto Rico claims many world records in this area: the world's largest blue marlin, caught in 1997, weighed in at 488 kg (1,075 lb).

⑯ Maspalomas

🏙 36,000. 🚌 ⓘ Avda. Touroperador
Tui. **Tel** 928 769 585. 🎪 Wed, Sat.
🎭 San Bartolomé (24 Aug).

The biggest resort in Gran Canaria has more than 500 hotels, apartment blocks and chalets, capable of accommo-dating 300,000 guests at a time. Tourists flock here, attracted by miles of sandy beaches, as well as hundreds of restaurants, bars and shops. Maspalomas is in fact a conglomeration of three separate resorts, reached by three different exits from the south-coast motorway.

The furthest east is **San Agustín**. This quiet, tourist town, full of greenery, with dark sand beaches, is aimed at an upmarket clientele, rather than mass tourism. It has a number of luxu-rious hotels, exclusive clubs, a casino and scenic promenades.

In the middle of the Maspalomas coastline is **Playa del Inglés**. This is the most crowded and liveliest resort, with Yumbo, a multi-storey shopping/restaurant centre, in the middle of town.

To the south of Playa del Inglés are the **Dunas de Maspalomas** – a vast, 4-sq km (1.5-sq miles) expanse of dunes and now a national park with a salt-water lake and palm grove, which can only be explored on foot or by camel. The dunes provide a habitat for lizards, rabbits and naturists.

Maspalomas is popular with surfers and windsurfers, as well as deep-sea fishing and diving enthusiasts. The resort offers **Aqualand**, the biggest water park on the island, with over 20 slides. There is also **Holiday World** – an amusement park occupying 14,000 sq m (150,695 sq ft) and featuring a traditional ferris wheel, 27 m (89 ft) high.

This large, modern resort, criss-crossed with numerous palm-lined boulevards, has an excellent golf course – the biggest on the island – while spiritual needs are served by the ecumenical church – **Templo Ecuménico**.

🏛 Aqualand
Ctra. Palmitos Park, km 3. **Tel** 928 140 525. **Open** Jul–Aug: 10am–6 pm daily; Sep–Jun: 10am–5pm daily. 🎫
W aqualand.es/maspalomas

🏛 Holiday World
Avda. Touroperador Tui. **Tel** 928 730 498. **Open** 6pm–midnight Fri–Sat (5pm–midnight in winter), 6–11pm Sun–Thu (5–11pm in winter). 🎫
W holidayworldmaspalomas.com

The spectacular dunes of Maspalomas

Colourful parrots in Palmitos Park

Environs

About 15 km (9 miles) north of Maspalomas, set in a mountain valley, is **Palmitos Park**. Amid its lush, tropical vegetation live 1,500 birds, including birds of paradise from New Guinea, miniature humming birds and toucans, with their colourful beaks. The park is also home to a Komodo dragon, Canarian lizards and spectacled caiman (alligator). Other attractions include the Casa de las Orquídeas, which houses around 1,000 orchids. The huge aquarium, with its vast tanks of water, has a large variety of fish from all over the world, including the Atlantic Ocean, Indian Ocean and South American waters. A further attraction of the park is the butterfly house – the largest of its kind in Europe. The park also boasts white-handed gibbons, whose natural habitats are the Malayan Peninsula and Burma, and who have been bred successfully here: the first time in captivity.

A little further to the north is **Mundo Aborigen** – a recon- struction of an ancient Canarian village. Set on a gentle slope, with a splendid view over the Barranco de Fataga, it consists of several crofts. Life-sized Guanche figures and recorded domestic animal noises give the setting some realism. A marked trail leads to a series of lifelike scenes including: a butcher gutting a goat, a doctor operating on a patient and wrestlers fighting in a small stadium. Nearby, a farmer is shown sowing a field, while the local executioner can be seen smashing a convict's head

with a rock. A sentry, poised at the highest point above the village, keeps watch over the surrounding area.

Over to the east, at the end of a rocky valley, is the small theme park **Sioux City**, which represents a ragbag of familiar associations with American culture. At the entrance, next to a wooden cart contain- ing models of the first settlers travelling west, we come across "Cadillac Café" with a genuine 1960s American car.

Visitors drinking in the saloon can enjoy dramatic interruptions from actors staging fights. There is also the "foam party" – a club night where participants throw foam at each other. The narrow streets of Sioux City Park provide the setting for scenes from westerns, including mock fistfights, gunfights and bank robberies. The air is filled with country and western music.

Palmitos Park
Barranco de los Palmitos.
Tel 928 797 070.
Open 10am–6pm daily.
W palmitospark.es

Mundo Aborigen
Macizo de Amurga. **Tel** 928 172 295.
Open 9am–6pm daily.
W mundoaborigen.es

Sioux City Park
Cañon del Águila. **Tel** 928 762 573.
Open 10am–3pm Tue–Fri (to 4pm Sat & Sun). **W** siouxcitypark.es

Statue of a native at Sioux City Park

⑰ San Bartolomé de Tirajana

56, 700. Carnival (Feb), Santiago (25 Jul).

Founded in the 16th century by the Spanish, this picturesque little town was once a shepherd settlement. Situated in the lush green valley of Tirajana, it is known for its orchards of almonds, plums, peaches and cherries, which are used in the production of vodkas and liqueurs. The local speciality is cherry liqueur, *guinda*.

The first chapel in San Bartolomé was built in the 16th century. In 1690, work started on its site to build a much grander, triple-nave parish church, which was not, in fact, consecrated until 1922. Its noteworthy features include the Mudéjar-style wooden vaults and carved statues of the saints. It is also worth visiting the old cemetery, set on a hill, where – contrary to the Spanish tradition – the dead were buried in the soil rather than being entombed in the cemetery wall.

Environs

Some 7 km (4 miles) to the south of San Bartolomé, in a beautiful setting of tall cliffs, palms and fruit trees, is **Fataga**, a mountain village with old houses and the 1880 church of San José. Next to the church are reservoirs – Embalse de Tirajana and Embalse de Fataga – both of which are excellent hiking destinations.

Children's water slide at Aqualand, Maspalomas

⓲ Around Pico de las Nieves

An all-day tour through the mountains of Gran Canaria can start from any point. The diverse character of the island's landscape makes it an unforgettable experience. The scenic road follows a serpentine course as it climbs mountain slopes and passes through enchanting villages and deep ravines. Lush sub-tropical vegetation, including exotic fruit trees and terraced fields, can be seen along the way. There are also numerous viewpoints en route that offer spectacular panoramas, even to the peak of Mount Teide on Tenerife. Some of the less accessible places can be reached by minor roads and tracks.

⑦ **Artenara**
One of the caves in this village houses a small chapel, another an unusual restaurant – Mesón de la Silla.

⑥ **Caldera Pinos de Gáldar**
On the road leading to Artenara, surrounded by the conifer forests of Pinos de Gáldar, stands a picturesque viewpoint. From here you can see the whole northern coast of the island.

⑧ **Tejeda**
This quiet little town, occupying a particularly scenic location on the mountain slopes, provides a good stopping place for lunch when touring the area.

⑨ **Roque Bentayga**
Along with nearby Roque Nublo, this basalt rock, rising to 1,412 m (4,633 ft) above sea level, was regarded as a holy place by the Guanches, who left rock inscriptions, granaries and ceremonial sites in this area.

⑩ **Roque Nublo**
This 60-m- (197-ft-) tall basalt monolith tops a 1,700 m (5,577 ft) peak. Thought to have been held sacred by the Guanches, this finger of rock was formed by erosion, and is often shrouded in clouds.

Map labels:
GC75
Artenara ⑦
⑥ Caldera Pinos de Gáldar
Fuente Carco de la Arena
GC210
Guardaye
Tejeda
Cuevas del Huerto
⑨ Roque Bentayga
La Aldea de San Nicolás
GC60
Montaña del Aserrad
Montaña del Humo
GC60
La Candelill
Maspalomas

Key
◼ Suggested route
◼ Scenic route
═ Other roads
❋ Viewpoint

0 kilometres   2

0 miles   2

⑤ **Cruz de Tejeda**
Carved in stone, this cross – from which the area takes its name – marks the central point of Gran Canaria. The view from this point on the mountain pass (altitude 1,450 m/4,757 ft) was described as a "petrified storm" by artist Miguel de Unamuno.

Tips for Tourists

Starting point: San Bartolomé de Tirajana.
Length: 80 km (50 miles).
Stopping places: The best place to stop for lunch is the parador at Cruz de Tejeda, which has an excellent restaurant. There are also restaurants in Artenara and San Bartolomé de Tirajana.

④ **La Degollada de Becerra**
This viewpoint offers a spectacular view to the west and of the Roque Bentayga peak.

③ **Pico de las Nieves**
Also known as Pozo de las Nieves (the Well of Snow), this is the highest peak on Gran Canaria at 1,949 m/6,394 ft. It is often cold and misty here, with occasional snowfall in winter. At the top stands a military radio station.

① **San Bartolomé de Tirajana**
The town is surrounded by a lush valley of orchards. The fruit from plum, cherry and peach trees is used to make vodka and liqueurs.

② **Presa de los Hornos**
The best view of the highest reservoir on the island can be seen near the summit of Roque Nublo *(see p64)*.

Map labels:
Teror
GC21
Montañón Negro
Ariñez
GC400
Cruz de Tejeda
⑤
Galás
Las Palmas de Gran Canaria
GC130
La Degollada ④ de Becerra
GC60
GC150
Mirador de Becerra
Montaña del Andén del Toro
Cruz Llanos de la Paz
GC130
Roque Nublo
Presa de los Hornos ②
GC600
El Salado
③
Pico de las Nieves
Ayacata
Los Tabuquillos
Los Caideros
GC60
Paso de la Herradura
San Bartolomé de Tirajana ①
Santa Lucía
Santa Lucía

⓭ Santa Lucía

🚌 ℹ️ Avda. de Canarias – Plaza de la Era, 928 125 260. 🎉 Fiesta de Ansite (29 Apr), Santa Lucía (13 Dec).

Located in the high country, this village stands 700 m (2,397 ft) above sea level, in the fertile palm valley of Santa Lucía de Tirajana. Set on top of the hill is the church of **Santa Lucía**, which was built in 1898 on the site of a former 17th-century chapel.

Various archaeological finds, unearthed from the surrounding hills and dating from the time of the Guanches, can be seen in the local **Museo del Castillo de la Fortaleza**. This ethnography/archaeology museum is housed in a modern pseudo-castle with turrets and battlements. The museum also features a reconstructed bedroom, typical of a 17th-century Canarian home, and displays of pottery (including a 3rd-century amphora), leather goods, basket-work and skeletons.

Environs

About 4 km (2 miles) south of Santa Lucía is the Fortaleza de Ansite. The volcano fortress, with numerous caves, is said to have been a refuge for native Canarians. A scenic road leads 5 km (3 miles) south to the viewpoint of Mirador de Guriete, with its spectacular views of the area.

🏛️ **Museo del Castillo de la Fortaleza**
Calle Tomás Arroyo Cardoso. **Tel** 928 798 310. **Open** by appoinment. 🔲

⓮ Agüimes

🔺 30,200. ℹ️ Plaza de San Antón, 928 124 183. 🚌 🎉 Nuestra Señora del Rosario (early to mid-Oct).

The old part of this town, with its narrow streets and beautiful houses, is overshadowed by the two huge towers of **San Sebastián** Church, standing in the Plaza del Rosario. The basilica has three naves and a barrel vault, and was constructed between 1796 and 1808. Along with the cathedral in Las Palmas de Gran Canaria, this is one of the best examples of the Canary

Picturesque narrow streets in Agüimes

Islands' Neo-Classical architecture. The vast dome lends an oriental touch to the building. The statues of saints inside the church are by Canarian sculptor José Luján Pérez (1756–1815).

Another attraction of Agüimes is the **Parque de los Cocodrilos**. This mini-zoo is home to crocodiles that have been rescued by SEPRONA (Servicio de Protección de la Naturaleza).

The town comes to life every July during the theatre festival, Festival del Sur. Groups from Europe, Africa and South America come to participate in this lively event.

🐊 **Parque de los Cocodrilos**
Carretera General Los Corralillos, km 5.5. **Tel** 928 784 725. **Open** 10am–5pm Sun–Fri. 🔲 🌐 cocodriloparkzoo. com/es/cocodriloparks

⓯ Ingenio

🔺 30,000. 🚌 🎉 Virgen de la Candelaria (Jan & Feb); Bajada del Macho (2nd Sat in Oct).

Situated in the eastern region, near Barranco Guayadeque, this small town is one of the oldest on Gran Canaria. It owes its name to the local sugar-cane industry, which flourished here in the 17th century (*ingenio* means sugar mill). Later, the region turned towards rum

production, but now it is a largely agricultural area, its main crop being tomatoes. Ingenio is, however, best known for its embroidery. There is a School of Embroidery housed in the **Museo de Piedras y Artesanía** – a white, bougainvillea-covered building with decorative turrets. The museum also houses a collection of rocks and minerals, agricultural tools, pottery and basketwork.

The imposing church of **Nuestra Señora de la Candelaria** looms over an attractive square, bordered by pretty houses with wooden balconies.

Environs

On the slope of a mountain, halfway along the road between Ingenio and Telde, is an archaeological site discovered in the 19th century. It consists of four caves, including **Cuatro Puertas**, with four openings (hence the name), which used to be the home of Telde rulers, or the site of sacrifices. The other caves, which face the sea, were used by the Guanches to bury the embalmed bodies of their dead.

🏛️ **Museo de Piedras y Artesanía**
Camino Real de Gando, 1. **Tel** 928 781 124. **Open** 9:30am–6pm Mon–Sat. 🔲

Entrance to Museo de Piedras y Artesanía in Ingenio

Painted houses in Plaza de San Juan – the main square in Telde

㉒ Barranco de Guayadeque

2 km (1.2 miles) north of Ingenio.

A scenic, winding road runs 7 km (4 miles) along the bottom of the Guayadeque Ravine, whose name in the Guanche language means "place of the flowing waters". The stream flowing along the canyon supplies water to the neighbouring towns of Ingenio and Agüimes.

Guayadeque is overgrown with cacti, agaves, palms and Canary pines, in addition to about 80 species native to the Canary Islands. In spring, the parched, rough terrain of the ravine is softened by the blossoming almond trees.

This region is one of the most important prehistoric burial grounds, where the dead, often wrapped in animal skins, were interred in inaccessible caves. Many of these graves were plundered in the 19th century by the local population, who sold the mummies to the Museo Canario in Las Palmas. Local caves were also used by the Guanches as dwelling places, food stores and as sites used for fertility rituals.

Barranco de Guayadeque is popular with modern-day people, who, following in the footsteps of the Guanches, have made their homes in the caves. This small troglodyte population has a chapel carved into the rock to meet their spiritual needs, while more earthly delights are provided by cave bars serving the strong local wine, bread and Temisas olives in green mojo sauce.

Guayadeque is also popular for Sunday picnics. The road running along the ravine ends at Restaurante Tagoror. Further on, the route is impassable for cars and ends up with a narrow footpath. During the summer, the sun's rays on the rocks dazzle spectators. In winter, the place can be cold, and clouds often cover the high ridges of the ravine.

Peaks shrouded in clouds above Barranco de Guayadeque

㉓ Telde

🏠 102,200. 🚍 ℹ Calle Conde de la Vega Grande, 9, 828 013 312. 🎎 San Juan (24 Jun). 🌐 teldeturismo.es

During pre-colonial times, Telde was the seat of the local king of the Guanches. Following the conquest of the island, it became known as a port for loading sugar cane.

Towards the end of the 15th century, the Spanish built a small chapel here. In 1519, work commenced on the site to build the present church of **San Juan Bautista**. The highlights of this large basilica are the Mannerist altar and a Flemish triptych dating from the first half of the 16th century.

From **Plaza de San Juan**, home to the church, runs **Inés Chemida**, a street connecting San Juan with another historic part of town – San Francisco. Here, the two-storey buildings are painted white and green. The narrow streets are lined with houses adorned with balconies of wrought iron and timber.

Fernando de León y Castillo (1842–1918)

León y Castillo, an engineer and diplomat born in Telde, played an important role in the regeneration of Gran Canaria. It is thanks to him that the island can boast the Las Palmas harbour, gaining Gran Canaria equal status with Tenerife. Opposed to Tenerife's domination, he was an advocate of the archipelago's division into two provinces. In 1881, he became Minister of Foreign Affairs, and also served as Spanish ambassador to France. In recognition, he was awarded the title of Marqués del Muni.

Bust of León y Castillo, in Telde

FUERTEVENTURA

Fuerteventura is blessed with sun and sand in equal measure. Much of its interior, consisting of arid dunes and rocky mountain ridges, is reminiscent of the western Sahara, which lies only 100 km (62 miles) to the east. Most of the island's tourists stick to the coast, where the fine sandy beaches are irresistible to sun worshippers, and strong winds provide ideal conditions for surfing.

With a distance of 97 km (60 miles) between Punta de la Tiñosa, in the north, and Punta de Jandía, in the south, Fuerteventura is the longest and the second largest of the Canary Islands. Yet despite its size, it is one of the most sparsely populated, and its 103,000 or so inhabitants are outnumbered by the many goats that scratch a meal from the island's dry scrub.

An island known as Forte Ventura first appeared on a map drawn by the cartographer Angelino Dulcert in 1339. Between 1402 and 1405 it was invaded by conquistadors, led by Jean de Béthencourt and Gadifer de la Salle. The village that grew up around the camp of Jean de Béthencourt, Betancuria, subsequently became the island's capital. Territorial expansion in the mid-17th century extended to the region of

El Cotillo and included the seat of the former kingdom of Maxorata. Volcanic eruptions and sand carried from the Sahara desert, as well as frequent droughts during the 18th and 19th centuries, caused the collapse of Fuerteventura's agriculture, once called the granary of the Canaries, and today most of the island's revenue comes from tourism.

The climate is harsher here than on the other islands thanks in part to a cooler prevailing wind called *gota fría*. The annual temperatures rarely exceed 25° C (77° F).

The arid climate and deforestation are responsible for the limited vegetation found here. An almost total absence of rain means that drinking water must be obtained either by desalination or shipped over from the mainland.

Long stretches of unspoiled golden beaches, south of Corralejo

◀ The attractive exterior of Iglesia de Santa María, in the town of Betancuria

Exploring Fuerteventura

Fuerteventura was discovered by tourists later than the other islands in the region, and as a consequence the local tourist industry is still in its infancy. The number of visitors is increasing, however, as news gradually spreads of the island's scenic landscape, and the peace and quiet to be found here. The vast stretches of white beach are a particular draw for sunbathers – the more accessible beaches are found in the northern part of the island, near Corralejo, the wilder ones around Cofete. The shores of Jandía provide perfect conditions for surfing and wind-surfing, while rich underwater life is a tempting attraction for divers. Fuerteventura is also an excellent area for walking and cycling. Those interested in history will find many interesting places to visit, including Betancuria and Pájara.

Locator Map

Mountain view on the road from
Pájara to La Pared

Sights at a Glance

- **❶** Puerto del Rosario
- **❷** Parque Natural de Corralejo
- **❸** Corralejo
- **❹** Isla de los Lobos
- **❺** El Cotillo
- **❻** La Oliva
- **❼** Tefía
- **❽** Antigua
- **❾** Betancuria
- **❿** Ajuy
- **⓫** Pájara

- **⓬** La Pared
- **⓭** Costa Calma
- **⓮** Morro Jable
- **⓯** Península de Jandía
- **⓰** Cofete
- **⓱** Gran Tarajal
- **⓲** Malpaís Chico and Malpaís Grande
- **⓳** Caleta de Fuste

Herds of goats, the main livestock on Fuerteventura

Punta del Penón Blanco

AJUY ⓰

Playa de los Muertos

Playa de Garcey

0 kilometres   5
0 miles   5

Playa de la Pared **⓬ LA PARED** 🏖

La Lajita

⓭ COSTA CALMA 🏖❌

Playa de Barlovento

Playa de Cofete

⓰ COFETE

PENÍNSULA DE JANDÍA FV2

Playa de Sotavento

⓯ 🏖❌

Puerto de la Cruz

Punta de Jandía

Playa de las Pilas

MORRO JABLE 🚶🏖 **⓮** 🚢 *Casas del Matorral*

Punta de la Tiñosa

🚩 ISLA DE LOS LOBOS ④

El Río

🚩🕭 CORRALEJO ③

Punta la Barra

🚩🏠 EL COTILLO ⑤   Lajares

PARQUE NATURAL ②
DE CORRALEJO

Montaña Roja
312 m △

Punta Paso
Chico

🏛🏠 LA OLIVA ⑥   △ Montaña de
Escantraga
529 m

FV1

FV10   Tindaya

Monumento a
Miguel de Unamuno

Punta de
la Tiñosa

Tetir

FV10

sas Los
Molinos

🏛 TEFÍA ⑦

PUERTO ①
DEL ROSARIO

Casillas del
Ángel

FV20

Playa Blanca

FV30   La Ampuyenta

✈

BETANCURIA ⑨   Triquivijate

Playa de
las Caletillas

FV2

ANTIGUA ⑧

🏛 CALETA ⑲
DE FUSTES

Pico de
ncuria
725 m △

FV20

Casas de
las Salinas

🏠 Vega de
Río Palmas

PÁJARA   Tiscamanita

MALPAÍS CHICO &
MALPAÍS GRANDE ⑱

FV50

Tuineje   FV2   Casas de
Pozo Negro

Punta Gorda

Tesejerague   FV20

FV2   Playa de
los James

GRAN TARAJAL ⑰   Las Playitas

rajalejo

The lush garden of the Casa de Santa
María, in Betancuria

Getting There

Fuerteventura has direct air
links with Lanzarote, Gran
Canaria and Tenerife, and
connects via Tenerife to the
western islands. There are also
flights from mainland Spanish
cities as well as a number of
European centres. Regular ferry
links connect Puerto del
Rosario with Arrecife (Lanzarote)
and Las Palmas de Gran Canaria,
and Corralejo with Playa Blanca
(Lanzarote). A hydrofoil runs
from Morro Jable to Las Palmas
de Gran Canaria. The local
transport is limited.

Key

▬▬ Motorway
━━ Major road
═══ Minor road
▬▬ Scenic route
△ Summit

Scenic approach road leading to the centre of La Pared

The altar at Nuestra Señora del Rosario, Puerto del Rosario

Reminiscent of the Sahara desert, the Parque Natural de las Dunas de Corralejo is almost totally devoid of any vestiges of civilization. Even when the tourist season is at its height, there is plenty of solitude and open space to be found here (don't forget to take a hat). The only signs of life are the stone walls built as windbreaks on the sandy hills. The area was declared a National Park in 1987.

❶ Puerto del Rosario

🏙 37,400. ✈ ⛴ 🚌 *i* Avda. Reyes de España, 928 850 110. 🚣 Nuestra Señora del Rosario (7 Oct).
🌐 visitfuerteventura.es
🌐 turismo-puertodelrosario.org

Puerto del Rosario, the capital of Fuerteventura, was first established in 1797 as a port for locally produced soda and grain. The port began to grow in the mid-19th century and by 1860 had become the capital of the island. Until 1957, the town, whose name means Port of the Rosary, was Puerto de Cabras – Port of Goats – in reference to the watering hole in the nearby canyon.

Today the port has a thriving cargo and passenger harbour, with ferries sailing to Gran Canaria and Lanzarote. It also has a yachting marina. Not far from the town – which is the largest on Fuerteventura and inhabited by more than a third of the island's population – is an international airport.

Highlights in Puerto del Rosario include the church of **Nuestra Señora del Rosario**, with its Classical façade. Standing opposite it is **Casa Museo de Unamuno**, which will interest lovers of Spanish literature, as it was the home of the writer and philosopher Miguel de Unamuno during his exile. Part of the house is furnished with period pieces, including the original desk used by the writer, as well as a collection of personal objects and documents. It represents a typical interior from his times.

🏛 **Casa Museo de Unamuno**
C/Virgin del Rosario 11. **Tel** 928 862 376. **Open** 10am–2pm Mon–Fri, 10am–1pm Sat. 🌐 **unamuno.usal.es**

Environs

Just 12 km (7 miles) to the west is a small village, **Casillas del Angel**, with pretty houses. The beautiful church of Santa Ana (St Anne), dates from 1781 and has a black, volcanic-stone façade.

❷ Parque Natural de Corralejo

🚌

In the northeast corner of the island is the Parque Natural de de Corralejo, which spans south to the base of the Montaña Roja volcano (312 m/ 1,024 ft). Occupying 27 sq km (10.4 sq miles), this belt of seemingly endless sand encroaches on the road between Puerto del Rosario and Corralejo and sweeps to the sea.

❸ Corralejo

🏙 14,900. 🚌 *i* Avda. Maritima, 2, 928 866 235. 🚣 Mon, Fri, Sun. 🚣 Carnival (Mar), Nuestra Señora del Carmen (16 Jul).
🌐 visitcorralejo.com

This northernmost town of Fuerteventura has a passenger harbour, with ferries sailing several times a day to Playa Blanca in Lanzarote. Small cruising boats also take tourists to the neighbouring island of Los Lobos. Weather-beaten fishing boats moored at the quayside and several fish restaurants add a touch of charm to this old fishing village.

Corralejo has become one of Fuerteventura's most popular resorts, along with the Jandía peninsula. Visitors come here not so much for the town but for its setting, with striking views of Lanzarote and Los Lobos and the wonderful beaches to the south of the centre. Thanks to a year-round stiff breeze, the El Río strait between Corralejo and

Kitesurfing at the Corralejo Flag Beach

For hotels and restaurants in this region see pp158–9 and pp171–2

Jet-skis and sailing school in Corralejo harbour

Lanzarote is an ideal place for water sports. The clear water teems with a rich variety of fish. Angling, diving and glass-bottomed boat trips are popular.

The town's most interesting sights are its modern church in **Plaza de la Iglesia** and sand-sculpting – on a small beach by the harbour, giant dragons and camels can be conjured up before your eyes.

Environs
11 km (7 miles) to the southwest, in Lajares, is the Escuela de Artesanía Canaria. The school sells authentic craft products from all the Canary Islands.

❹ Isla de los Lobos

This small volcanic island, occupying only 4.4 sq km (1.7 sq miles) is situated in the El Río strait,

Miguel de Unamuno (1864–1936)

Unamuno, the "Philosopher from Salamanca", played a major part in the rebirth of Spanish literature and in the intellectual life of Spain in the early 20th century. He was the rector of Salamanca University from 1900 to 1924, and from 1930 until his death. Having spoken out against the dictatorship of Primo de Rivera, he was forced into exile in the Canary Islands for a few months. His opposition to Franco led to his being put under house arrest. In his work, he advocated the view that philosophy should express the tragedy of the human dilemma. His *Spanish Travels and Scenes* (1922) is a testament to the author's love for his homeland.

Miguel de Unamuno, outspoken and defiant

between Fuerteventura and Lanzarote. It can be reached by small cruising boat from Corralejo or by glass-bottomed motor-yacht. The island of Los Lobos is little more than 6,000–8,000 years old, and owes its name to the seals – *lobos marinos* – which once made their home on its sandy shores.

According to the history books, the French adventurer Gadifer de la Salle dropped anchor by the island of Los Lobos in 1402. He and his crew were saved from starvation by seal meat. In the early 15th century, Jean de Béthencourt built a hermitage on the island. Later on, the island served as a base for pirates raiding the neighbouring islands of the archipelago. It was also a centre of the slave trade.

The island was inhabited by its only residents – the lighthouse keeper and his family – until 1968. Thanks to the fact that the island remained uninhabited for so long, it has retained its original ecosystem. The natural botanical garden on the slopes of the Montaña Lobos is used as a resting place by migrating birds.

The whole of the island of Los Lobos is a nature reserve. The sandy coves offer ideal conditions for swimming and relaxing, while angling is limited to a few allocated spots. There are also well-marked trails for walking and cycling. There is no accommodation on the island, but day visitors can enjoy peace, tranquillity and great views of Fuerteventura.

Isla de los Lobos, a fine destination for picnics, swimming and hiking trips

Fishing harbour in El Cotillo, with the mighty Fortaleza del Tostón guarding its entrance

❺ El Cotillo

🏘 1,100. 🚌 ℹ️ 609 207 967.
🎉 Nuestra Señora del Buen Viaje
(mid–late Aug).

The early days of this small fishing town are associated with the Guanches. This was once the seat of the tribal chiefs of Maxorata – the ancient kingdom that encompassed the northern part of Fuerteventura.

The round fortified tower – **Fortaleza del Tostón** – dates from more recent times. A small fort, it was built in 1797 as a defence against British and Arab pirates. Thanks to restoration work, it is now well preserved. Approached via stone steps with a drawbridge, this is a two-storey structure. Originally the upper floor housed a water tank, while the lower level was used as soldiers' quarters.

The small harbour features a **giant rock** rising out of the water. Although picturesque, it is hard for fishermen to navigate during rough weather. El Cotillo also offers scenic coves and sandy beaches.

❻ La Oliva

🏘 25,200. 🚌 ℹ️ 928 866 235. 🎉
Nuestra Señora de la Candelaria (2 Feb),
Nuestra Señora del Rosario (7 Oct).

Situated at the northern end of Fuerteventura, La Oliva is one of the prettiest towns on the island and a popular excursion destination. It stands in the shadow of Montaña de Escantraga (527 m/ 1730 ft). The first European settlers arrived here in the early 14th century. In 1709, the newly established military governor of the island (the "Colonel") selected La Oliva as his seat. The town soon became the military capital of the island and, along with Betancuria, a centre of Fuerteventura's political life.

The military headquarters were at the **Casa de los Coroneles**.

Sculpture, Centro de
Arte Canario

The "House of Colonels", built in the 18th century, is a large austere edifice featuring two low towers at the corners and numerous windows: it is said to have one window for each day of the year, though this is inaccurate. The nearby **Casa del Capellán** (Chaplain's House) is a modest single-storey building with an ornately decorated portal and window frames. In the town centre stands the **Iglesia de Nuestra Señora de la Candelaria**. The white walls of this attractive church, which dates from 1711, stand in stark contrast to its square belfry, built of black volcanic stone and visible from miles away. The interior of the church houses a Mudéjar ceiling, a large painting of The Last Judgement, a Baroque altar painting and various other sculptures and paintings by the 18th century artist Juan de Miranda.

Art lovers will enjoy Casa Mané's **Centro de Arte Canario**, which holds exhibitions of local artists' work. The **Museo del Grano La Cilla** – with an exhibition on grain production in an early 19th-century granary, is worth a visit.

🏛 **Museo del Grano La Cilla**
Tel 928 868 729. **Open** 10am–6pm
Tue–Sat. **Closed** Sun, Mon. 🎫

The triple-naved Iglesia de Nuestra Señora de la Candelaria, La Oliva

For hotels and restaurants in this region see pp158–9 and pp171–2

❼ Tefía

230.

This village, which lies on the road from La Oliva to Betancuria, has an interesting open-air museum – the **Ecomuseo de la Alcogida** – featuring seven reconstructed houses typical of traditional Fuerteventura architecture. The exhibition illustrates the former life of the islanders, their occupations relating to farming and crafts, and also explains the process of the houses' reconstruction.

Reconstructed farm buildings in the Ecomuseo de la Alcogida, Tefía

Ecomuseo de la Alcogida
Tel 928 175 434. **Open** 10am–6pm Tue–Sat.

Environs
Some 12 km (7 miles) northeast is the small village of **Tetir**. It's worth visiting for its traditional houses with balconies and the local church, Santo Domingo de Guzmán (1745). The square in front of the church features a bust of Juán Rodriguez y Gonzáles (1825–93), the founder of the Banco de Canarias, who was born here.

A further 8 km (5 miles) north, on the slopes of **Montaña Quemada**, stands a monument to Miguel de Unamuno. Reaching over 2 m (6.5 ft) in height, it was carved in 1970 by Juan Borges Lineres.

❽ Antigua

2,300. 928 163 286.
Nuestra Señora de Pino (8 Sep).

Antigua, in the centre of Fuerteventura at the foot of the mountains, is – true to its name – one of the oldest towns on the island. It was established in 1485 by the settlers arriving from Andalusia and Normandy, who began cultivating the soil and breeding animals. Many windmills erected at the time were used to irrigate the fields. In 1812, Antigua was granted municipal rights and in 1835 it became the capital of the island.

Its more interesting features include the small, single-nave church of **Nuestra Señora de**

Antigua (1785), which has wooden vaults and a high altar incorporating folk motifs.

The **Centro de Artesanía Molinos de Antigua**, situated on the town's outskirts and surrounded by a low wall, is a museum village, built under the supervision of César Manrique. It includes a craft centre, a reconstructed windmill, and a gallery and

Façade of the late 18th-century church, Antigua

exhibition halls devoted to ethnography and archaeology.

Centro de Artesanía Molinos de Antigua
Tel 928 878 041. **Open** 10am–6pm Tue–Sat.

Environs
Travel 5 km (3 miles) or so to the north for **La Ampuyenta**, a small village with a 17th-century chapel, Ermita San Pedro de Alcántara. This picturesque sanctuary is surrounded by a fortification erected by Norman settlers.

About 14 km (9 miles) south is the village of **Tiscamanita**, with the 17th-century chapel of San Marcos. At the **Centro de Interpretación de los Molinos**, visitors can learn about the island's windmills.

Centro de Interpretación de los Molinos
Tel 928 164 275. **Open** 10am–6pm Tue–Sat.

Jean de Béthencourt (c.1362–1425)

On 1 May 1402, Jean de Béthencourt, together with Gadifer de la Salle, set sail from La Rochelle in France, at the head of a small expedition intent on conquering the Canary Islands. He left some of his men on Lanzarote and sailed to Spain to seek support. He returned not only with ships, soldiers and money, but also with a title – he was now the lord of four of the islands: Fuerteventura, Lanzarote, El Hierro and La Gomera. The furious de la Salle immediately returned to France. Béthencourt, having handed over the power to his nephew, Maciot de Béthencourt, also returned to France in 1406. He died at his castle in Normandy in 1425.

Jean de Béthencourt, Norman conqueror

Betancuria's lush vegetation, a contrast to the stark mountains beyond

⑨ Betancuria

🗺 730. 🚌 ℹ C/Juan Béthencourt, 6, 928 878 092. 🎭 San Buenaventura (14 Jul). 🌐 aytobetancuria.org

Nestling in a volcanic crater sheltered from the winds, Betancuria lies in the central region of the island, where the rugged peaks of extinct volcanoes punctuate the wide, fertile valleys. Practically all of this area is within the Parque Natural de Betancuria. The highest peak, Pico de Betancuria, offers a splendid vantage point.

The town was founded in 1404 and was given its full name, Villa de Santa María de Betancuria, by Jean de Béthencourt. The Normans made the town the island's capital, and it remained so until 1834. Betancuria's inland position was intended to protect it against pirate raids. However, in 1593 the Berber pirate Xabán de Arráez pillaged it mercilessly, destroying virtually every building and taking 600 of its inhabitants captive.

Today, Betancuria is the prettiest village on Fuerteventura. At its centre stands the **Iglesia de Santa María**. The first church built on this site in 1404 was elevated to the status of a cathedral and bishopric by Pope Martin III in 1425, but no bishop ever arrived to take up the post. In 1593, the church was burned by Arráez; it was rebuilt in 1620. Noteworthy features include the Baroque altar, the original stone floor set in a wooden frame, the carved stalls and the coffered ceiling. The space behind the choir contains a vast painting, *Nava de La Iglesia*, depicting the

church as a ship, and painted by Nicolás Medina in 1730.

On the northern outskirts of the village is the Franciscan abbey of **San Buenaventura** – the oldest abbey on the island. Its roof collapsed in the mid-19th century, and what remains today are merely scenic ruins. Next to the abbey stands the **Pozo del Diablo** – Devil's Well. According to legend, Satan was chained to this rock and forced to carry stones used in the building of the abbey.

Betancuria has two small museums. The **Museo de Arte Sacro**, established in a former parish house, has a collection of sacred art and photographs showing almost every church on the Canary Islands. The **Museo Arqueológico** has a collection dating from the time of the Guanches, as well as antique items of everyday use. Visitors to the restored 16th-century town house of Casa de Santa María can pick up souvenirs in the craft shop.

🏛 **Museo de Arte Sacro**
Alcalde Carmelo Silvera, s/n. **Tel** 928 878 003. **Open** 10am–4:30pm Mon–Fri, 10am–1:30pm Sat. 🎟

🏛 **Museo Arqueológico**
Roberto Roldán, 12–35. **Tel** 928 878 241. **Closed** closed for renovation.

Environs
Some 2 km (1 mile) north of Betancuria, Mirador de Morro Velosa offers a fine view over the island's lunar-like landscape.

⑩ Ajuy

30 km (19 miles) southwest of Betancuria.

Ajuy perches on the shores of a small bay and is surrounded by steep cliffs. Jean de Béthencourt, accompanied by Gadifer de la Salle, landed here in 1402 and embarked on the conquest of the island. For many years the bay served as a harbour for settlers arriving in Betancuria.

Today Ajuy is a quiet fishing village. The fishing season lasts from May until October, and during this time the simple beach-side restaurants serve up the day's catch. The dark sands of Playa de los Muertos are also worth visiting. The beach gained its name, "beach of the dead", from pirate attacks. Be warned, the waves can be powerful.

With its rocky seabed, vast underwater caves and shoals of darting fish, Ajuy is a paradise for scuba divers.

Waves battering the steep cliffs around Ajuy

Old irrigation equipment, Pájara

⑪ Pájara

🏠 21,500. 🚌 ⛪ Virgen del Carmen (16 Jul). 🌐 **pajara.es**

To the south of Betancuria lies the small town of Pájara, linked with the island's former capital by a scenic road. This is one of the oldest settlements on Fuerteventura. It was founded by fishermen and goatherders who settled here in the 16th century.

Historic attractions include the church of **Nuestra Señora de la Regla**. Built in 1684, the church is worth seeing for its Latin American influences. The stone reliefs above the main portal depict stylized images of fish, lions, birds and snakes devouring their own tails. The origin of these motifs, said to be inspired by Aztec art, is unknown. The church's interior features two wooden altars, including a smiling figure of the Madonna and Child, and one of Our Lady of Sorrows (Nuestra Señora de los Dolores), the patron saint of the island.

Portal of the church in Pájara

Environs

Some 11 km (7 miles) northeast lies **Vega de Río Palmas**. Here, perched among high rocks is the hermitage of Nuestra Señora de la Peña, which features another image of Our Lady of Sorrows. Each year on the third Sunday in May a feast is held here in her honour. The church (1666) contains statues of saints, believed to have been brought here by Béthencourt for the first church built in Betancuria.

⑫ La Pared

🏠 600. About 21 km (13 miles) south of Pájara.

This small tourist resort has undergone a fair degree of development. It is worth visiting both for its historical associations and for its landscape.

Before the Spanish conquest, a land wall (*la pared*) running around here marked the boundary between two rival Guanche kingdoms: Maxorata and Jandía. Much of the wall may have been dismantled to use as building material; today no trace of it remains.

La Pared has the most extensive dunes in Fuerteventura and separates the Jandía peninsula from the remaining part of the island. It also forms a natural border between two beaches of completely different sand colour – the southern Playa del Viejo Rey has golden sand, while Playa de la Pared to the north consists of black sand.

A trek of several hours along volcanic formations leads to a ravine at the foot of the Risco del Pasco mountain, where it joins the road leading to Morro Jable.

⑬ Costa Calma

🏠 5,200. 🚌

Costa Calma is an upmarket modern resort distinguished by its tasteful architecture. It lies at the northern end of Playa del Sotavento, which is the longest and most scenic beach on the island, with excellent conditions for windsurfing.

The first private homes appeared here in the late 1960s, and the first hotel was built in 1977. The rapid growth of Costa Calma contributed to the construction of an asphalt road connecting Puerto del Rosario with Morro Jable. The building of a sea-water desalination plant followed in 1986. Large-scale construction works began in the mid-1990s to provide tourist facilities, including hotels, restaurants and shops.

To the southwest of Costa Calma lies Risco del Gato, which offers beautiful views of Costa Calma and its stretch of coast. The wind farm at Cañada del Río is an interesting spot to stop at, and the prevailing winds throughout the year provide perfect conditions.

Environs

The small village of **La Lajita** lies some 8 km (5 miles) north. Visitors come here for the **Oasis Park**, home to 200 species of exotic birds and mammals from around the world. A local garden centre sells specimens of tropical and subtropical flora, as well as native plants.

🌳 **Oasis Park**
Tel 928 161 102. **Open** 9am–6pm daily. 🌐 **fuerteventuraoasispark.com**

An eerie lunar landscape, the mountainous region north of La Pared

Virtually uninhabited northern coast, the Península de Jandía

⓮ Morro Jable

🗺 7,800. **Tel** 928 540 776. 🚌 🚢

Set amid long sandy beaches, on the southern end of Fuerteventura, Morro Jable is an old fishing village with narrow streets and lively taverns, which serve dishes of freshly caught seafood. Once a sleepy little place, the village has grown to become the biggest resort on the island.

The modern part of town is geared for tourists and includes countless hotels and apartments, shopping malls, restaurants and bars. Hydro foils and ferries sail from the local harbour to Las Palmas on Gran Canaria, while the marina is full of yachts. Morro Jable is also a good starting point for hikes on the Península de Jandía.

⓯ Península de Jandía

The Jandía Peninsula is surrounded by miles of scenic beaches with fine white sand. The longest beaches with the highest waves to be found on the island, they are particularly attractive to surfers, while the secluded beach of Barlovento, on the northwestern shore, is popular with scuba divers.

The area around Puerto de la Cruz, near Punta de Jandía – the southwestern headland of the island with rocky shores and a solitary lighthouse – has in recent years become a Mecca for caravanning holiday-makers. In this remote region, it is possible to escape from most of the noise and bustle of mass tourism.

A considerable part of the peninsula, with its rugged hills, is a conservation area and forms part of the **Parque Natural de Jandía**. Covering 140 sq km (54 sq miles), it features many species native to the island. In the remote mountain valleys, it is still possible to see wild goats and donkeys.

During World War II, this was a closed area and belonged to the German industrialist Gustav Winter (1893–1971). Rumour has it that he ran a secret submarine base in southwest Fuerteventura during the war, and stories about spies and buried Nazi treasure persist to this day.

⓰ Cofete

🗺 20.

Judging by the surroundings of this small, windswept hamlet, Fuerteventura appears to be a desert island. Only a roughly surfaced road connects it with Morro Jable. At the height of Playa de Juan Gómez, the road forks: one side leads to the southwestern end of the island; the other winds up at Cofete. The end of the line, Cofete marks the starting point for hiking trails along the ridge of Gran Valle and the pass between the peaks of Pico de Zarza and Fraile.

Beyond the village, perched below the Degollada de Cofete, is the imposing villa of Gustav Winter (1893–1971). There has been speculation that Winter was involved in the construction of a secret submarine port in World War II, but this has not been proved.

Gustav Winter's villa, on land given to him by General Franco

Windmills

Windmills of all types, driven by the steady trade winds, form an important element of the Canary Islands' landscape. Introduced in the 17th century, they came to replace the horse-driven mills – *tahonas*. The oldest type of windmill is the *molino*. Built of local stone, plastered in white, with a round body and conical roof, the *molino* has four to six sails. The 19th century saw the arrival of a second type of windmill – the *molina*. This differed from the previous design in the way its structure was exposed. Modern turbines were later introduced for use in desalination plants. There are now also many wind farms all over the island, which are used for generating electricity.

Wind turbines – the latest generation of powerful hi-tech wind farms is used to generate electricity for the island on an industrial scale.

Old-style windmills, used in the generation of electricity, were also employed for pumping water in desalination plants.

Sails, or wings, of the molino are made of strong slats.

Rigid sail panels

Molino

A typical feature of the islands' landscape, this kind of windmill is Spanish in origin. Such windmills were used to grind flour from wheat, barley and maize. The milling mechanism is mounted in the upper section.

Grain was poured by hand onto the grindstone. The flour passed into a funnel-shaped dispenser from which it was sent by chute to sacks placed on a lower level.

Chute used for pouring flour into sacks

Long rods turned the head of the windmill and were also used to stabilize the milling mechanism.

Entrance to the lower floor of the molino

The molino's grinding mechanism is simple: rotating sails turn a vast cogwheel, which connects directly with the grind wheel.

The molina's structure, unlike the molino, is visible on the outside and sits on top of the building that houses the grinding mechanism.

⑰ Gran Tarajal

🗺 8,000. 🚌 ℹ 928 162 723.
🎉 Fiesta de San Diego de Alcalá
(13 Nov).

The second-largest town on
Fuenteventura, and an important
trade centre, is Gran Tarajal lacks
much of the gloss typical of
modern resorts. Due to its strategic importance, a fort was built
here at the time of the island's
invasion by Jean de Béthencourt.
From the early 20th century,
the local port played a more
important role than that of the
island's capital and is used today
for shipping goods from the
Península de Jandía.
Apart from the single-nave
church of **Nuestra Señora de la
Candelaria**, built in 1900, there
are virtually no historical sights
found in the town centre.

Environs

A detour 6 km (4 miles) to the
east leads to a small fishing village
– **Las Playitas**. The peaceful

Waterfront at the harbour, Las Playitas
near Gran Tarajal

atmosphere contrasts with that
of the crowded resorts. Instead
of vast hotels and apartments,
guests are invited to stay in old
fishermen's cottages, clad with
bougainvillaea and peppers,
boasting fantastic sea views.
Local bars and restaurants serve
fresh fish daily and there is a small
stony beach near the harbour.
Some 6 km (4 miles) to the east

is **Punta de la Entallada**, which
is the point of Fuerteventura
closest to Africa and is reached
by a narrow, winding road. On
top of 300-m- (984-ft-) tall cliffs
is a lighthouse. Built in 1950, it
resembles a fortress. The site
offers a splendid view across the
mountainous part of the island
and the Atlantic.

⑱ Malpaís Chico and Malpaís Grande

The inhospitable Regions of
Malpaís Chico and Malpaís
Grande bear witness to the
island's volcanic past, and
occupy the south-central part
of Fuerteventura. It would be
pointless to look for any traces
of human activity here.
Don't look for any roads either.
The bleak landscape is traversed
by two hiking trails. One leads
around Malpaís Chico, which

Fuerteventura's Beaches

Fuerteventura, one of the least populated
of the Canary Islands relative to its size,
features the archipelago's most beautiful
beaches, which stretch for miles. The
loveliest of these are on the Península de
Jandía, where sunseekers will readily find
peace and quiet. There are more than 150
of these remote beaches, of which some
are popular with nudists *(see p181)*.

② Cofete
It takes a determined effort to reach the
remote and windswept beach of white
sand near the village of Cofete.

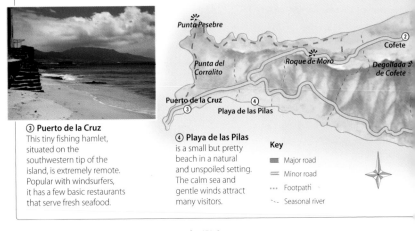

③ Puerto de la Cruz
This tiny fishing hamlet,
situated on the
southwestern tip of the
island, is extremely remote.
Popular with windsurfers,
it has a few basic restaurants
that serve fresh seafood.

④ Playa de las Pilas
is a small but pretty
beach in a natural
and unspoiled setting.
The calm sea and
gentle winds attract
many visitors.

Key

▬ Major road
═ Minor road
••• Footpath
⌇ Seasonal river

was formed by lava flowing from the Caldera de Gaíra. The other, leading to Malpaís Grande, passes through the national park, declared a conservation zone in view of its unique geological features. Wildlife is scarce; one of the few creatures to inhabit this desert area is the Egyptian vulture.

⑲ Caleta de Fuste

🏠 6,000. 🚌 ℹ️ Calle Juan Ramón Soto Morales, 10, 928 163 286. 🎭 Nuestra Señora del Carmen (16 Jul). 🔗 **caletadefuste.es**

Caleta de Fuste is one of the island's main holiday resorts. Though not the most attractive, it is a quiet place. Located in the middle of the eastern coast, it is convenient for the airport. It features sprawling, low-built apartments, built around a horseshoe bay with a safe, sandy beach. The resort is a good choice for visitors with small children.

At its centre is **Pueblo Majorero** – a modern, village-like complex of shops, bars and restaurants. One of the bungalow estates, the Barceló Club El Castillo, is built round the old **El Castillo** watchtower near the harbour. Built in 1741, it bears witness to the strategic importance of this place during the 18th century.

Around 4 km (2 miles) to the south are the Salinas del Carmen,

where salt was recovered before the 1980s. Today, in the Open Air Museum, visitors can see how seawater is accumulated in small basins before evaporating, leaving salt crystals behind. In Pozo Negro, 10 km (6 miles) to the south, is the excavation site at La Atalayita. It is an ancient settlement of indigenous Canarians, with an informative information centre.

El Castillo, the watchtower in Caleta de Fuste

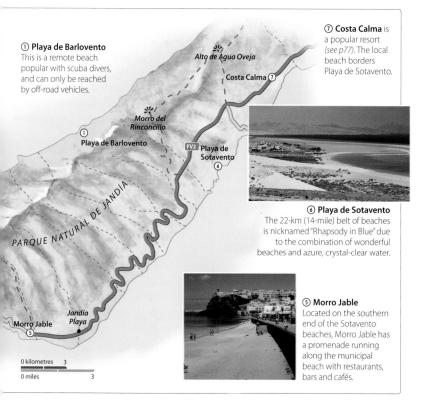

① Playa de Barlovento
This is a remote beach popular with scuba divers, and can only be reached by off-road vehicles.

Alto de Agua Oveja

Costa Calma ⑦

Morro del Rinconcillo

①
Playa de Barlovento

FV2 **Playa de Sotavento**
⑥

PARQUE NATURAL DE JANDIA

Jandía Playa

Morro Jable
⑤

0 kilometres   3
0 miles   3

⑦ Costa Calma is a popular resort *(see p77)*. The local beach borders Playa de Sotavento.

⑥ Playa de Sotavento
The 22-km (14-mile) belt of beaches is nicknamed "Rhapsody in Blue" due to the combination of wonderful beaches and azure, crystal-clear water.

⑤ Morro Jable
Located on the southern end of the Sotavento beaches, Morro Jable has a promenade running along the municipal beach with restaurants, bars and cafés.

LANZAROTE

This is volcano country, known as the Isla del Fuego, or Fire Island. Indeed, most of Lanzarote's 795 sq km (307 sq miles) are covered with solidified lava in tones of black, pink, purple and ochre, and peppered with around 300 volcanic peaks. Many tourists stick to the coast, especially the southern shores. Others prefer to head inland to trek through Lanzarote's breathtaking lunar landscape.

Much of the local architecture is in harmony with the island's unique landscape. The inhabitants continue to build in the traditional style, and, as a result of strict planning controls, Lanzarote is almost totally free of high-rise buildings. This trend has been influenced by the artistic concepts of the late architect and artist César Manrique, who sought for the island's architecture to harmonize with the natural environment. In 1993, UNESCO declared Lanzarote a Biosphere Reserve to support the local population's efforts to preserve the natural landscape.

The island's name probably derives from the distorted name of the Genoese sailor Lanzarotto (or Lancelotto) Malocello, who first arrived here in 1312. In 1402, the island was conquered by Jean de Béthencourt.

The proximity of the African coast made the island prone to attacks by Algerian and Moroccan pirates, who often plundered the capital at that time, Teguise. In the 16th and 17th centuries, the island was also raided by English and French pirates. These attacks, combined with years of droughts and catastrophic volcanic eruptions, led at one time to the almost total depopulation of the island.

In the absence of the island having any natural resources, the main occupations of its inhabitants were agriculture and fishing. Large plantations of prickly pear and vineyards still flourish. Other crops include tomatoes and sweet potatoes. Tourism is the dominant industry, generating 80 per cent of the island's revenue. The development of agriculture and tourism resulted in a severe water shortage, and, at one stage, drinking water had to be shipped in. It wasn't until 1964, that the first desalination plant was opened, and today most of the larger estates have their own water unit.

Traditional white-and-green houses in Yaiza village

◄ An idyllic volcanic lagoon in the hamlet of El Golfo

Exploring Lanzarote

Although Lanzarote is almost totally devoid of
vegetation, many tourists, enchanted by the shapes
and colours of its unique volcanic landscape,
regard the island as the most picturesque in
the archipelago. Visitors chiefly come here for the
beaches. Lanzarote's northern shores are good for
surfing; the waves are especially good at La Santa.
César Manrique's strange architectural designs,
which merge with the natural landscape, are
another of the island's attractions.

Locator Map

Sights at a Glance

1. Arrecife
2. Costa Teguise
3. Tahiche
4. Guatiza
5. Jameos del Agua
6. Cueva de los Verdes
7. Malpaís de la Corona
8. Órzola
9. La Graciosa
10. Mirador del Río
11. Guinate
12. Haría
13. Teguise
14. La Caleta de Famara
15. Tiagua
16. San Bartolomé
17. *Parque Nacional de Timanfaya pp94–5*
18. Yaiza
19. El Golfo
20. Salinas de Janubio
21. Playa Blanca
22. Femés
23. La Geria
24. Puerto del Carmen

Fountain and church in the main square,
San Bartolomé

Mosaic in Tahiche's César Manrique Fundación

Getting There

Lanzarote has air links with the other islands of the
archipelago and with mainland Spain. Regular
charter flights also bring in visitors from all over
Europe. Frequent ferries connect Lanzarote with
nearby Fuerteventura and Gran Canaria. The capital
and other main towns have reasonable public
transport. Not all places on the island are as well
served, however. Many places, even those that
are particularly attractive to tourists, cannot be
reached by bus, and it is advisable to make use of
organized coach tours or to hire a car. Though the
main roads are well surfaced, some remote
beaches require an all-terrain vehicle.

Punta Gaviota

PARQUE NACIONAL
DE TIMANFAYA 17

EL GOLFO 19

Los Hervideros

YAIZA 18

Ug

SALINAS 20
DE JANUBIO

FEMÉS 22

L72

PLAYA BLANCA 21

*Castillo de
las Coloradas*

*Playa de las
Mujeres*

*Punta del
Papagayo*

For keys to symbols *see back flap*

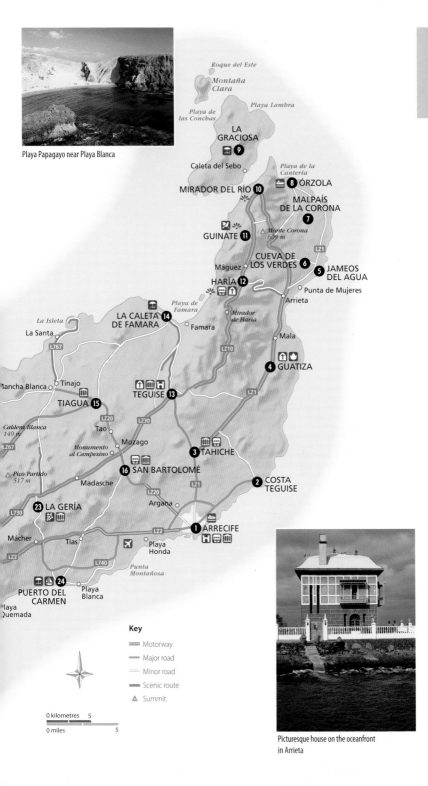

Playa Papagayo near Playa Blanca

Roque del Este

Montaña Clara

Playa de las Conchas

Playa Lambra

LA GRACIOSA

9

Caleta del Sebo

Playa de la Cantería

8 ÓRZOLA

MIRADOR DEL RÍO 10

MALPAÍS DE LA CORONA

7

Monte Corona 609 m

LZ1

GUINATE 11

CUEVA DE LOS VERDES 6

Máguez

5 **JAMEOS DEL AGUA**

HARÍA 12

Punta de Mujeres

Arrieta

Playa de Famara

Mirador de Haría

LA CALETA DE FAMARA 14

Famara

Mala

La Isleta

La Santa

L767

LZ10

4 **GUATIZA**

Mancha Blanca

Tinajo

LZ21

TIAGUA 15

TEGUISE 13

Caldera Blanca 149 m

LZ220

LZ230

LZ267

Tao

Mozago

Monumento al Campesino

3 **TAHICHE**

Pico Partido 517 m

Madasche

16 **SAN BARTOLOMÉ**

2 **COSTA TEGUISE**

23 **LA GERÍA**

Argana

LZ20

LZ1

L730

1 **ARRECIFE**

Mácher

Tías

LZ2

LZ2

L740

PUERTO DEL CARMEN

24

Playa Honda

Playa Blanca

Punta Montañosa

Playa Quemada

Key

▬▬ Motorway

▬▬ Major road

▬▬ Minor road

▬▬ Scenic route

△ Summit

0 kilometres 5

0 miles 5

Picturesque house on the oceanfront in Arrieta

Boats on the water at Charco de San Ginés, in Arrecife

❶ Arrecife

🏘 56,880. ✈ 5 km (3 miles) west of Arrecife. 🚌 ℹ Parque José Ramírez Cerdá, s/n, 928 813 174. 🚢 Sat. 🎭 Carnival (Feb), San Ginés (Aug). 🌐 arrecife.es

Arrecife has genuine Spanish character. With modern houses and a palm-lined promenade, it has been the capital of Lanzarote since 1852, as well as the island's main seaport and commercial centre. It is not as picturesque as the rest of the island, but there are some interesting sights and no high-rise apartment blocks; instead the one-storey houses are built in the traditional style. The attractive main shopping street, León y Castillo, has goods at much cheaper prices than at the major tourist resorts, plus a number of cafés and restaurants.

The first harbour, protected by small islands and reefs, existed here as early as the 15th century. Two forts, the **Castillo de San Gabriel** (1574) and **Castillo de San José** (1771) were built to protect the island from seaborne raiders and have survived to this day.

The castle of St Gabriel, situated on a small island, is reached by a long drawbridge – Puente de las Bolas, or "Balls Bridge". Destroyed during a pirate attack in

1586, the castle was restored by Italian engineer Leonardo Torriani.

The San José fortress, restored by César Manrique, was turned into a modern art gallery, the **Museo Internacional de Arte Contemporáneo,** in 1976. Four rooms are used for temporary exhibitions of the great masters, including Pablo Picasso, Joan Miró, Oscar Dominguez or Manrique himself. Recitals of chamber and modern music are held in the concert hall. Manrique designed the spacious and stylish gallery as well as the castle restaurant.

Also worth visiting are the **Casa de la Cultura Agustín de la Hoz** and **Casa de Los Arroyo**, dating back to 1749 and featuring a courtyard with wooden galleries and a well at its centre.

Arrecife's Iglesia de San Ginés

Quite different in character is the area around **Charco de San Ginés**, with its pretty fishermen's cottages overlooking a small lake that connects to the sea. The **Iglesia de San Ginés**, completed in 1665, is dedicated to the patron saint of Arrecife. This triple-naved church with timber vaults features late-Baroque statues of San Ginés and the Virgen del Rosario, which were brought from Cuba.

🏛 **Museo Internacional de Arte Contemporáneo**
Castillo de San José, Carretera de Naos. **Tel** 928 812 321. **Open** 10am–8pm daily. 🚫 📷

❷ Costa Teguise

🏘 7,981. 🚌 ℹ Avenida Islas Canarias, s/n, 928 592 542. 🌐 turismoteguise.com/en

This is the third-largest resort on the island, after Puerto del Carmen and Playa Blanca. Just 9 km (6 miles) northeast of Arrecife, it is fairly new and dates back to 1977, when the five-star Gran Meliá Salinas hotel was built here with the assistance of Manrique.

This large resort, with low-rise holiday developments of white bungalows, has a golf course, a marina and a shopping centre. It also has some pleasant sandy beaches. The largest and most scenic of these is Playa de las Cucharas. Smart and modern, Costa Teguise once attracted an elite clientele (King Juan Carlos of Spain has a private villa here), though it is now fairly similar to other resorts on the island.

Constant breezes mean that the place is popular with windsurfers. Those preferring less strenuous water activities can enjoy the water park located just outside town.

Monument at Playa de las Cucharas, Costa Teguise

❸ Tahiche

8 km (5 miles) north of Arrecife. 🚌

Just outside the town, on the lava fields created by the 1730–36 volcanic eruptions, stands **Taro de Tahiche**. This house was built in 1968 by César Manrique, who lived here until 1988. Upon moving to Haría, he donated Taro de Tahiche to the **Fundación César Manrique**. Founded by himself and a circle of his friends, this organization aims to promote architecture that is in harmony with the natural environment.

In keeping with this goal, Manrique built his house amid the island's characteristic blue-black lava flows. The cubic forms above ground draw on the traditional style of the island, though the space is opened out with contemporary touches such as large windows and wide terraces. Below ground, the design becomes more dramatic still. The lower floor features five volcanic "bubbles" – interconnected by tunnels. These vast compartments, 5 m (16 ft) in diameter, were formed by solidifying lava.

Each of the "bubbles" has its own basalt staircase leading from the lower floor to the upper level. In one of the rooms, the upper and lower spaces are linked by a fig tree, which rises from the lower floor and into the drawing room above.

The house, which became the embodiment of the artist's dream to live near and in harmony with nature, now houses a modern art museum, which has examples of Manrique's own works and project designs, plus other modern art, including works by Pablo Picasso, Antonio Tàpies, Joan Miró and Jesús Soto.

The broad terraces and garden are an essential part of the house. Situated within the garden, near the café, is a giant mural created by Manrique in 1992, using volcanic rock and ceramic tiles.

🏛 **Fundación César Manrique**
Taro de Tahiche, Calle Jorge Luis Borges, 10. **Tel** 928 843 138.
Open 10am–6pm daily. 🅿
ⓦ fcmanrique.org

Inside Taro de Tahiche, Manrique's former home

Environs

On a plateau located 2 km (1 mile) west of Tahiche lies the well-preserved **Quesera de Zonzamas**, a block of stone-like porous basalt into which the Guanches carved five deep and wide channels. Although their exact function is still unclear, a theory suggests that the channels may have been used for the production of cheese. There are also several petroglyphs nearby.

César Manrique (1919–1992)

Painter, sculptor, architect, town-planner and art restorer César Manrique was born in Arrecife. Having volunteered in Franco's artillery unit in the Spanish Civil War, he later devoted himself to art. His abstract paintings were exhibited across Europe as well as in Japan and the United States, and he won international acclaim. In 1968, he returned to Lanzarote and brought his talent to bear on the task of protecting the natural environment against the uncontrolled development of the island for tourism. Manrique's efforts paid off, and rules were introduced for developers, dictating the height, style and colour of buildings. In addition, Manrique's own designs incorporating volcanic forms helped to create many architectural masterpieces on all the Canary Islands. Manrique died in a car accident in 1992, but he left his mark on Lanzarote, both in terms of his bold designs and in the restrained way traditional island life has adapted to tourism.

César Manrique, against the backdrop of immense lava fields

Giant metal cactus at the entrance to Guatiza's Jardín de Cactus

❹ Guatiza

🗺 810. 17 km (11 miles) northeast of Arrecife.

The small town of Guatiza, to the northeast of Lanzarote and featuring the lovely 19th-century chapel of **Santa Margarita**, is surrounded by vast plantations of prickly pear. The plant is host to the cochineal insect – a source of vermilion or crimson dye.

Situated at the very centre of the cactus fields, on the outskirts of Guatiza, is the **Jardín de Cactus**, designed by César Manrique. At the entrance to the garden, established in 1990, stands an 8-m- (26-ft-) tall metal statue of a cactus. The large garden, which has a good restaurant, was built in an enormous pit, originally dug by the villagers, who were excavating volcanic ash to fertilize their fields.

The Jardín de Cactus is arranged in the form of a giant amphitheatre, dominated by a white windmill. Growing on the terraces are about 10,000 specimens, representing over 1,000 varieties of cactus.

🌵 **Jardín de Cactus**
Carretera General del Norte, s/n. **Tel** 928 529 397. **Open** Jul–Sep: 9am–5:45pm daily; Oct–Jun: 10am–5:45pm daily. 🖼

❺ Jameos del Agua

Carretera de Orzola. 🚌 **Tel** 928 848 020. **Open** Jul–Sep: 10am–6:30pm Sun–Fri (to 12:30am Sat); Oct–Jun: 10am–6:30pm Sun–Fri (to 10pm Sat). 🖼

In the late 1960s, César Manrique turned these natural caves into a complex of entertainment venues. Situated in the northeastern part of the island, the caverns are well worth visiting. A staircase leads down to an underground restaurant and, further on, to a giant cave, 62 m (203 ft) long, 19 m (62 ft) wide and 21 m (69 ft) high.

The cave features a salt lake, connected to the ocean (look out for the unique blind species of crab). The bed is below sea level, and the water level rises and falls with the tide.

Above the caves is Jameo Grande. This picturesque, irregularly shaped swimming pool is surrounded by artistically arranged tropical flora and opens to an underground auditorium, seating 600. This unique setting is famous for its outstanding acoustics. Apart from the natural features in the caves, another point of interest is the exhibition on volcanoes.

At night one of the caves is used as a nightclub – a striking setting for a dancefloor.

A palm beside the pool in one of Jameos del Agua's sunken craters

❻ Cueva de los Verdes

26 km (16 miles) north of Arrecife. **Tel** 928 848 484. **Open** 10am–6pm daily (summer: to 7pm). 🖼 🎫

Cueva de los Verdes is a 7-km- (4-mile-) long underground volcanic tunnel, created by the eruption of the nearby Monte Corona, more than 5,000 years ago. One of the world's longest volcanic tunnels, it is formed from a tube of solidified lava. The cave's name has nothing to do with any green colour; it derives from the name of a shepherd family, the Verdes (Greens), who inhabited it in the 18th and 19th centuries. The cave's walls and vaults are in fact

Exploring the Cueva de los Verdes

red and ochre due to iron oxidation and water seeping from the suface. From the 17th century, the cave was used by the local population as a shelter from pirates and slave traders.

In 1964, artificial lighting was installed, and 2 km (1 mile) of the cave was opened to visitors. The tour takes about an hour. One of the caves included in the tour features a small lake. Although only 20 cm (8 inches) deep, the stone vaults reflected in the water make it appear far deeper. Another cave has been converted into a concert hall.

Lichen growing on the volcanic debris in Malpaís de la Corona

❼ Malpaís de la Corona

These volcanic badlands bear testimony to the extreme volcanic activities that shook this northernmost point of the island some 5,000 years ago. This wild terrain, strewn with volcanic rock and slowly being colonized by sparse vegetation, occupies 30 sq km (12 sq miles) between the village of Orzola

and the headland of Punta de Mujeres, near Arrieta.

On the western end of Malpaís, visible from far and wide, stands the mighty Monte Corona volcano. This measures 1,100 m (3,609 ft) in diameter at its base, 450 m (1,475 ft) at its top section and 609 m (2,000 ft) high. The eruptions of this volcano produced the wide belt of strange lava formations (the Malpaís de la Corona), which include the Cueva de los Verdes and Jameos del Agua.

❽ Órzola

🏔 290. 🚌 ⛴

This fishing village, lying at the northern tip of Lanzarote, is a haven of peace. It is known mainly for its excellent seafood restaurants, which stretch along the coastal seafront.

Órzola is also famous for the picturesque **Playa de la Cantería**, situated to the west. This beach is not suitable for bathing, as strong sea currents create unfavourable conditions.

A frequent ferry service provides links with the neighbouring island of **La Graciosa**. From here, you can travel by fishing boat as far as the islands of **Montaña Clara** and **Alegranza**.

You won't be allowed to explore, however, as these two small and uninhabited islands form part of the national park, which was founded in 1986 and is off-limits to visitors.

La Graciosa, from the Mirador de Guinate

❾ La Graciosa

🏔 720. ⛴

The smallest inhabited island of the archipelago has an area of just 27 sq km (10 sq miles). Separated from Lanzarote by the straits of El Río, it was dubbed the "gracious island" by Jean de Béthencourt, and it fully meets the expectations of visitors looking for a quiet rest. An ideal place for scuba divers, anglers, hikers or anyone wishing to escape the brasher elements of tourism, La Graciosa plays to its strengths and offers a slow pace and a minimum of amenities. The island is fringed by long beaches of golden sand dunes.

The most beautiful of these is **Playa de las Conchas**, stretching over many kilometres of the northern shore. It is regarded as one of the most picturesque of all the beaches of the archipelago and provides a good view of the uninhabited smaller islands: **Montaña Clara, Roque del Este** and **Alegranza**.

There are no hotels on La Graciosa itself, but the village of **Caleta del Sebo**, linked by a ferry service to Órzola, has a few guesthouses and restaurants.

Fishing village of Órzola, on the northern end of Malpaís de la Corona

❿ Mirador del Río

Tel 928 526 548. **Open** 10am–5:45pm daily (Jul–Sep: to 6:45pm).

The most famous panoramic viewpoint on Lanzarote is situated at the northernmost point of the island, 474 m (1,555 ft) above sea level. This spot, hidden among rocks, provides a breathtaking view over the high cliffs of the northern shore. Clearly visible is the island of **La Graciosa** and, beyond it, **Montaña Clara** and Alegranza.

In 1898, when Spain was at war with the United States over Cuba, a gun emplacement was built here, guarding the straits of El Río, which separate Lanzarote from La Graciosa.

In 1973, the former gun emplacement was transformed by César Manrique to provide a belvedere, which combines nature and art in a unique architectural design, and visitors have been coming here ever since. Built into the rock, with an enormous window stretching the length of the room, is a minimalist bar and restaurant. Its stone walls are painted white. The only significant decorations inside are the huge mobiles by César Manrique. Their function is not merely decorative; they are also meant to dampen noise, because of the poor acoustics of the place.

Haría's town square with its restored, whitewashed houses

⓫ Guinate

 40.

Situated at the foot of the Monte Corona volcano, Guinate is a small village that is popular with bird lovers.

The **Guinate Tropical Park**, spread out on terraces, features waterfalls, ponds and gardens. Here you can see some 1,300 exotic birds, representing about 300 species, as well as many small apes. The park also has a penguin pool with an underwater viewing area.

Guinate Tropical Park
Tel 928 835 500. **Open** 10am–5pm daily.

Sign at the Mirador del Río

Environs
Just outside the village, the **Mirador La Graciosa** provides fine views over La Graciosa, Alegranza and Montaña Clara.

⓬ Haría

4,800. ℹ Plaza de la Constitución, s/n, 928 835 2541. 🚌 🏛 Sat. 🎉 San Juan (23 Jun), San Pedro (24 Jun).

Cubic, whitewashed houses, reminiscent of North African architecture, along with numerous palms, give this picturesque village an almost Middle-Eastern flavour. The scenic valley in which Haría is situated, known as the "valley of a thousand palms", was once home to far more of these trees. Many of

them were burned during a pirate attack in 1856.

The shady, tree-lined **Plaza León y Castillo** is surrounded by restored historic houses. At one end of the square stands the church of **Nuestra Señora de la Encarnación**.

Environs
Not far south of Haría is the **Mirador de Haría**. A winding road leads to the mountain pass, providing a fine view over the village, the surrounding volcanoes, the high cliffs, and Arietta. Ermita de las Nieves, on the road to Teguise, also offers wonderful views over the village of Los Valles.

⓭ Teguise

1,800. 🚌 ℹ Plaza de la Constitución, s/n, 928 845 398. 🏛 Sun. 🎉 Nuestra Señora del Carmen (16 Jul), Virgen de las Nieves (5 Aug).

Teguise is one of the oldest towns on Lanzarote. It was founded in 1418 by Maciot – nephew and successor of Jean de Béthencourt – who, it is said, lived here with Princess Teguise, the daughter of the Guanche king, Guadarfía.

Spacious squares and well-kept cobbled streets lined with beautifully restored houses are testimony to Teguise's former glory. A good time to visit is on

Tourists enjoying the wonderful view from the Mirador del Río

Sundays, when there is a craft market and folk dancing.

For centuries the town was one of the largest and richest on the island. Until 1852, it was its capital city. The fame and the wealth of Teguise, bearing the proud name of La Villa Real de Teguise (the Royal City of Teguise), attracted pirates who raided it repeatedly. The Callejón de la Sangre ("Street of Blood") owes its name to the worst of these raids and commemorates the victims of the massacre that took place in 1596.

The eclectic church of **Nuestra Señora de Guadalupe** stands in the town square. Since its construction in the mid-15th century, it has been rebuilt many times. The interior furnishing is Neo-Gothic and features a statue of the Virgin Mary of Guadalupe. On the opposite side of the square stands the **Casa-Museo del Timple Palacio Spínola**. This beautiful residence, with its small patio and a well, was built between 1730 and 1780. The reconstruction work, supervised by César Manrique, has restored the palace interiors to their former glory. The museum showcases the Canarian equivalent of the ukulele – the *timple*.

Also of interest are two conventual churches. The 16th-century **Convento de San Francisco**, better known as La Madre de Miraflores, was used

Castillo de Santa Bárbara, high above Teguise

as a burial site for the most prominent citizens of Lanzarote, and is now a venue for cultural events. Inside the 17th-century **Convento de Santo Domingo** is the original main altar. Now the abbey houses a modern art gallery – the Centro Arte.

Towering over the town is the **Castillo de Santa Bárbara**. The castle was built in the early 16th century on top of the 452-m- (1,483-ft-) high Guanapay peak, and provides a view over almost the entire island. Within the castle is the **Museo de la Piratería**, which tells the story of piracy in the Canary Islands.

Lion from
Teguise Palace

🏛 **Casa-Museo del Timple Palacio Spínola**
Plaza de la Constitución, s/n. **Tel** 928 845 181. **Open** 9am–4:30pm Mon–Sat (to 3:30pm Sun). 🖼
W **casadeltimple.org**

🏛 **Museo de la Piratería**
Castillo de Santa Bárbara. **Tel** 928 845 001. **Open** Jul–Sep: 10am–4pm Mon–Sun; Oct–Jun: 9am–4pm Mon–Sat, 10am–4pm Sun. 🖼
W **museodelpirateria.com**

⓮ La Caleta de Famara

🏠 1,100. 35 km (22 miles) north of Arrecife. 🚌

A small fishing village, with a handful of restaurants and one of the most beautiful beaches on Lanzarote, **Playa de Famara** is popular with visitors. **Urbanización Famara**, situated to the north, is a cluster of holiday chalets.

The beautiful 3-km- (2-mile-) long sandy beach stretches along the base of tall cliffs formed during the most recent volcanic eruption in 1824. Behind the beach, which provides a wonderful view over **La Graciosa**, runs a long band of dunes. This is a popular surfing beach, though the strong currents can be dangerous. The village also attracts quite a few painters and has been declared a conservation area.

Environs
Club La Santa, 13 km (8 miles) west, offers around 400 apartments and some 30 sports, so it is popular with professional sportsmen in off-season.

Playa de Famara, one of Lanzarote's most beautiful beaches

Windmill and camel at the Museo Agrícola El Patio, Tiagua

⓫ Tiagua

🗺 302. 🚌

This modest village offers visitors an insight into local history and tradition. The **Museo Agrícola El Patio** provides a glimpse of past agricultural practices. The complex is on the site of a farm dating back to 1845, when a group of impoverished farmers began to cultivate the fertile land. A century later, it was the biggest and best-run estate on the island.

Environs
Some 5 km (3 miles) to the west, in Mancha Blanca, stands the church of **Nuestra Señora de los Dolores**, where the Madonna is said to have brought lava streams to a halt on two occasions.

🏛 **Museo Agrícola El Patio**
Tel 928 529 134. **Open** 10am–5:30pm Mon–Fri, 10am–2:30pm Sat. 📷

⓰ San Bartolomé

🗺 18,500. 🛈 928 522 351 🚌 📷
San Bartolomé (15 Aug).
🌐 sanbartolome.es

Known to the Guanches as Ajei, San Bartolomé has some fine examples of traditional Canary architecture, including the 18th-century **Casa Perdomo**, with its beautiful courtyard and tiny chapel of Nuestra Señora del Pino. Today it houses the **Museo Etnográfico Tanit**. Various exhibits, such as musical instruments, agricultural tools, furniture and wine-production

equipment, illustrate the island's economic history. In the town centre is a large, stylish square, containing the parish church of **San Bartolomé** (1789).

🏛 **Museo Etnográfico Tanit**
C/Constitución, 1. **Tel** 928 802 549.
Open 10am–2pm daily. 📷
🌐 **museotanit.es**

Environs
A short way north, towards Mozaga, stands the **Monumento al Campesino** (Peasant's Monument). This 15-m (50-ft) tall construction was designed by César Manrique, and built in 1968 by Jesús Soto. Made of old water containers once used on fishing boats, the monument is devoted, in Manrique's own words, "to the nameless farmers, whose hard work helped to

Manrique's homage to peasant life

create the island's unique landscape". The nearby **Casa-Museo Monumento al Campesino** houses workshops devoted to various crafts, illustrating former rural life on Lanzarote. Its restaurant is good for lunch.

🏛 **Casa-Museo Monumento al Campesino**
Carretera Arrecife. **Tel** 928 520 136
Open 10am–5:45pm daily.

⓱ Parque Nacional de Timanfaya

See pp94–5.

⓲ Yaiza

🗺 720. 🚌 🛈 Playa Blanca, Calle, Limones, 1, 928 518 150. 📷 San Marcial (Jun), Nuestra Señora de los Remedios (1st week in Sep).

Nestling at the foot of the Montañas del Fuego, Yaiza is regarded, along with Haría, as one of the most picturesque towns on the island. In the 19th century, rich merchants settled here, and to this day some houses with palm-shaded façades bear evidence of this former wealth. The parish church of **Nuestra Señora de los Remedios** dates from the 18th century. This triple-naved church was built on the site of a former chapel dating back to 1699 and has a number of fine 18th-century paintings.

One of the former residences in Yaiza, now a hotel

Los Hervideros, south of El Golfo

The Baroque vault decorations, which incorporate folk elements, give the church its unique atmosphere. Numerous shops along the main street sell embroidery, pottery and other craft items.

Environs
Just 2 km (1 mile) east of Yaiza, **Uga** is the departure point for camel trips across the volcanic landscape.

⑲ El Golfo

130. 8 km (5 miles) northwest of Yaiza.

The sleepy hamlet of El Golfo is home to a small crater lagoon, **Lago Verde**, which was created by an underwater volcano. Its emerald-green colour is due to the sea algae that thrive in it. El Golfo's restaurants make it popular with tourists, while the presence of olivine (an olive-green semi-precious stone) attracts geologists and jewellery makers to the area.

Taking the path from the village, you get the best view of the lake, which is surrounded by dramatic, volcanic rocks resembling a petrified wave, and separated from the ocean by a narrow strip of black volcanic sand.

Environs
South of El Golfo are **Los Hervideros** ("the kettles"). As the name suggests, the waves "boil" inside the vast caves of the 15-m (50-ft) high cliffs.

⑳ Salinas de Janubio

9 km (6 miles) north of Playa Blanca.

The greenish waters of a natural lagoon are used to produce salt. Long used to preserve fish, the salt is still extracted by the traditional method of evaporation. The sea-salt plant is believed to be the largest operating on the archipelago and currently produces about 2,000 tonnes of salt per annum. Years ago, the water was pumped into the lagoon by windpower; today the pumps are electrically driven.

Local salt is still bought by fishermen, with a small portion sold as table salt. Each year, during the Corpus Christi festival, locals use dyed salt to create

Sunset over the checkerboard salt pans of Salinas de Janubio

magnificent decorations for the streets and squares.

㉑ Playa Blanca

🏠 8,000. 🚌 🚐 🛈 Pza. de Los Remedios, 1, 928 836 220. 🖪 Wed & Sat. 🎭 Nuestra Señora del Carmen (Jul).

A former fishing village, Playa Blanca is one of the largest resorts on the island, with regular ferry links to nearby Fuerteventura.

One of the best beaches is situated near the centre, with clear water and wonderful views over neighbouring Fuerteventura and Los Lobos. The **Playas de Papagayo** beaches, situated 4 km (2 miles) south of Playa Blanca, are also popular for sunbathing and swimming, due to their sheltered location.

Castillo de las Coloradas, one of Playa Blanca's former defences

Environs
The **Castillo de las Coloradas**, in Punta del Águila, is a watchtower dating from 1741–8. Between here and Punta de Papagayo is a string of scenic coves with sandy beaches: **Playa de las Mujeres**, **El Pozo** and **Papagayo**. Their fine sand and warm, clear waters attract an ever- increasing number of visitors.

This area is a part of the **Los Ajaches** nature reserve, created in 1994, which includes a bird protection zone. There is an entrance charge and the only access from Playa Blanca is by a minor road. Nearby, on the very edge of a cliff, are the remains of the island's first Norman settlement, **San Marcial del Rubicón**, founded in 1402 by Jean de Béthencourt.

⑰ Parque Nacional de Timanfaya

Between 1730 and 1736 the Montañas del Fuego – or Fire Mountains – belched forth smoke and molten lava, burying entire villages, and turning the island's fertile lowlands into a sea of solidified lava, grey volcanic rock and copper-coloured sand. Today, the lava remains are Lanzarote's greatest attraction. Situated to the southwest, they have become the heart of the national park, established in 1974, and include the 517-m (1,700-ft) Pico Partido. For the time being, the area is quite safe, though the lava still bubbles away under the surface, and a whiff of sulphur hangs in the air.

Park Logo
This mischievous little devil, designed by César Manrique, marks the boundaries of the national park.

La Mesa
Piedra Alta
Islote de los Betancores
Bermeja
El Volcán
Mar de Lavas
Halcones
103 m
Islote d Hilari
Buna de los Volcan
Encantada
Pedro Perico
258 m
Casas de Juan Perdomo

Montañas del Fuego
Femés offers a stunning view of the Fire Mountains. However, it is only at close range that it is possible to appreciate the awesome landscape. The lava fields can be visited on foot with a guide, by coach or as part of a camel tour.

0 kilometres 1
0 miles 1

Pedro Perico and Encantada
These two mountains, flecked with gorse shrubs and fig trees, are typical of the national park.

Fire in a Crater
Dry pieces of lichen, thrown into a shallow rock hollow, begin to burn quickly, demonstrating the continuing volcanic activity of this area.

Geyser
Water poured into underground pipes turns to steam within seconds. Islote de Hilario has the highest underground temperature in the park, reaching 600° C (1,112° F) at a depth of 12 m (40 ft).

★ Volcanic Grill
Taking advantage of the 300° C (572° F) temperatures, the volcanic grill is used to cook meat and fish at El Diablo, a restaurant designed by César Manrique (1970).

Caldera Blanca
149 m

Tiagua
ⓘ

Caldera Roja
427 m

LZ67

Pico Partido
517 m

Caldera de los Cuervos
502 m

Yaiza

Key
═══ Minor road
═══ Other road
··· Footpath
━━━ Park boundary

★ Ruta de los Volcanes
A really interesting part of the national park open to visitors. However, there is a wide variety of different landscapes and volcanic formations elsewhere in the park.

㉒ Femés

🏔 200. 🎪 San Marcial (7 Jul).

Overlooked by the 608-m (1,995-ft) high volcanic peak of Atalaya de Femés, this village once boasted one of the island's oldest religious buildings – the **Ermita San Marcial del Rubicón** cathedral, devoted to the patron saint of the island and destroyed in the 16th century by pirates. The present church, built on the site in 1733, is devoted to the same saint. Its white-painted walls are decorated with models of sailing ships, testimony to the seafaring heritage of the Canary Islands. Unfortunately, the church is open only during services.

In the centre of Femés, by the side of the road, is a fine viewpoint, which provides a scenic panorama of Montaña Roja and the ocean. The opposite side of town overlooks the panorama of Montañas del Fuego.

Ermita San Marcial del Rubicón, in Femés

㉓ La Geria

🏔 20. Northeast of Uga.

Stretching on both sides of the road from Masdache to Uga, the valley of La Geria is the main vine-growing area on Lanzarote. Set within this black cinder landscape that once featured only the occasional palm tree, the vineyards look as if they have been transplanted whole-sale from another planet. They occupy 52 sq km (20 sq miles) and have been declared a protected area. The valley, right up to the volcanic slopes, is dotted with small hollows, sheltered from the drying wind by low, semicircular walls. Each hollow *(gería)* is covered with volcanic cinder that absorbs dew at night and maintains the required humidity. Each contains a single vine. There are over 10,000 such hollows here.

The grapes are used to produce the very sweet and aromatic Malvasía – an excellent-quality wine, for

Lanzarote's Beaches

Lanzarote's 250-km- (155-mile-) long shoreline offers only 30 km (19 miles) of sandy beaches, some of which are popular with nudists *(see p181)*. In contrast to the long beaches of Fuerteventura, these are usually fairly small and consist of golden or white sand. Particularly beautiful beaches are found north of Arrecife.

③ **Puerto del Carmen** has several easily accessible but built-up beaches. The main ones are Playa Blanca and Playa de los Pocillos, both over a kilometre (half a mile) long with golden sand.

① **Playas de Papagayo**
A dirt track leads to several lovely sandy beaches, situated in a picturesque cove at the foot of a high cliff, on the southern shore of the island. The journey is rewarded by the sheer beauty of the area.

Key

━ Motorway

▬ Main road

═ Minor road

which Lanzarote is famous. This, as well as other brands of local wine, can be purchased cheaply in one of the many local *bodegas* (wine shops). All visitors coming to *bodegas* may sample the wines on offer before buying.

The vineyards tend to be small. El Grifo, situated at the northern end of La Geria, is a good example. Its outbuildings house a wine museum, the **Museo del Vino de Lanzarote**, arranged in an old *bodega* dating from 1775. Apart from the old equipment used in the production and storage of wine, the museum has a library with more than 1,000 books, plus several 17th- and 18th-century manuscripts devoted to winemaking. The area was declared an official natural park in 1987 and reclassified as a Natural Space of the Canary Islands in 1994.

🏛 **Museo del Vino de Lanzarote**
Tel 928 524 951. **Open** 10:30am–6pm daily. 🔲 elgrifo.com

㉔ Puerto del Carmen

🏔 11,000. 🚌 🚢 ⓘ Avda. de las Playas, 928 510 542. 🎉 Nuestra Señora del Carmen (Aug).
🔲 **puertodelcarmen.com**

This former fishing village is now established as the island's top resort. Visitors come for the beaches along the Avenida de las Playas, which are some of the island's most beautiful.

In Puerto del Carmen, which is densely filled with hotels, guesthouses and white villas,

there is no shortage of shops, nightclubs, banks and restaurants. Numerous agencies encourage visitors to sample the local attractions, such as windsurfing, diving, fishing and trips by catamaran to Fuerteventura and Lobos.

Environs
Just 9 km (6 miles) north, **Puerto Calero** has the island's loveliest marina. It offers boat rides to the Papagayo beaches and submarine trips for glimpses of life beneath the Atlantic waves.

The harbour district, the oldest part of Puerto del Carmen

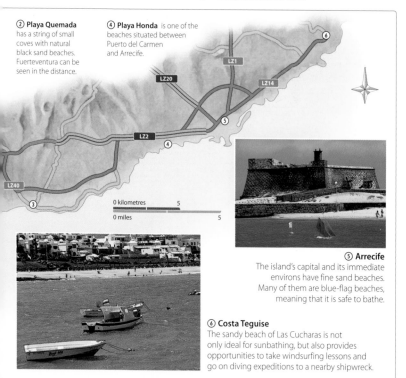

② **Playa Quemada** has a string of small coves with natural black sand beaches. Fuerteventura can be seen in the distance.

④ **Playa Honda** is one of the beaches situated between Puerto del Carmen and Arrecife.

LZ1
LZ20
LZ14
LZ2
LZ40

0 kilometres 5
0 miles 5

⑤ **Arrecife**
The island's capital and its immediate environs have fine sand beaches. Many of them are blue-flag beaches, meaning that it is safe to bathe.

⑥ **Costa Teguise**
The sandy beach of Las Cucharas is not only ideal for sunbathing, but also provides opportunities to take windsurfing lessons and go on diving expeditions to a nearby shipwreck.

TENERIFE

In the language of the Guanches the name Tenerife meant "white mountain". This referred to the looming Pico del Teide – Spain's tallest peak. The 3,718-m (12,198-ft) volcano is at the heart of the island and forms part of the national park, attracting many thousands of visitors every year. Depending on the season, its summit is enveloped in clouds, sulphur or a good dusting of snow.

Covering an area of 2,034 sq km (785 sq miles), Tenerife is the largest of the archipelago's islands. Situated between La Gomera and Gran Canaria, 300 km (186 miles) from Africa, it has about 908,000 inhabitants. The northern areas are the most densely populated, in particular around Santa Cruz – the island and provincial capital.

Pico del Teide divides the island into two distinct climate zones. Sheltered by the crater, the northwestern area is humid, covered in lush tropical vegetation and supports evergreen vineyards. The southern part is hot, rocky and arid. Because of this, Tenerife, like Gran Canaria, is often referred to as a "miniature continent".

By far the most important element of the island's economy is tourism. Its beginnings date back to the late 19th century when the first tourists arrived in search of blue skies, sun and clean air. The first hotel – the Grand Hotel Taoro in Puerto de la Cruz – opened in 1889 and was then one of the largest hotels in Spain.

However, the real boom in tourism began in the late 1960s. At first, tourists came mainly to the fertile, northern region of the island. Soon, tourism reached the south, and, before long, its rocky shores were covered with many truck-loads of sand imported from the Sahara. Investment was stepped up with the addition of smart hotels and a dash of greenery. The gamble paid off, and today most of the visitors to Tenerife prefer the southern resorts, such as Playa de las Américas and Los Cristianos.

The seafront boulevard, Playa de las Américas

◀ The charming Taganana village at the foot of the Anaga mountains

Exploring Tenerife

Attracted by the mild climate and an average coastal temperature of 21° C (70° F), Tenerife attracts thousands of tourists. Most visitors stay in large resorts where they have the opportunity to indulge in a variety of sports. The rocky, volcanic terrain of the national park, with its rivers of solidified lava, is fabulous for walking, and there are still some relatively remote villages within the region of the Anaga Mountains. In February and March, the island explodes in a riot of colour for the carnival, which in terms of its exuberance ranks alongside that of Rio de Janeiro.

Atlantic Ocean

Santa Cruz de Tenerife

Las Palmas de Gran Canaria

Locator Map

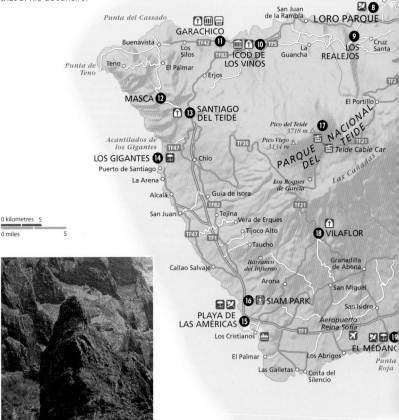

Punta del Cassado

PUERTO DE LA CRUZ **7**

San Juan de la Rambla

LORO PARQUE **8**

GARACHICO

Buenavista

Los Silos

TF42

11

TF82

ICOD DE LOS VINOS

10

La Guancha

TF5

9

LOS REALEJOS

Cruz Santa

Punta de Teno

Teno

El Palmar

Erjos

El Portillo

TF2

MASCA **12**

13 SANTIAGO DEL TEIDE

Pico del Teide 3718 m

17

PARQUE NACIONAL DEL TEIDE

TF21

Acantilados de los Gigantes

TF47

Pico Viejo 3134 m

TF36

Telde Cable Car

LOS GIGANTES **14**

Chío

Las Cañadas

Puerto de Santiago

La Arena

Los Roques de García

Alcalá

Guía de Isora

TF82

San Juan

Tejina

Vera de Erques

TF21

18 VILAFLOR

TF47

TF1

Tijoco Alto

Taucho

Callao Salvaje

Barranco del Infierno

Granadilla de Abona

Arona

San Miguel

16 SIAM PARK

San Isidro

PLAYA DE LAS AMÉRICAS **15**

Aeropuerto Reina Sofía

Los Cristianos

TF1

19

EL MÉDANO

El Palmar

Los Abrigos

Punta Roja

Las Galletas

Costa del Silencio

0 kilometres 5

0 miles 5

Masca, one of the most beautiful villages on Tenerife

Getting There

Tenerife has two airports: Reina Sofía in the south and Tenerife North (formerly Los Rodeos) in the north. Both airports receive international and charter flights. Ferries from Tenerife sail to all the islands of the archipelago and to Cadiz. TITSA lines provide bus transport, although not the entire island has bus links. Visitors can take organized coach tours or hire a car and use the tram that runs throughout Santa Cruz and La Laguna.

For keys to symbols see back flap

Punta del Hidalgo

Punta del Hidalgo
Chamorga
Benijo
Faro de Anaga

Taganana
Taborno
El Balladero

BAJAMAR 4

Mesa del Mar

Tegueste

TF13

PARQUE RURAL DE ANAGA

TF12 3

CORONTE 5

Aeropuerto Tenerife Norte

TF5

auzal

TF24

2 **LA LAGUNA**

San Andrés

La Esperanza

1 **SANTA CRUZ DE TENERIFE**

La Matanza

Taco

La Victoria

Santa María del Mar

OROTAVA

TF1

Tabaiba

Las Caletillas

Arafo

20 **CANDELARIA**

North Atlantic Ocean

GÜIMAR 21

servatorio Teide

Puerto de Güimar

Fasnia

El Tablado

Los Roques

TF28

Arico

Las Eras

o de Arico

Poris de Abona

Abades

TF1

San Miguel de Tajao

El Médano, a favourite destination for windsurfers

Key

━━ Motorway

── Major road

══ Minor road

── Scenic route

▲ Summit

The picturesque town of Los Realejos

Sights at a Glance

① Santa Cruz de Tenerife

Santa Cruz de Tenerife took its name from the conquistadors' Holy Cross, which Alonso Fernández de Lugo erected after landing on Añaza beach in 1494. During the 16th century, this former fishing village became an important port for land-locked La Laguna. Since 1723, the town has been the administrative centre of Tenerife; it was also the capital of the entire archipelago from 1822 to 1927. Today, the economic life of Santa Cruz is dominated by its deep-water harbour, which can accommodate luxury liners, tankers arriving from Venezuela and the Middle East, and container ships loaded with bananas and tomatoes ready for export.

The imposing bell tower of Nuestra Señora de la Concepción

Exploring Santa Cruz de Tenerife

Though it does not have many historic sights, the capital of Tenerife has many attractions. The town's unique atmosphere is provided by the 19th-century, colonial-style architecture. Visitors come for the plentiful shopping opportunities, the museums and art galleries, the musical repertoire of the Tenerife Auditorium, the annual classical music festival and, above all, the carnival.

🏛 Museo de la Naturaleza y el Hombre

C/Fuente Morales, s/n. **Tel** 922 535 816. **Open** 9am–8pm Tue–Sat, 10am–5pm Mon & Sun. **Closed** 1 & 6 Jan, Shrove Tue, 24–25 & 31 Dec. 🅿

The natural history museum occupies a classical building that was once a military hospital. The exhibition is a colourful multimedia show dedicated to the geology, archaeology, and flora and fauna of the Canary Islands.

In addition to the ever-popular mummies and skulls of the Guanches, it also displays a small collection of artifacts (including pottery, African carvings and pre-Columbian art) as well as fossils from around the world.

🏛 Iglesia de Nuestra Señora de la Concepción

C/Domínguez Alfonso.
Though this church was built in 1498, its present appearance is the result of reconstruction work carried out in the second half of the 18th century. Its richly furnished interior features paintings and sculptures, including the magnificent main altar by José Luján Peréz.

The church serves as a pantheon and houses mementoes of the island's history, including a silver cross (Santa Cruz) of the conquistadors and British flags captured during Nelson's attack on the city in 1797.

Madonna at Plaza de la Candelaria

🏛 Plaza de España

The circular Plaza de España is in the town centre near the harbour. The giant monument standing in the middle of the square – **Monumento de los Caídos** – featuring bronze figures, is the work of Enrique César Zadivar and commemorates the victims of the 1936–9 Spanish Civil War.

The vast building on the south side of the square, the Cabildo Insular, was designed by José Enrique Marrero. An example of the Fascist architecture of the 1930s, it houses Tenerife's council building and Santa Cruz's main tourist office.

🏛 Plaza de la Candelaria

Laid out in 1701 and adjoining the Plaza de España on the west, the Plaza de Candelaria is a popular local meeting place and promenade. Its official name is Plaza de la Constitución. The monument standing at its centre – **El Triunfo de la Candelaria** – depicts the patron saint of the island. Carved in white Carrara marble and unveiled in 1787, it is the work of the Italian master, Antonio Canova. Another landmark on the square is the **Palacio de Carta** (1742). Formerly the Prefecture, it now contains a branch of the Banco Español de Crédito. It is worth seeking out for its fine example of a traditional Canarian patio.

Plaza de España, a good orientation point when exploring the town

Calle Castillo, the main shopping street, also good for handicrafts

🏛 Calle Castillo

Many visitors come to Santa Cruz with the sole purpose of spending a few hours in the little shops in and around Calle Castillo – the main pedestrianised shopping precinct.

Bargains are to be had in the local shops lining this attractive narrow street, whether they be electronic goods, watches or designer-label clothes, except during the siesta, which takes place between 1–4:30pm. Several large handicraft centres sell embroidery, wickerwork and pottery.

🏛 Iglesia San Francisco

C/Villalba.

Opposite the Museo Municipal de Bellas Artes stands the monumental Franciscan abbey founded around 1680. It was restored and extended in the 18th century and acquired an additional chapel.

Inside the church there is a 17th-century wooden altar and pulpit with beautifully painted decorations. The chapel became the parish church in 1869.

🏛 Museo Municipal de Bellas Artes

C/José Murphy, 12. **Tel** 922 609 446. **Open** 10am–8pm Tue–Fri, 10am–3pm Sat & Sun (Jul–Sep: to 2pm). 🅿 ⓦ santacruzdetenerife.es

Founded in 1898, the Museo has prize possessions from the Prado, including works by Old Masters. As well as works by Spanish painters from the 17th and 18th centuries, and collections of coins and armour, there is an exhibition of paintings depicting local events and landscapes, such as Santa Cruz Harbour or Landscape around Laguna, by Valentín Sanza y Carta (1849–98).

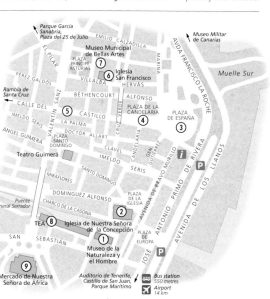

Baroque portal of the Iglesia San Francisco

🏛 TEA (Tenerife Arts Centre)

Avenida de San Sebastián, 10. **Tel** 922 849 057. **Open** 10am–8pm Tue–Sun.

This innovative building showcases contemporary photography, painting and sculpture exhibitions, both temporary and permanent.

🏛 Mercado de Nuestra Señora de África

Avenida de San Sebastián, 51. **Open** Market: 6am–3pm Mon–Sun. Mall: 9am–9pm Mon–Fri (to 3pm Sat), 10am–3pm Sun. Blue Rambla: 9am–1:30pm Mon–Sun.

This market-hall was built in 1946 in the style of North African architecture and sells fruit, vegetables, flowers, fresh fish, poultry and cheese.

Santa Cruz de Tenerife

1. Museo de la Naturaleza y el Hombre
2. Iglesia de Nuestra Señora de la Concepción
3. Plaza de España
4. Plaza de la Candelaria
5. Calle Castillo
6. Iglesia San Francisco
7. Museo Municipal de Bellas Artes
8. TEA (Tenerife Arts Centre)
9. Mercado de Nuestra Señora de África

0 metres 200
0 yards 200

For keys to symbols *see back flap*

The palm-shaded Plaza del 25 de Julio

🔊 Auditorio de Tenerife
Avenida de la Constitución, 1.
📧 auditoriodetenerife.com
The Auditorio de Tenerife opened in 2003 and is home to the Symphony Orchestra of Tenerife. The building, designed by Spanish architect Santiago Calatrava, has a futuristic style and has become one of the landmarks of the island's capital.

🏰 Castillo de San Juan
Situated on the waterfront, the protective fort of Castillo de San Juan was built in 1641. One of its functions was to guard the safety of the port, once famous for the trade in African slaves that was carried out on the Los Llanos wharf.
    The nearby small chapel of **Nuestra Señora de Regla** dates from the same period. Now both these buildings are overshadowed by the colossal edifice of the **Auditorio de Tenerife**, the island's leading performing arts venue. Every year on 25 July, a re-enactment of the Battle of Santa Cruz de Tenerife is held, marking Admiral Nelson's unsuccessful attempt to take the city.

🏙 La Rambla de Santa Cruz
This is one of the most elegant streets in Santa Cruz, stretching from the Plaza de la Paz to Avenida de Anaga. With its smart houses, numerous restaurants and cafés, the street sweeps in a semi-circle through most of the city. Its wide central reservation, exclusively for pedestrians separates two busy traffic lanes. Planted with tall palms, Indian laurel trees and lilac jacaranda, it is a veritable "art boulevard". Modern sculptures are set amid the trees, which are illuminated at night and bear plaques with the names of famous artists from around the world, including Michelangelo, Vermeer, Piranesi, Warhol and Pollock. Every Sunday, a lively antiques fair takes place here.

Lush, green avenue in the peaceful Parque García Sanabria

🏙 Plaza del 25 de Julio
The 25th of July Plaza is a green oasis at the centre of the crowded, buzzing city. Its charm is enhanced by the central fountains and landscaped areas of trees and shrubs. The place, popular with the inhabitants of Santa Cruz, has a circle of original benches made of stone imported from Seville. Note the backrests decorated with ceramic tiles featuring old advertisements.

💠 Parque García Sanabria
Established in the 1920s, this attractive and peaceful park was named after the mayor of Santa Cruz. The park is full of lush tropical plants and has a wonderful collection of trees. It has since been improved by the addition of a fountain and a number of modern sculptures. Besides being a good place to cool off, the park provides a brief lesson in Tenerife's history. The backrests of three benches depict the arrival of the conquistadors, the daily life of the Guanches and their defeat at the second Battle of Acentejo.

🏛 Museo Militar
C/San Isidro, 2. **Tel** 922 298 557.
Open 9am–3pm Mon–Fri, 10am–2pm Sat. 🅿
Founded in 1988, the museum occupies the former premises of the Cuartel de Almeida, a fortress dating back to 1884. The exhibition features ancient weapons of the Canary Islands, 17th-century Spanish militaria, and weapons dating from the 19th century.
    Banners, uniforms and the personal belongings of many famous soldiers form a major part of the exhibition. A separate section is devoted to the July 1797 battle against the British fleet under Nelson. The most famous exhibit – El Tigre – is a cannon that fired the grapeshot that tore into Nelson's arm during the attack on Santa Cruz.

Henry Moore sculpture in La Rambla de Santa Cruz

❷ La Laguna

🏛 153,000. 🚌 ℹ Casa Alvarado Bracamonte, Calle La Carrera, 7, 922 631 194. 📅 daily. 🎭 San Benito Abad (1st Sun in Jul), Santisimo Cristo (7–15 Sep). 🌐 **aytolalaguna.com**

Officially named Ciudad de San Cristóbal de la Laguna, La Laguna is Tenerife's second-largest city and a UNESCO World Heritage Site. Situated in the middle of the fertile valley of Aguere, it owes its name to the lagoon on whose shores it stood, and which was drained in 1837.

Founded in 1496 by the conquistador Alonso Fernández de Lugo, the town was the original residence of the Adelantados – the island's military governors. Until 1723, La Laguna was capital of the island, but moving the capital to Santa Cruz has not reduced the city's importance.

La Laguna is a university city, and its academic traditions go back to the first half of the 18th century. **San Fernando University**, still in existence, opened its doors for the first time in 1817. Since 1818, the city has been a bishopric.

St Christopher, La Laguna's patron saint

Despite its dynamic development (with some of the suburbs virtually merging with Santa Cruz), the old town has a layout that has maintained its traditional form with a network of narrow streets and alleys following a chequerboard pattern. The district includes several noteworthy houses that have wooden balconies and lavish portals crowned with crests. They include **Casa del Corregidor** and **Casa de la Alhondiga** (both dating from the 16th century), the 17th-century **Casa Alvarado Bracamonte**, also known as Casa de los Capitanes and the 18th-century **Casa Mesa**.

The meticulously restored **Casa Lercaro**, built in 1593 by Genoese merchants, now houses the **Museo de Historia y Antropología de Tenerife**. Opened in 1993, it presents the history of the island from the times of the Spanish conquest through to the 20th century. The collection includes old documents, tools and 16th-century paintings. Among the collection's highlights are some of the oldest maps of the archipelago.

Nearby is another noteworthy building, the **Palacio Episcopal**. The bishop's palace features a beautiful stone façade dating from 1681. Of equal interest are some 19th-century buildings, such as the **Casino de la Laguna** (1899), whose creators drew on French designs, and the **Ayuntamiento**, the town hall of 1829 that houses the banner under which de Lugo fought during his conquest of Tenerife (see p34).

The present town hall, with its interior frescoes illustrating the island's history, stands in the **Plaza de Adelantado**. The adjacent church of **San Miguel** (1507) was founded by de Lugo himself. Also in the tree-shaded square is the **Convento de Santa Catalina de Siena**, with its original cloisters, and the **Palacio de Nava** – a good example of Spanish colonial architecture. Behind the square is a large market hall, where fruit, cheese and flowers are sold.

Patio of the Palacio Episcopal

Portal of Iglesia de Nuestra Señora de la Concepción

To the east of the Plaza de Adelantado stands the **Cathedral** (1904–15). The building features a twin-towered façade dating from 1825. The main feature of the interior is the magnificent retable (or altarpiece) at the back of the altar, dating from the first half of the 18th century. Behind the main altar stands the simple tomb of Alonso de Lugo.

In the Plaza de la Concepción stands the **Iglesia de Nuestra Señora de la Concepción** (1502) – an example of the architectural style dating from the time of the conquest. This triple-naved Gothic-Renaissance church has a magnificent reconstructed wooden vault. Each year, in August, thousands of pilgrims flock to the **Santuario del Cristo** – a small church at the northern end of La Laguna's old quarter – to pay homage to a statue of Christ carved in the late 15th century. This Gothic sculpture by an unknown artist was brought to Tenerife in 1520, by Alonso de Lugo.

🏛 **Museo de Historia y Antropología de Tenerife**
C/San Agustín, 22.
Tel 922 825 949. **Open** 9am–8pm Tue–Sat, 10am–5pm Mon & Sun. **Closed** 1 & 6 Jan, Shrove Tue, 24–25 & 31 Dec. ♿
🌐 **museosdetenerife.org**

❸ Anaga Mountains

A picturesque range of volcanic peaks, the Anaga Mountains (Parque Nacional de Anaga) are lush and green thanks to a cool, wet climate. Narrow tracks lead through craggy, inaccessible valleys, and wind among steep rock faces and dense forests. For walkers, the effort required to deal with arduous paths is amply rewarded by the breathtaking views of the rocky coast below and by the chance to see a wide variety of birds and plants.

⑩ Cliffs

These tall, rugged cliffs, which run west of Taganana, thrust their way into an often rough ocean, creating picturesque nooks and inlets. They are difficult to reach and are best admired from the deck of a cruising boat.

⑨ Taganana

This enchanting village lies at the foot of the mountains, amid palm trees. The access road runs in the shadow of the Roque de las Animas (Spirit Rock).

Cliffs ⑩

Taganana (

Taborno

Las Casas de Afur

Ermita Cruz del Carmen

⑪   TF12

Road to La Laguna

Las Mercedes

⑪ Road to La Laguna

Known as the gate to the Anaga Mountains, the road to La Laguna runs from Mirador Pico del Inglés, through the plateau of Las Mercedes.

↓ *La Laguna*

0 kilometres   2

0 miles   2

TF1   Bufader●

Valle Seco ●

Santa Cruz de Tenerife
①

Flora and Vegetation

The lush, evergreen vegetation of this remote region, including forests of laurel and juniper trees, and heather, ferns and herbs, gives the air its spicy scent. This area is deservedly popular with nature lovers. Dense bushes shelter the twisting roads from the wind, but they are difficult to trek through for anyone straying from a trail or path. Although the weather is not very warm, the humid air encourages the growth of vegetation.

Heather and ferns on the roadside near Chinobre

① Santa Cruz de Tenerife

The capital of Tenerife, in the northeastern part of the island is the start of the two motorways – del Norte and del Sur.

⑧ Roque de las Bodegas

The bay and the rocky beach are popular with surfers. Further to the east are Almáciga and Benijo, two fishing villages poised on top of the cliffs, which have a handful of restaurants.

⑦ Faro de Anaga

From Chamorga, one of the loveliest villages on Tenerife, a steep path, 2 km (1 mile) long, runs eastwards to the Anaga lighthouse, which stands on a high peak.

Punta
Bajo Las Palmas

Faro de Anaga
⑦

Roque de
⑧ las Bodegas

134

Chamorga

⑥ Chinobre

Punta de
Anaga

⑤ Barranco de
las Huertas

Punta de
Antequera

Igueste de San Andrés

TF12   TF11   ④

Playa de
las Teresitas

③

② San Andrés

⑥ Chinobre

The road leading from the El Bailadero Pass to Chinobre is where, according to folk legend, witches used to hold their Sabbaths. Some 13 km (8 miles) to the west, at the foot of the Taborno summit, is the Mirador Pico del Inglés.

④ Igueste de San Andrés

The inhabitants of this quiet village, at the mouth of a ravine, grow mangoes, avocados and bananas. The plantations stretch all the way to the ocean.

⑤ Barranco de las Huertas

The road from San Andrés to El Bailadero runs along the bottom of a ravine. On both sides are isolated farms standing in the cool shade of palm trees and mountain valley terraces, planted with crops.

② **San Andrés** This former fishing village is now a resort. It has narrow, shady streets and is justly famous for its selection of little seafood restaurants.

③ Playa de las Teresitas

The fine sand for this 2-km-(1-mile-) long beach was imported from the Sahara. Lined with palm trees, which lend the place an exotic character, the beach is a favourite spot with people from Santa Cruz.

Key

▬ Suggested route
═ Other road
••• Footpath
☀ Viewpoint

The scenic coastline of Bajamar in the northern part of Tenerife

❶ Bajamar

🗹 2,100. 🚌

The inhabitants of Bajamar once made their living from fishing and cultivating sugar cane. It is now popular as a resort and is a well-known tourist centre for Tenerife's northern coast. The high coastal cliffs and the soaring peaks of **Monte de las Mercedes** provide a picturesque backdrop for the numerous hotels and bungalows. The main road is lined with restaurants and cafés. Visitors who like bathing will enjoy the large complex of saltwater swimming pools.

Environs
About 2.5 km (2 miles) to the northeast is **Punta del Hidalgo**, a headland offering a fine view of the rocky coast and banana plantations. Strong winds create excellent conditions for windsurfing, though the currents make it dangerous for novices. Punta del Hidalgo is a starting point for a marked hiking trail to the cave dwellings at Chinamada.

❺ Tacoronte

🗹 3,700. 🚌 🚎 Sat, Sun. 🎭 Cristo de los Dolores (1st Sun after 23 Sep).

A coastal village, set 450 m (1,476 ft) above sea level, Tacoronte dates back to the Guanche times. The town and its environs are famous for their excellent wines. When in the area, you should visit one of the many wineries to sample some of the fine local vintages, known as Tacoronte-Acentejo.

Tacoronte is notable for its two churches. The **Iglesia del Cristo de los Dolores** features a revered 17th-century statue of Christ, which during the harvest festival, is carried through the streets of the town. Also noteworthy are the Baroque woodcarvings decorating the interior. The **Iglesia de Santa Catalina** (1664) has a fine wooden vault and rich interior furnishings.

Environs
Famed for its wine, **El Sauzal** is a short way to the south. Its main attraction is La Casa del Vino La Baranda – a complex in a renovated country house, which comprises a wine museum, wine-tasting hall, bar and store, as well as an excellent restaurant.

❻ La Orotava

See pp110–13.

❼ Puerto de la Cruz

See pp114–15.

❽ Loro Parque

See pp116–17.

❾ Los Realejos

🗹 36,000. 🚌 🎭 San Sebastián (22 Jan).

A sprawling town overlooked by the peak of the Tigaiga Mountain, and crisscrossed with a network of steep and winding streets, Los Realejos consists of two parts: Realejo Bajo (the lower town) and Realejo Alto (the upper town).

The town played an important part in Tenerife's history. It was here that the last five chieftains of the Guanches surrendered to the Spanish invaders in 1496.

In the upper part of Los Realejos stands the **Iglesia de Santiago Apóstol** (1498). The oldest church on the island, it has a beautiful *Mudéjar* (Spanish-Moorish) wooden vault. At the entrance to the town, from the direction of Puerto de la Cruz, stands **El Castillo de los Realejos**, built in 1862. This square structure, with four almost round towers at its corners, is set in a beautifully tended garden. Unlike other fortresses on the Canary Islands, built during the 16th and 17th

Tacoronte, situated on the coast and surrounded by vineyards

The Castillo de los Realejos, with its palm-decorated gardens

centuries on the ocean coast for defence, was never used for military purposes.

⓾ Icod de los Vinos

🏘 23,000. 🛈 C/San Sebastián, 6, 922 812 123. 🚌 🚕 San Antonio Abad (22 Jan), San Marcos (Mar), Fiestas del Cristo del Drago (1st Sun after 17 Sep).

As its name suggests, this small town is in the heart of a fertile wine-growing region. However, tourists visit Icod mainly in order to see the legendary symbol of the islands – the **Drago Milenario**. Reputed to be over 1,000 years old, this dragon tree *(see p19)* is probably half that age. The biggest specimen in the archipelago, it is best seen from the Plaza de la Iglesia.

The triple-naved church of **San Marcos** was built in the 15th and 16th centuries. Its interior features a beautiful coffered ceiling and a silver high altar. Other interesting items include the painting of Santa Ana, attributed to Bartolomé Murillo, and a fine marble baptismal font (1696).

One of the chapels houses the **Museo de Arte Sacro**. The jewel of its collection is an enormous filigree silver cross. Made in Cuba in 1663–8, by Jerónimo de Espellosa, it is 2.45 m (8 ft) high. Weighing 48.3 kg (106 lb), this gleaming filigree silver cross is thought

Huge dragon tree, in Icod de Vinos

to be the largest ever made. At **Mariposario del Drago**, close to the dragon tree, you can learn about the life cycle of butterflies. Many tropical butterflies flutter freely here, among jungle vegetation and water gardens.

🏛 **Museo de Arte Sacro**
Iglesia de San Marco. **Tel** 922 810 695. **Open** 9am–1:30pm, 4–6:30pm daily.

🏛 **Mariposario del Drago**
Avenida de Canarias, s/n. **Tel** 922 815 167. **Open** 10am–7pm daily (winter: to 6pm). 🚕 🌐 **mariposario.com**

⓫ Garachico

🏘 5,000. 🚌 🚕 San Sebastián (20 Jan), Romería de San Roque (16 Aug).

Established in the 16th century by Genoese merchants, Garachico, on the north coast of Tenerife, is a jewel of a town, with historic buildings and traditional-style houses providing a sense of architectural unity.

Garachico was once the most important port on the island (later developing into a centre of sugar production) until the eruption of the Volcán Negro in 1706 put an end to its prosperity. Lava buried whole districts and most of the harbour, with only a handful of

houses escaping destruction, together with the **Castillo de San Miguel** (1577). The castle currently houses the Heritage Information Centre and guards Garachico Bay. The only portion of the former **Santa Ana** church to escape is the 16th-century façade. The restored interior has a Baroque font and a crucifix attributed to Martín de Andújar.

Another relic of the town's former glory includes the partially restored **Palacio de los Condes de la Gomera** (Palace of the Counts of Gomera). It stands in the Plaza de la Libertad and seems more like a fortress than a palace, due to its thick walls and stone façade. There are also several former convents, including the 17th-century **Santo Domingo**, now a modern art museum, and the convent of **San Francisco Nuestra Señora de los Angeles**. A section of this 18th-century convent is occupied by a modest museum, **Casa de la Cultura**. Also in the Plaza de la Libertad is a **monument** to **Simón Bolívar**, liberator of South America.

Every winter, Garachico is battered by Atlantic gales. The huge waves are truly spectacular, especially when the water level drops to reveal the vast **Roque de Garachico**.

🏛 **Museo de Arte Contemporáneo**
Plaza de Santo Domingo. **Tel** 922 830 000. **Open** 10am–1pm, 3–6pm Mon–Sat, 10am–1pm Sun. 🚕

Entrance to the Castillo de San Miguel, Garachico

⑥ La Orotava

Prior to the conquest of the island, the town of La Orotava, situated on Teide's northern slopes, belonged to Taoro – the richest of the Guanche kingdoms on Tenerife. Soon after the Spanish conquest, settlers from Andalusia populated the Orotava valley, and the first churches and residences were built here in the 16th century. The beauty of their wooden decorations is reminiscent of the Arabian palaces of southern Spain. After gaining its independence from La Laguna in 1648, La Orotava began to develop rapidly to become one of the loveliest towns in the entire archipelago.

Exploring La Orotava

La Orotava is one of the best-preserved old towns on Tenerife. Its steep, narrow, cobbled streets captivate most visitors, as do the enchanting 17th- and 18th-century town houses. Their wooden, exquisitely carved balconies, fashioned from dark wood, represent the quintessence of Canarian architecture.

Most of the interesting buildings are found in the compact old town. Excellent signposting makes it easy to find all of the sights.

🏛 Iglesia de la Concepción

Plaza Casañas. **Open** daily.
The Iglesia de la Concepción, or Church of the Immaculate Conception, located in Plaza Casañas, has a unique atmosphere. Its magnificent interior, with wooden sculptures by several local artists, including Fernando Estévez and José Luján Pérez, is enhanced by recordings of Mozart's music, which are played here almost all day long.

The original church, built in the 16th century, was destroyed by earthquakes in 1704 and 1705. The present triple-naved church is the result of restoration work carried out between 1768 and 1788 by two architects – Diego Nicolás and Ventura Rodríguez – who together produced this fine example of Canary Baroque architecture, which takes much of its inspiration from the sacral buildings of Latin America. In 1948, the church was listed as a national monument.

🏛 Calle Carrera Escultor Estévez

The town's defining feature is the chain of streets, including Calle Doctor Domingo González García, Calle San Francisco and Calle Carrera Escultor Estévez, which run in a semicircle through the old part of La Orotava. Lined with charming houses built mostly in the second half of the 19th century, the streets wind up the hill toward the Plaza del Ayuntamiento.

Carrera Escultor Estévez, the main street in La Orotava

The tourist office at Calle Carrera Escultor Estévez 2 can supply free town maps indicating the must-see sights along this street. One interesting stopping-off point is El Pueblo Guanche (C/Carrera, 7), an ethnographic museum occupying a renovated town house. The museum has a shop selling handicrafts and food products and also a restaurant.

🏛 Plaza del Ayuntamiento

During Corpus Christi, this pleasant square, which is situated at the very heart of the old town and towered over by its Neo-Classical town hall, becomes the focus of religious celebrations. At this time, the paving stones of the tree-lined square are covered with unusual, colourful "carpets", created from volcanic ash, soil and sand. Visitors can take home images of these fleeting works of art because they are recorded on colourful post-cards that can be found on sale throughout the town all year round.

The imposing façade of the Iglesia de la Concepción

The tree-lined Plaza de la Constitución

🏛 Palacio Municipal

The town's administration centre is the *ayuntamiento* – the late Neo-Classical town hall, built in 1871–91, which has a modest façade virtually free of decoration. Its vault is painted with the heraldic arms of other towns on Tenerife, and with wall carvings depicting allegorical figures, which represent agriculture, history, morality and the law. Its patio once featured the oldest and largest dragon tree in the Canary Islands, which was destroyed during a storm in 1868.

🌿 Hijuela del Botánico

C/Tomás Pérez. **Open** 9am–2pm daily.
La Orotava's botanical garden was established in 1923 using shoots and cuttings taken from the Jardín Botánico in Puerto de la Cruz, which is famous throughout the Canary Islands. This process gave the garden its name, Hijuela del Botánico, meaning "daughter of the botanical garden". Today, the relatively small garden is blooming and features over 3,000 species of tropical and subtropical plants.

🏛 Plaza de la Constitución

This is a good place to sit down and admire La Orotava from the comfort of one of the bars and cafés, which come to life in the evenings. The Plaza, a relic of the old town's merchant past, has a tree-lined terrace, offering fine views over the buildings below. The multicoloured roof tiles and slender church towers combine to produce a memorable panorama of the town and valley that is reminiscent of Florence.

⛪ Iglesia de San Agustín

The north side of the Plaza de la Constitución is occupied by the church and abbey of St Augustine. Dating from the 17th century, this building features a beautiful façade with a Renaissance-Baroque portal. The church has many fine historic remains and a panelled ceiling, which was renovated between 2009 and 2011. The former abbey was once a music school, then an office and is now the Casa de la Cultura.

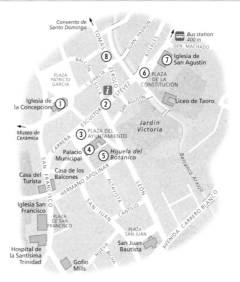

Decorations on the Iglesia de San Agustín

La Orotava

① Iglesia de la Concepción
② Calle Carrera Escultor Estévez
③ Plaza del Ayuntamiento
④ Palacio Municipal
⑤ Hijuela del Botánico
⑥ Plaza de la Constitución
⑦ Iglesia de San Agustín
⑧ Calle Tomás Zerolo

0 metres   200
0 yards   200

Calle Tomás Zerolo

Almost every street or alley in La Orotava offers some historic interest. Calle Tomás Zerolo, which passes through the lower part of the old town, is no exception. It features the **Convento de Santo Domingo**, which has a small museum of Latin American handicrafts, and, opposite it, the **Casa Torrehermosa**, a colonial-style house built in the 17th century for the Hermosa family. Today, this residence houses the Empresa Insular de Artesanía, a small workshop and museum devoted to local handicrafts.

Wooden galleries around the patio of the Casa de los Balcones

Casa de los Balcones

C/San Francisco, 3. **Tel** 922 330 629.
Open 8:30am–6:30pm daily.
W casa-balcones.com

The "House of Balconies", also known as the Casa de Fonseca, is a major landmark of La Orotava. Its light-coloured façade is adorned with a heavy, carved door, smart windows and long teak balconies. The palm-shaded patio, brimming over with greenery, is surrounded by the first- and second-floor galleries, which rest on slender wooden columns.

The house, built in 1632–70, has its own small museum of Canary art and handicrafts. Here, visitors can view and buy local products, including embroidery, lace, pottery, regional costumes and other souvenirs. Don't miss the miniature balconies of La Orotava.

Casa del Turista

C/ San Francisco, 4. **Tel** 922 330 629.
Open 9am–7pm Mon–Fri, 8:30am–5pm Sat.

Standing on the opposite side of the road to the Casa de los Balcones is the Casa del Turista, the former Convento Molina. This is a magnificent Canarian town house once belonging to a wealthy family. It was known collectively (with the 17th-century Casa Mesa and the Casa de los Lercaro) as the Doce Casas or "twelve houses". The house is built in a style similar to that of Casa de los Balcones, but is older, dating from 1509. It also offers the chance to view and purchase local handicrafts. Its prize exhibit is a religious scene made from coloured volcanic sand. This type of decoration, for which the town is famous, is made during Corpus Christi. The terraces at the back of the house provide a fine view over the Orotava valley.

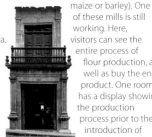

Stone portal of the Casa del Turista

Iglesia San Francisco

C/San Francisco.

The church of San Francisco, with its Baroque portal and rather plain interior, stands in the palm-shaded Plaza de San Francisco and serves as hospital chapel.

The church stands next to the **Hospital de la Santísima Trinidad** (Hospital of the Holy Trinity), which has occupied the 18th-century Convento de San Lorenzo since 1884. The interior is closed to visitors. Note the revolving drum on the door, where foundling babies were placed to be cared for by the nuns.

Gofio Mills

C/Doctor Domingo González García.

In the south, Calle San Francisco becomes Calle Doctor Domingo González García. The street features a number of 17th- and 18th-century mills that once produced *gofio* (a roasted mixture of wheat, maize or barley). One of these mills is still working. Here, visitors can see the entire process of flour production, as well as buy the end product. One room has a display showing the production process prior to the introduction of electrical machinery.

Iglesia San Juan Bautista

C/San Juan Bautista.

The single-nave church of St John the Baptist was built in the 18th century. Its modest façade, with a monumental belfry, does nothing to hint at the magnificence of its interior. Thanks to the beautiful *artesonado* – the wooden coffered ceiling – and the opulent interior decorations featuring sculptures by Luján Peréz and Fernando Estévez, the church is regarded as one of the most precious historic sites in La Orotava. The fine altars deserve special attention.

In front of the church is a bust of the Venezuelan President, Rómulo Betancourt (1908–81).

The simple façade of Iglesia San Juan Bautista

🏛 Museo de Cerámica – Casa de Tafuriaste

C/León, 3. **Tel** 922 333 396.
Open 10am–6pm Mon–Sat,
10am–2pm Sun. 🗚

The island's passion for ceramics reached its peak even before the advent of the European conquerors, and remains alive to this day, particularly among the local population of La Orotava. The primitive designs, which are based on old Guanche forms, are popular with many tourists, as are items representing a more modern style of pottery.

La Orotava's Museo de Cerámica was founded to cater for this interest. The museum is housed in the Casa de Tafuriaste – a much-restored Canary townhouse from the 17th century, which is about 2 km (1 mile) west of La Orotava's old town on the La Luz–Las Candias road.

The collection includes nearly 1,000 vessels from the Canary Islands and Spain. Down on the ground floor there is a pottery workshop, where visitors can see demonstrations of how modern jugs and bowls are made. On the museum's first floor, there is a fine display of antique ceramics.

The gift shop sells a wide variety of items to take home as souvenirs.

Modern pottery from Casa de Tafuriaste

🏛 Liceo de Taoro

C/San Agustín. 🗚
Above the Plaza de la Constitución stands the charming, eclectic building of the former grammar school, with a well-maintained 100-year-old garden. These days, it houses a club with elegant reception rooms, a bar (which is open to non-members), a games room and a library.

🌳 Jardín Victoria

Plaza de la Constitución.
Open 8am–6pm daily. 🗚
Bordering the Liceo de Taoro is the 19th-century Jardín Victoria, which is full of beautiful flowers and palm trees, arranged on terraces along a shallow ravine with a stream running at the bottom. The main architectural feature of this garden is the mausoleum of **Diego Ponte del Castillo**, made of Carrara marble.

🏛 Ex-Convento Santo Domingo

C/Tomás Zerolo, 34.
On the outskirts of La Orotava's old town stands a 17th- to 18th-century Dominican convent, which has a triple-naved church featuring a magnificent polychromatic wooden coffered ceiling. The remaining rooms of

Jardín Victoria, situated in a ravine

the former convent are arranged around a patio with lovely balconies resting on wooden columns. These rooms are occupied by the compact **Museo de Artesanía Iberoamericana**, which opened in 1991. This ethnographic museum has an interesting exhibition of handicrafts from Spain and Latin America. The collection includes traditional musical instruments (look out for the Canarian *timple*, a kind of ukulele), pottery, textiles, wickerwork and some fine locally produced furniture.

🏛 Museo de Artesanía Iberoamericana

Tel 922 321 746. **Open** 10am–3pm
Mon–Fri. 🗚

Environs
The **Mirador de Humboldt** is 5 km (3 miles) northeast. This splendid viewpoint overlooks the entire Orotava valley and is named after the Prussian geographer, traveller and naturalist, Alexander von Humboldt, who visited Tenerife in 1799.

Some 30 km (19 miles) south, along a scenic road that crosses the Orotava valley, is the **Izaña Atmospheric Research Center**. This research centre is near the entrance to the Parque Nacional del Teide, and occupies a picturesque spot 2,200 m (7,218 ft) above sea level, close to the top of the Izaña mountain.

Corpus Christi

Apart from Epiphany, Corpus Christi is the most celebrated religious festival in the Canary Islands. In Tenerife, extravagant festivities are held in La Orotava and La Laguna, which try to outdo each other in the splendour of the occasion. The streets are lined with floral decorations, and the Plaza del Ayuntamiento is adorned with pictures and "carpets" made of volcanic sands, which can take months to prepare. The large size of the carpets has been recognised by the Guinness World Records.

Preparing a floral picture from volcanic sand

❼ Puerto de la Cruz

Rising up from the sea front, Puerto de la Cruz was the principal port of the island after the destruction of Garachico. By the late 19th century, it had already become a resort and a popular destination for upmarket British visitors, and it remains so to this day. The hotels tower above banana plantations, shopping arcades, casinos, restaurants, cafés and nightclubs, as well as numerous historic sites. An artificial lagoon and warm, clear water attracts over 100,000 visitors each year to the area.

Portal of the Iglesia de Nuestra Señora de la Peña de Francia

🏛 Iglesia de Nuestra Señora de la Peña de Francia
The triple-naved cathedral was built in 1684–97. Its tall tower was added in the late 19th century. In the dark interior of the church the eye is drawn to Baroque sculptures – the work of the local artist Fernando Estévez and José Luján Pérez, a well-known island artist. No less precious are the paintings by Luís de la Cruz. The cathedral's organ was brought from London in 1814.
A bust of Agustín de Betancourt (1758–1824), founder of the Engineering College in Madrid, stands in front of the church.

🏛 Calle Quintana
The street leads to Punta del Viento, a terrace poised on the edge of the ocean and affording a fine view over the rocky coast and **Lago Martiánez**. Branching off eastwards is the **Calle de San Telmo**, a seaside promenade with stone seats and numerous bars. The **Monopol Hotel** – one of the oldest hotels in Puerto de la Cruz – stands in Calle Quintana.

🏛 Plaza de Europa
Hugging the shoreline, this square was laid out in 1992, but is based on 18th- and 19th-century European-style town planning. Its features include the **town hall** (1973) and the **Casa de Miranda** (1730), a fine old town house, which now accommodates a restaurant specializing in local fare.

🏛 Casa de la Real Aduana
Calle de las Lonjas. **Tel** 922 378 103. Tourist Office: 9am–8pm Mon–Fri (to 5pm Sat & Sun).
This house was built in 1620 for Juan Antonio Lutzardo de Franchy and is the oldest in town. After the destruction of Garachico, it became the seat of the governor and from 1706 to 1833 served as the customs house. The building was restored in the 1970s and now houses the Museum of Contemporary Art Eduardo Westerdahl and a shop selling local crafts. The tourist information office is here too.

🏛 Puerto Pesquero
The history of this picturesque fishing harbour, situated on a small, stony beach, goes back to the 18th century, when the town was the main exporter of the island's agricultural produce. Today you can buy freshly caught fish direct from the fishermen.

🏛 Iglesia de San Francisco
C/San Juan.
The church of St Francis is built around the Ermita de San Juan, which was constructed in 1599. One of the oldest buildings in Puerto de la Cruz, it is decorated with sculptures and paintings, from the 16th century up to modern times.
This modest building now serves as an ecumenical church, and holds services for all Christian denominations in the town.

🏛 Plaza del Charco de los Camerones
Many of the town's most historic buildings are found in Plaza del Charco, a square shaded by palm and laurel trees, which were imported from Cuba. The centre of the square is occupied by a huge yam plant within a fountain. The plaza is a pleasant place to sit and watch the world go by, particularly on Sundays, when locals promenade in their Sunday finery.

Town crest at Plaza de Europa

🏛 Museo Arqueológico
C/El Lomo, 9A. **Tel** 922 371 465. **Open** 10am–1pm & 5–9pm Tue–Sat, 10am–1pm Sun.
Opened in 1991, this museum is devoted to the history and cultural heritage of the Canary Islands. Its exhibits include a collection of Guanche products and the mummified remains of the island's original inhabitants.

View of the entrance to Puerto Pesquero fishing harbour

Lush banana plantations south of Parque Taoro

🏰 Castillo de San Felipe
This small 17th-century fort once guarded the harbour entrance against attacks from pirates and the ships of Spain's two maritime rivals: France and England. Now the fort, situated in the western part of town, often serves as a venue for temporary exhibitions. To the west of the fort is the **Playa Jardín** – the town's longest beach.

🌳 Parque Taoro
This park is an enchanting spot and a good place to escape the bustle of town. The park has cascades, waterfalls, streams crossed with bridges, small ponds and viewing terraces. At the centre of the park lies the **Jardín Risco Bello Acuático** – a tropical water garden that is home to many varieties of fish, as well as ducks and swans.

🏊 Lago Martiánez
Playa Martiánez. **Tel** 922 385 955. **Open** 10am–5pm daily (24 & 31 Dec: to 3pm). **Closed** May. 🦆

This artificial lagoon, designed by César Manrique, was built in 1969. Conjuring up a subtropical paradise, it consists of a complex of seawater swimming pools and gurgling fountains, which contrast with the surrounding lava field. There is also an ultra-smart casino here.

🌿 Jardín Botánico
C/Retama, 2. **Tel** 922 383 572. **Open** 9am–6pm daily. **Closed** 1 Jan, Good Fri, 25 Dec. 🌿

The local botanical garden is one of the oldest in the world. It was established in 1788 at the request of Carlos III of Spain, by Alonso de Nava y Grimón.

The lush garden is crammed with over 1,000 species of plants and trees from the Canary Islands, as well as flora from all over the world.

Playa Jardín, a popular beach with tourists

Puerto de la Cruz
① Iglesia de Nuestra Señora de la Peña de Francia
② Calle Quintana
③ Plaza de Europa
④ Casa de la Real Aduana
⑤ Puerto Pesquero
⑥ Iglesia de San Francisco
⑦ Plaza del Charco de los Camerones

0 metres   200
0 yards   200

8 Loro Parque

From the day it opened in 1972, this tropical plant complex has been hugely popular and has established itself as a firm favourite with tourists, despite recent controversy over the welfare of its orcas. The sprawling park is home to many species of birds, mammals and fish from around the world. Attractions include the aquarium, which has more than 100 aquatic species, an impressive free flight aviary, where you can watch birds in their natural habitat, the children's playground "Kinderlandia," and the park's beautiful gardens of orchids and dragon trees.

★ **Main Entrance**
The entrance to the park leads through an authentic Thai village. Built in 1993, it consists of six buildings that were built in Thailand and shipped in sections to Tenerife, where they were reassembled by Thai craftsmen.

Jaguars
These big cats live in a reconstructed volcanic landscape. You can see them through a series of large windows.

Flamingos
These elegant birds were among the first animals introduced to the Loro Parque, and the colony still flourishes today.

★ Penguin House
With frost-covered rocks and a water temperature of 8° C (46° F), the Penguin House recreates a natural habitat, enabling its inhabitants to forget that they are living on Tenerife.

Tower of Fish
A school of fish swim inside an illuminated glass cylinder, more than 8 m (26 ft) tall, which stands next to the Penguin House.

Entrance

0 metres   50
0 yards   50

Gorillas
A sizeable number of gorillas live out their days in relative freedom in the park, in an area of 3,500 sq m (37,674 sq ft).

★ Shark Aquarium
Several species of shark can be viewed in the aquarium. A glass-tunnel walkway allows visitors to watch sharks swimming directly overhead.

KEY

① "Natural Vision" cinema complex

② Parrot hatchery

③ Alligators

⑫ Masca

🗺 95. 🚌

Masca, with its scenic position at an altitude of 600 m (1,970 ft), is a popular destination for day trips from many of the big resorts. Just above the small village is a terrace, which offers an impressive outlook, especially at sunset, towards Mount Teide on one side, and the Atlantic on the other.

Masca was once a refuge for pirates and accessible only by mule. Even today, it can only be reached via a steep, winding road. Though narrow, the road is a feat of modern engineering and uses small laybys along the roadside to allow vehicles to pass each other. The incredible views as the road winds through the mountains are reason enough to visit.

The village is charming and consists of a handful of old, red-tiled, stone houses clinging to the sides of the gorge, and surrounded by lush palm trees. Roadside vendors offer prickly pears and oranges to passers-by.

Crops are grown in small fields on terraces, which descend towards the Barranco de Masca ravine. The villagers also keep bees that gather nectar from the surrounding flowering meadows. The village is an excellent starting point for hikers. One of the best routes leads along the Masca ravine, to the seashore. A fit mountain walker should be able to get there

The green square of Plaza de la Iglesia in Los Silos

and back again in under four hours. Take care, however, as the return hike is steep and fairly arduous.

Environs
Past the village, the road leads north through the Macizo de Teno massif, towards the coastal flatland. Some 12 km (7.5 miles) along the route is the scenic village of **El Palmar**. The nearby **Montaña de Talavera** has had chunks cut out of it to provide soil for the banana plantations.

Another 5.5 km (3.5 miles) further on is **Buenavista**, the island's westernmost village, which has a small fishing harbour and a pebble beach.

A short way eastwards in the midst of banana plantations, **Los Silos** is a quiet little town with a compact 19th-century layout. In the town centre is a typical tree-shaded square, with a coffee pavilion. The shady square is idyllic and has traditional Canarian houses with wooden balconies.

⑬ Santiago del Teide

🗺 10,690. 🚌 ℹ Avda. Marítima, Playa de la Arena, 922 860 348.

Should you visit Santiago del Teide in February, when the countless almond trees are in bloom with pink and white blossom, you will see it is particularly lovely. The small town is surrounded by vineyards and cornfields, and nestles among the foothills of the Teno massif. La Gomera can be seen in the distance.

The pride of the town is the Baroque parish church of **San Fernando**, which was built in the mid-16th century and stands at the end of the main street. Its asymmetric façade is adorned with a wooden, grill-shaded balcony. A tall belfry has been added at the northern end of the church. The small, Moorish-looking domes give the building its distinctive look.

Look out for the strange figure in front of one of the side altars: it represents Christ on horseback, wearing a black Spanish hat and carrying a sword.

Environs
Branching off from the southern approach road to the village is a path to **Camino de la Virgen de Lourdes**. The path, dedicated to the Virgin Mary of Lourdes and with a shrine and an ornamental bridge, leads along the slope of the mountain to a grotto decorated with flowers.

The façade of San Fernando with its wooden balcony, Santiago del Teide

⑭ Los Gigantes and Puerto de Santiago

The giant cliffs, known as the **Acantilados de los Gigantes** ("Cliffs of the Giants"), form the ridge of the Teno massif. Some 10 km (6 miles) long, this steep cliff-face plunges 500 m (1,640 ft) into the ocean. The dark rocks are best seen by boat. Trips often leave from Puerto Deportivo and usually travel further north to include a wonderful view over the **Barranco de Masca**.

Situated beneath the cliffs, the small town of **Los Gigantes** is a typical Canarian holiday resort, the biggest on the northwest coast of Tenerife, with apartment complexes sprawling over the slopes. Its yachting marina has diving clubs and offers angling trips.

The town itself, with its concentrated development, gives the impression of being overcrowded. Only narrow alleys separate small hotels and apartment blocks.

A seaside boulevard connects Los Gigantes with nearby **Puerto de Santiago**, which has long been a resort, although on a smaller scale. The main attraction here is the dark volcanic-sand beaches, including the most popular of them, **Playa de la Arena**, situated to the south. Most of the fishermen here have traded in their rods and nets and take tourists out for boat trips instead.

Boulevards along the beach in Playa de las Américas

⑮ Playa de las Américas and Los Cristianos

20,300. Avda. Rafael Puig Llivina, 19, 922 797 668. Fiesta del Carmen (beg. of Sep).

You would not think so to look at it now but Los Cristianos was once a sleepy fishing village. Today, it is a year-round provider of fun and sun with artificial beaches, sprawling hotel-apartments, and countless bars, clubs and souvenir shops. Many people embrace the noise and kitsch good humour of the place, and Los Cristianos is one of the most popular resorts in the archipelago. It extends into the virtually identical Playa de las Américas, which merges in turn with **Costa Adeje** a little further up the coastline.

A promenade, running alongside the crowded beaches and the harbour wall, has shops, restaurants and bars.

In Las Américas the promenade turns into a palm-shaded boulevard several miles long, which runs above numerous sheltered beaches. The most exclusive among them is the **Playa del Duque**. Ferries and hydrofoils make regular trips from Los Cristianos' port to La Gomera and El Hierro.

Environs
A short way northeast, **Parque Ecológico Las Águilas del Teide** has displays of condors in flight, evening variety shows and a floodlit pool full of crocodiles. Some 7 km (4 miles) north, and a 2-hour walk from the town of Adeje, is the **Barranco del Infierno**, a wild gorge with an impressive waterfall.

⑯ Siam Park

TF-1, 38660. **Tel** 922 691 429. **Open** 10am–6pm daily (winter: to 5pm). siampark.net

Enjoy an exhilarating wet and wild experience at Tenerife's greatest water park. Owned by the same company that runs Loro Parque *(see pp116–17)*, this theme park offers a wealth of attractions that are aimed at giving visitors a white-knuckle ride. The Tower of Power, The Dragon and The Volcano are among the most popular with thrill-seekers, but there are some more relaxing options too, as well as rides suitable for the whole family. There are also several restaurants and a shop.

Harbour in Puerto de Santiago, against the steep cliffs of Los Gigantes

⑰ Parque Nacional del Teide

Some 3 million years ago volcanic subsidence left behind the 16-km (10-mile) Las Cañadas depression with the island's emblematic volcano, Teide, standing 3,718 m (12,198 ft) high at its centre. In 1954 the area was turned into one of Spain's largest national parks. Marked paths guide visitors round the best of this awesome wilderness of ash beds, lava streams and mineral tinted rocks. The national park has been a UNESCO World Heritage Site since 2007, and it offers a funicular, visitor's centre and a hotel.

Echium wildpretii (tajinaste rojo) This striking plant, a kind of viper's bugloss, has bright red stalks. It can grow up to 2m (6.6 ft) high and is one of the symbols of Tenerife.

Los Roques de García Close to the parador is a much-photographed set of strangely shaped rocks, rising some 150 m (492ft) above the crater floor.

A special permit is required if you are ascending the summit of Pico del Teide from the La Rambleta mountain station (www.reservasparquesnacionales.es). Ascent to the viewpoints at La Fortaleza and Pico Viejo, however, does not require a permit.

Pico Viejo
3135 m
①

Pico del Teide
3718 m
②

La Rambleta
3555 m

Chío

Mirador de Chío

TF38

Roques de García

Mirador de la Ruleta

Mirador de Boca Tauce
⑥

Llano de Ucanca

Vilaflor ↓

TF21

Mirad
Ucanc

KEY

① **Pico Viejo** The crater of this volcanic cone, which last erupted in the 18th century, measures 800 m (2,625 ft) in diameter.

② **Pico del Teide** is an active volcano.

③ **Refugio de Altavista** This modest shelter is located along the trail leading to Pico del Teide, at an altitude of 3,270 m (10,728 ft).

④ **The visitor centre** includes a video and various exhibits explaining the park's evolution and history.

⑤ **Cable-Car** Built in 1971, the cable-car takes only eight minutes to whisk tourists to within 200 m (656 ft) of Teide's summit.

⑥ **Mirador de Boca de Tauce** This lookout provides great views of the national park's gulleys and slopes.

Key
=== Major road
— Minor road
-- Footpath

Llano de Ucanca This treeless plain contains the rocks of Los Azulejos. Their blue-green glitter is due to the copper deposits within them.

Observatorio del Teide

The observatory, at the entrance to the park, is used primarily for solar observation and houses the THEMIS solar telescope.

0 kilometres 2
0 miles 2

P 🄸 El Portillo ⟶ *Santa Cruz de Tenerife*
④

TF21

Montaña Blanca
2748 m

Montaña Bajada
2509 m

Mirador de San José

⑤

Mirador del Tabonal Negro

1

Las Cañadas

rador de
ñadas del
ide

Las Cañadas

The seven *cañadas* (sandy plateaus) are the result of the collapse of ancient craters. Only a few species of plant can grow in this dusty, arid wasteland.

Parador

A mountain lodge, the Parador de Cañadas del Teide is an ideal base for exploring the surreal and spectacular landscape of the National Park.

Roque Cinchado

One of the Roques de García, the Cinchado is this strange shape because it is wearing away faster at the bottom than the top.

Pico del Teide

At 3,718 m (12,198 ft), Pico del Teide is the highest mountain in Spain, and the snow-capped peak is often visible from across Tenerife. Visitors can only reach its peak if they have a permit. The viewing platform in La Fortaleza, reached by a footpath leading from the top cable-car station, affords (on a clear day) an incredible view of the entire archipelago, stretching hundreds of miles. The most recent eruption of Mount Teide occurred on 18 November 1909.

Early map showing Teide as the world's highest mountain

⑱ Vilaflor

🏔 1,700. 🚌

With an elevation of 1,400 m (4,593 ft), Vilaflor is the highest village in the Canaries. In the 19th century the village became famous for its lacework. Close to the village, which is surrounded by pine forests, is "Pino Gordo", a

The giant "Pino Gordo" located just outside Vilaflor

pine tree over 70 m (230 ft) tall. In the plaza at the top of the village is the **Iglesia de San Pedro** (1550), which has a statue of the church's patron saint.

Environs
Hikers can set out from Vilaflor on the well-marked footpath, Camino de Chasma, for the so-called **Paisaje Lunar** ("Lunar Landscape"). It is a curious volcanic rock formation made of weathered cones of sandstone.

⑲ El Médano

🏔 8,000. 🚹 Plaza de los Príncipes de España, 922 176 002. 🚌 🚢 San Antonio de Padua (13 Jun).

El Médano, a former fishing village, is now famous for its bay, fringed by long, sandy beaches. These stretch south to the **Punta Roja**, towered over by the **Montaña Roja** volcano (now a nature reserve). The strong winds (known as *alisios*)

make the place very popular with windsurfers (international competitions are held here). The winds are also utilized in the **Parque Eólico de Granadilla** – a wind farm, supplying electricity to over 3,000 homes.

Environs
Some 5 km (3 miles) to the northwest, at the end of the runway of Reina Sofía Airport, is the **Cueva del Hermano Pedro** – a cave converted into a sanctuary, dedicated to Father Peter, the first Canarian saint (1626–67).

⑳ Candelaria

🏔 26,490. 🚌 🚢 🚹 Avenida de la Constitución s/n, 922 032 230. 🚢 Sat, Sun. 🚢 Nuestra Señora de la Candelaria (15 Aug).

Candelaria is famous for its religious sanctuary, the most important in the archipelago. Every August, crowds of pilgrims come to the **Basílica de Nuestra Señora de**

Tenerife's Beaches

With the possible exception of Las Teresitas, near Santa Cruz, the beaches of Tenerife are not nearly as scenic as those of Fuerteventura, though they are nevertheless popular with tourists. Numerous diving packages are on offer to visitors, from courses aimed at beginners to expeditions into the depths of the ocean. Reliable winds make the place popular with windsurfers and conditions are also good for many other water sports, from paragliding to waterskiing.

④ **Playa San Blas** is situated near Los Abrigos. From here a modern road leads to Golf del Sur, the biggest golf course on Tenerife and one of the finest on the Canary Islands.

⑤ **Los Abrigos** is a fishing village next to a quiet, rocky beach. It is known for its many excellent fish restaurants.

① **Playa de las Américas**
The local volcanic beaches of black and grey sand are covered with light imported sand, to make them more attractive to visitors.

② **Los Cristianos**
is one of the Canary Islands' most popular resorts, with newly laid-out sand beaches close to its centre.

③ **Costa del Silencio**, as its name suggests, is quieter than many resorts, though it is right next to the international airport.

Playa de las Américas

Los Cristianos

TF1

Gua

TF66

Paraje Natural Malpaís de Rascia

Punta Saleme

Candelaria to pray to the Black Madonna – the patron saint of the Canary Islands.

According to legend, in 1390 two fishermen from a Guanche tribe miraculously found a statue that had been washed up on the beach – probably a figurehead from a shipwreck. The tribe placed it in one of the coastal caves as an object of veneration, and there it remained until 1826, when it was swept away during a violent storm. The basilica itself was built in 1958 on the site of an earlier 16th-century church. The present statue of the Madonna is the work of Fernando Estévez (1827). It has been placed inside a niche above the main altar. The wall around the niche has paintings by Jose Aguiar and Manuel Martín Gonzáles.

The church's main entrance features a

vast painting of the Black Madonna by Dimas Coello (1986).

The basilica adjoins the 17th-century church of **Santa Ana**. Both churches stand along the northwest frontage of **Plaza de la Patrona de Canaria**, a huge square that includes nine bronze statues depicting the legendary Guanche rulers, known as the *Menceyes*.

Imposing façade of the basilica, Candelaria

❷ Güímar

🏠 19,000. 🚌 🎭 San Pedro (29 Jun).

The largest town in southeast Tenerife, Güímar has an eclectic mix of 19th-century houses. On a small square in the town centre is the 18th-century church of **San Pedro Apóstol**. The town is famous for the

Statue of a Guanche chieftain, Candelaria

pyramids made from uncut stone that were unearthed in the suburb of Chacona in the 1990s. The anthropologist Thor Heyerdahl and the ship owner Fred Olsen persuaded the authorities to seal off the area and founded the **Parque Etnográfico** museum.

🏛 **Parque Etnográfico Pirámides de Güímar**
C/Chacona, s/n. **Tel** 922 514 510.
Open 9:30am–6pm daily.
Closed 1 Jan & 25 Dec.
🌐 **piramidesdeguimar.es**

---

⑥ **Playa del Confital**
This small village, situated midway between Los Abrigos and El Médano, is extremely popular with fans of water sports.

⑦ **Playa de la Tejita** is at the foot of the Montaña Roja volcano and just 10 minutes walk from El Médano. One of the island's most beautiful beaches, it is also popular with naturists (see p181).

San Isidro

TF1   TF64

TF65   TF643

0 kilometres 2
0 miles 2

⑧ El Médano

Cañada Blanca • Guargacho
Playa San Blas ④ Los Abrigos ⑤ Playa del Confital ⑥ Playa de la Tejita ⑦

Costa del Silencio ③ Las Galletas

Key
▬ Motorway
▬ Main road
▬ Minor road
••• Footpath
~- Seasonal river

⑧ **El Médano**
Thanks to steady winds blowing from Africa, the golden sand beaches around the resort are an irresistible magnet for windsurfers.

LA GOMERA

La Gomera, the Isla Redonda or Round Island, is the "alternative" Canary Island. A mere 378 sq km (146 sq miles), it has little tourism infrastructure and only small pebble-and-sand beaches. Many visitors treat it as a day trip. Some, however, come for this very absence of commercialism, drawn by the mountainous countryside and an ancient laurel forest that is perfect for hiking.

Despite the poor soil and the hilly conditions, the inhabitants of La Gomera, who lived on the island during the Guanche era as well as those who arrived after the Spanish conquest, made a living as farmers. Fields were set on terraces cut into the slopes of ravines. Crops included potatoes, tomatoes, bananas and grapes. To this day, many of the local people are engaged in farming and the island has maintained its agricultural character.

The isolation of the island, its inaccessibility and the difficulties in cultivating the fertile land all contributed to its poverty and often caused many of the Gomerans to leave for South America (though quite a few have returned). Signs of emigration are still visible in the form of numerous deserted villages.

In the 1960s, La Gomera was discovered by people seeking an alternative lifestyle, and the island became a symbol of unspoiled nature. This was the beginning of the development of tourism. Today, the island authorities try to maintain a balance between the traditional economy and the proceeds of tourism, and they strive to protect the historic scenery from the trappings of civilization that threaten it.

One of the outstanding features of La Gomera that attracts many visitors each year is the Garajonay national park. This is one of the world's oldest natural forests and provides an excellent area for walking. Sadly, 20 per cent of the Garajonay burned down in forest fires in 2012 and it could be as long as 30 years before the forest returns to its former glory.

Harbour entrance in San Sebastián de La Gomera

◀ The rocky landscape of Hermigua

Exploring La Gomera

Most visitors come to La Gomera on day trips, arriving from nearby Tenerife. This small island, though somewhat short of historical sites, such as those on Gran Canaria or Tenerife, is extremely attractive in terms of its landscape. Deep ravines, rocky summits, mist-shrouded laurel forests and valley slopes descending in terraces all compensate for the lack of long, sandy beaches. Rich in unspoiled areas and seemingly untainted by tourism, the island is an excellent place for hiking. With no industry and motorways, and few large hotels, La Gomera is a haven of peace and suits those wishing to escape the bustle of the larger resorts.

Locator Map

Sights at a Glance

1. San Sebastián de La Gomera
2. Hermigua
3. Agulo
4. Vallehermoso
5. Valle Gran Rey
6. El Cercado
7. *Parque Nacional de Garajonay pp132–3*
8. Alajeró
9. Playa de Santiago

The parador courtyard in San Sebastián de La Gomera

For keys to symbols *see back flap*

0 kilometres   3
0 miles   3

Getting There

The distance between La Gomera and Tenerife is 32 km (20 miles). The journey by ferry from Los Cristianos takes 1 hour 40 minutes, by hydrofoil it is 45 minutes. There are also ferry links with La Palma and El Hierro. The island has direct air links with Tenerife and Gran Canaria. All main routes on the island are served by buses, although these are not very frequent. It is therefore preferable to hire a car. A few unmade roads on the island are only suitable for a four-wheel-drive vehicle.

Black sand beach near the harbour in San Sebastián de La Gomera, one of the few beaches on the island

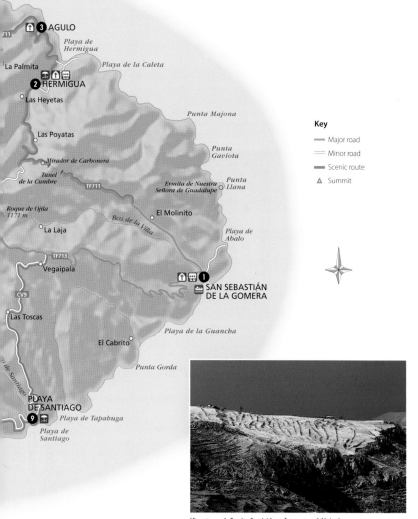

AGULO

Playa de Hermigua

La Palmita

Playa de la Caleta

HERMIGUA

Las Heyetas

Punta Majona

Las Poyatas

Punta Gaviota

Mirador de Carbonera

Tunel de la Cumbre

TF711

Ermita de Nuestra Señora de Guadalupe

Punta Llana

Roque de Ojila 1171 m

El Molinito

La Laja

Bco. de la Villa

Playa de Abalo

TF713

Vegaipala

CV9

SAN SEBASTIÁN DE LA GOMERA

Las Toscas

Playa de la Guancha

El Cabrito

Punta Gorda

de Santiago

PLAYA DE SANTIAGO

Playa de Tapahuga

Playa de Santiago

Key

— Major road

— Minor road

— Scenic route

△ Summit

View towards Ermita San Isidoro, from around Alajeró

Façade of the Iglesia de la Virgen de la Asunción in San Sebastián

❶ San Sebastián de La Gomera

🏔 9,000. ✈ 🚢 *i* C/Real, 4, 922 141 512. 🎉 Fiesta de San Sebastián (20 Jan), Bajada de la Virgen de Guadalupe (1st weekend in Oct, every 5 years: 2018, 2023).

With the daily arrival of tourists on the Tenerife ferry, the island's sleepy capital and main harbour comes alive. The road from the harbour into town passes through the laurel-shaded **Plaza de las Américas**, which is lined with street cafés.

To the west of the square stands the **Torre del Conde**. This Gothic tower was built in 1447 by the first Spanish governor of La Gomera, Hernán Peraza the Elder. Restored in 1997, it is the only remaining fragment of the town's fortifications. The Torre del Conde is a reminder of a tragic uprising in the town. In 1448, Beatriz de Bobadilla, wife of Hernán Peraza the Younger, barricaded herself within its walls after her husband was killed by a Guanche in revenge for his illicit affair with a native princess. When help arrived from Gran Canaria, Beatriz avenged herself by putting almost every male Guanche on Gomera to death.

The island's main church is the **Iglesia de la Virgen de la Asunción** in Calle Real. The foundations were laid in the mid-15th century and Christopher Columbus is said to have knelt down to pray in the church's dim interior before continuing on his first voyage.

Casa de Colón, at Calle Real 56, is where Columbus is said to have stayed before setting off for the New World, while the **Pozo de Colón**, a well standing in the courtyard of a former customs building, has the inscription "With this water, America was baptised." Another sight to look out for is the small **Ermita de San Sebastián**. Built around 1450, this is the oldest church

The Gothic defensive tower of the Torre del Conde

on the island; it is dedicated to La Gomera's patron saint.

Heading towards **Mirador de la Hila**, which offers views over the whole of San Sebastián, the road leads to the **Parador de San Sebastián**. This comfortable hotel was built in 1976 and is a modern replica of a Canarian colonial mansion.

Environs
Some 4 km (2 miles) north, the gravel road divides: one route descends towards the quiet beach at **Playa de Abalos**; the other leads to **Ermita de Nuestra Señora de Guadalupe** – every five years a statue of the Virgin Mary is carried to San Sebastián from here (the next "Bajada" is in 2018).

❷ Hermigua

🏔 1,800. 🚢

A winding road leads from San Sebastián to Hermigua. Along the route, the scenery is attractive and varied with weathered rocks, forests of willow and laurel, juniper groves, deep ravines and lush green valleys.

Hermigua, known as Mulagua during the Guanche times, was once an important town but is today little more than a village. The fertile soil in the lower regions of Barranco de Monteforte still allows cultivation of grapes, bananas and dates.

Today the only evidence of past glories is a handful of old buildings along the small scenic streets and the **Convento de Santo**

Christopher Columbus (1451–1506)

The name "Isla Colombina" evokes La Gomera's links with Christopher Columbus, who stopped here three times, in 1492, 1493 and 1498. The island provided his fleet with food and fresh water and was a good launchpad for his historic expeditions. The many stories surrounding his visits include an alleged romance with Beatriz de Bobadilla. Columbus will always remain an unofficial patron of the island, and September's Semana Colombina (Columbus Week) commemorates his first voyage.

Statue of Columbus in Playa de las Américas

Domingo de Guzmán in the Valle Alto district. Dating from the 16th century, the church's interior features a fine 19th-century image of the Madonna by Fernando Estévez.

Hermigua is famous for its handmade rugs and other woven products. These can be seen and purchased in **Los Telares**, the local handicraft centre. Nearby is **Playa de Hermigua** – covered with shingle, it is not the most beautiful of beaches and is subject to rough weather.

Environs
An hour's hike along the footpath, to the northeast of Hermigua , brings you to **Playa de la Caleta**, one of the best black sand beaches on the island.

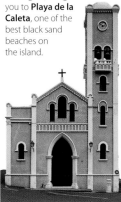

The pretty Iglesia de la Encarnación in Hermigua

❸ Agulo

🏘 950. 🚌

The 17th-century town of Agulo lies in the north-eastern part of the island, high above the sea at the foot of a natural rock amphitheatre and surrounded by banana plantations. Together with the nearby hamlet of Lepe, inhabited by hardly more than handful of crofters, this is a picturesque little place and a popular destination for sightseers around La Gomera.

One unique feature of Agulo's architecture is the **Iglesia de San Marcos** (1939). Moorish in design, it has four white domes, which are visible from far away. The town's best-known native son is the painter José Aguiar

Banana plantation on the coast near Agulo

(1895–1976) who was born in Cuba of Gomeran parents, and spent his childhood in Agulo.

Environs
A steep, twisting road leads upwards from Agulo to the **Mirador de Abrante**. This stone terrace offers a splendid view over the rocky coast and the ocean and is a fine spot to appreciate Mount Teide on Tenerife. A little further along the road, at the end of a ravine, is the village of La Palmita, renowned for its traditional lifestyle.

❹ Vallehermoso

🏘 2,900. 🚌 ℹ Plaza de la Constitución, 922 800 000.

Vallehermoso translates as "beautiful valley," and the surrounding agricultural landscape is evidence of the island's fertile soil. About 15 km (9 miles) along a winding road from Agulo, this compact town, with its bustling centre (including shops, a post office, a bank and a petrol station) is a good starting point for sightseeing and walking tours around this green and pleasant region.

At the centre of the town is the Iglesia San Juan Bautista, which was designed by the Tenerife architect, Antonio Pintor. One of the town's other attractions is a small park enlivened by bizarre groups of roughly hewn sculptural figures.

Facing the sea lies the impressive Castillo del Mar. This former banana offloading station dates back to

1890. After restoration, cultural events are scheduled to take place here. Information at www.castillo-del-mar.com.

Environs
A short way to the north is **Playa de Vallehermoso**, which is good for windsurfing. Those who prefer to swim in calmer waters can make use of the swimming pool built next to the pebble beach.

Some 4 km (2 miles) north is **Los Órganos** – an impressive section of steep cliff that can be seen only from the sea, on cruising trips from Valle Gran Rey, Playa de Santiago or San Sebastián. This basalt wall, 80 m (262 ft) high and 200 m (656 ft) wide, resembles the pipes of an organ and is one of the most unusual (and least accessible) attractions on La Gomera.

Just 2 km (1 mile) to the east, along the road to Agulo, is the **Roque Cano**. This 650-m (2,132-ft) high fang-shaped rock was created by erosion of a volcanic peak.

Las Rosas, situated just 11 km (7 miles) from Vallehermoso, is a popular stopping place for coach tours. It has a restaurant where tourists are treated to demonstrations of El Silbo – the island's famous whistling language *(see p130)*.

Mother and Father in Vallehermoso's park

Black sand beach at Valle Gran Rey

❺ Valle Gran Rey

🏙 4,200. 🚌 🚆 ℹ C/El Caidero, 16, 922 805 417. 🅦 **vallegranrey.es**

The centre of tourism on the island, Valle Gran Rey ("Valley of the Great King") was known even before the Spanish conquest of La Gomera, when it was named Orone after a Guanche leader. Today's Valle Gran Rey is really a complex of several seaside villages – **La Calera**, **La Playa**, **Borbalán**, **La Puntilla** and **Vueltas** – which are the measure of the tourism boom that has even reached La Gomera. The developing estates try hard to meet the demands of modern European guests, particularly Germans, who look for comfort but are also keen to sample a different lifestyle. The place attracts many visitors who come not only for the idyllic scenery, but also for the excellent guesthouses and restaurants. The magnificent Atlantic waves will satisfy even the most demanding of surfing fanatics.

La Calera, with its picturesque setting in the midst of banana plantations, is an upmarket part of La Gomera, thanks to its small boutiques and cosy restaurants. It is regarded as one of the archipelago's prettiest towns, and the house prices here are some of the highest on the island. Like La Playa, it also has a small beach.

The harbour at **Vueltas** offers hydrofoil links to Los Cristianos on Tenerife, as well as short cruises along the coast of La Gomera and to Los Órganos. It is also used by fishing boats and numerous yachts. Several restaurants tempt visitors with tasty dishes of freshly caught fish. The most scenic road on the island is surrounded by massive basalt rocks and runs through the valley, renowned for its fertility. Local crops include dates, bananas, papayas, avocados, mangoes and tomatoes. Small fields, cutting into the valley slopes in the form of terraces, are similar to Balinese rice fields.

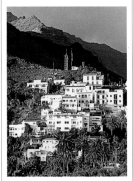

Suburbia, La Gomera style – in Valle Gran Rey

For hikers there are several walking trails, representing various degrees of difficulty. Above the town, at the entrance to the valley, is a **viewpoint** made according to a design by César Manrique, and featuring one of the island's best restaurants.

Environs
Perched above the valley, 11 km (7 miles) to the north, is the village of **Arure**, which prior to the island's conquest, used to be its main centre. Today the place has a desolate look about it and is known mainly for its excellent *miel de palma* – "palm honey". The palms from which the honey is made have flanges fitted around their trunks to protect them against hungry ants.

8 km (5 miles) northeast of Arure lies the sources of **Chorros de Epina**, surrounded by beautiful expanses of heather and a forest. The nearby **Mirador del Santo** offers a splendid view over the ravines and on to La Palma and El Hierro.

❻ El Cercado

🚌 Chipude.

This small village is best known for its handicrafts, especially the primitively shaped earthenware products that are made of dark Gomeran clay, without the use of a potter's wheel.

Local traditions are also being upheld by a small number of bars offering traditional cuisine.

El Silbo Gomera
Long before the invention of the telephone, La Gomera's inhabitants needed a way of communicating across the island. A unique whistling language, known as El Silbo, was the solution. Modulating the whistle by changing finger positions produced many different sounds, which could be transmitted up to 4 km (2 miles). Nowadays the whistle is mainly used to impress tourists but the local Guanches once relied on it when threatened or during hunting expeditions. The whistle has been deemed of important cultural heritage and is taught to children in school.

Cupping the hands to carry the sound further

The terraced fields of El Cercado

Environs

Some 3 km (2 miles) to the south, at the foot of **La Fortaleza** – a large basalt rock that is almost as flat as a table top – lies **Chipude**. At 1,050 m (3,445 ft) above sea level, this is the highest village on La Gomera. It is known for its 16th-century church, the **Iglesia de la Virgen de la Candelaria**. Like El Cercado, Chipude is renowned as a pottery village. A steep country road that later becomes a walking trail leads from El Cercado to **La Laguna Grande**, an information point at the entrance to the Parque Nacional de Garajonay.

Some 17 km (10.5 miles) to the south is **La Dama**. Surrounded by banana plantations, this small village is poised high above the ocean.

➐ Parque Nacional de Garajonay

See pp132–3.

➑ Alajeró

🗺 2,100. 🚌 ℹ 928 895 650.
🎊 Fiesta del Paso (Sep).

A typical Gomeran village, Alajeró sprawls along a mountain road in the southern part of the island. Most of the village's inhabitants make a living by growing bananas. The 16th-century **Iglesia del Salvador** is one of the few remains of the village's historic past.

From Alajeró a path leads westward, along a very deep ravine, to **La Manteca**. Though many of the people who were born here have left in search of a better life, this ghost village, set in a very picturesque spot, is one of the few villages to be totally abandoned.

Environs

In Agalán, 2 km (1 mile) north of Alajeró down a cobbled road, is the island's only surviving dragon tree (see p19). The **Drago de Agalán** was planted in the mid-1800s.

➒ Playa de Santiago

🗺 1080. 🚌 ℹ Edif. Las Vistas, Local 8, Avenida Marítima, s/n, 922 895 650.

Traditional pottery made in El Cercado

Playa de Santiago plays a vital role in La Gomera's transport system. It lies at the junction of two ravines – **Barranco de los Cocos** and **Barranco de Santiago** – and has a fishing harbour and an airport, situated on a bare stretch of land to the west. In addition, the town lies along the road that runs in a loop around the southern part of the island. During the 1960s Playa de Santiago was probably the busiest centre on the island, with a thriving food industry, a small shipyard and a harbour with facilities for the export of the local cash crops, including bananas and tomatoes. Then, in the 1970s, an economic crisis hit, and the town went into a steep decline.

Affordable holidays provided the town's route back to prosperity, and these days Playa de Santiago is orientated mainly towards tourism. It is the second-largest resort on the island, besides Valle Gran Rey, and is slowly but surely returning to its past glory.

Visitors are attracted mainly by the weather, since the place is believed to be the sunniest spot on La Gomera. Further temptations include the local beaches and the modern hotel and beach-club facilities.

If proof were needed of Playa de Santiago's tourist-friendly credentials then look no further than the **Jardín Tecina**. The complex has numerous bars, restaurants, tennis courts and a new golf course. Perched on top of cliffs, the complex consists of unobtrusive white bungalows, built in the local style. A lift, running in a shaft carved into the rock face, whisks guests to the beach and the Club Laurel beach club, which has a huge seawater pool and a restaurant. To the east of the hotel are other beaches, including **Tapahuga, Chinguarime** and **Playa del Medio**.

Shingle beach in Playa de Santiago

❼ Parque Nacional de Garajonay

Covering an area of 40 sq km (15 sq miles), La Gomera's national park is the largest intact area of ancient woodland in the archipelago, but one-fifth of it was destroyed by forest fires in 2012. The unique weather conditions, caused by the constant flow of mist produced when the cool Atlantic trade winds encounter warm breezes, ensure constant dew and humidity conducive to the growth of some 450 species of plants and trees. The vegetation often reaches unprecedented sizes, providing an idea of what a Mediterranean forest looked like before the last Ice Age. So precious is this region that it has been declared a UNESCO World Heritage Site.

Walking Trails
The high viewpoints situated along the park trails provide fabulous views over to Tenerife.

La Laguna Grande
Often shrouded in mist, La Laguna Grande is a good stopping-off point for walks around the park. It also features an excellent restaurant, a children's playground and a picnic area.

Vegetation

The term *laurisilva*, meaning "laurel grove", is used to describe the ancient laurel forest at the heart of the park. The evergreen laurel trees grow to 20 m (66 ft). These trees provide large areas of the park with a thick ceiling of green, which keeps in much of the mist and provides enough shade to keep walkers cool on the many hiking trails that wind through the forest. As well as laurel trees, the park has dense tree heather and juniper groves.

Lichen hanging from the branches of tree heather

0 kilometres 1
0 miles 1

Key

▬ Major road

═ Other road

••• Footpath

— Park boundary

-•- Seasonal river

Mirador de Vallehermoso
From this fine viewpoint, just inside the park boundary and surrounded by dense heather, you can enjoy a magnificent overview of the park and the north side of the island.

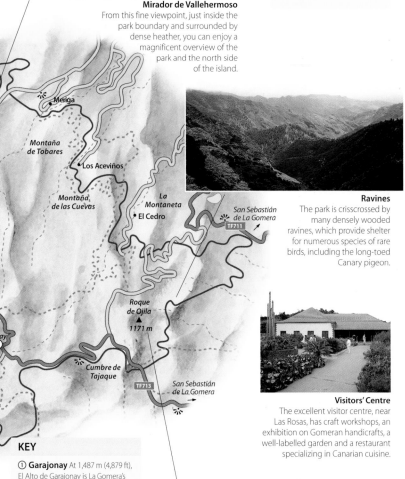

Ravines
The park is crisscrossed by many densely wooded ravines, which provide shelter for numerous species of rare birds, including the long-toed Canary pigeon.

Visitors' Centre
The excellent visitor centre, near Las Rosas, has craft workshops, an exhibition on Gomeran handicrafts, a well-labelled garden and a restaurant specializing in Canarian cuisine.

KEY

① **Garajonay** At 1,487 m (4,879 ft), El Alto de Garajonay is La Gomera's highest mountain. A marked trail leads to the summit.

② **Chipude** This village, on the outskirts of the park, has a small hotel and restaurant.

③ **El Cercado** The village, enjoying a scenic position and easily reached by bus, provides a starting point for walks around the park.

Los Roques
The volcanic formations, including Zarcita (1,236 m/4,055 ft), Carmen (1,140 m/3,740 ft) and Agando (1,250 m/4,100 ft), are situated just outside the park's boundaries, and are best seen from the Mirador El Bailadero.

EL HIERRO

El Hierro is the smallest and westernmost island of the archipelago. Known locally as "La Isla Chiquita" – the Small Island – it occupies a mere 278 sq km (107 sq miles). Rural and, for the most part, untouched by tourism thanks to its lack of sandy beaches, the entire island has only 11,000 or so inhabitants, half of whom live in the island's capital – Valverde. In 2000, UNESCO declared El Hierro a Biosphere Reserve and, in 2014, also named it a Geopark for its geological wealth and sustainable energy programmes.

The shape of El Hierro is the result of a strong earthquake that struck the island some 50,000 years ago. At that time one third of the island broke away from its northern side and sank beneath the ocean waves, creating the El Golfo bay. The most recent volcanic eruption on this mountainous island was in 2011, when an underground volcano spewed magma 20 m (66 ft) into the air.

Prior to the Spanish invasion of 1403, the island's population consisted of Bimbache tribes. Following the island's conquest, most of these tribes fell victim to slave traders, and their land was appropriated by Norman and Castilian settlers. A feudal system, introduced at that time, survived until the mid-19th century.

Today, the population lives mainly off agriculture, growing grapes and bananas, as well as almonds, peaches, potatoes and tomatoes. As elsewhere, fishing is another key element of the local economy, particularly on the southern coast.

Tourism plays little part in the economy of the island. The accommodation on offer consists mainly of *casas rurales* (rural houses). The pine-forest camp site of Hoya del Morcillo is also very popular.

There is no industry on El Hierro, but handicrafts thrive, particularly pottery, weaving and woodcarving. Many tourists shop for local products, particularly at village markets, where folk musicians and dancers entertain buyers and sellers alike.

Natural pools in Charco Manso near Valverde

◀ A juniper tree, bent out of shape by the wind, in El Sabinar

Exploring El Hierro

El Hierro's chief draw is its romantic wildness.
Before Columbus's voyages, this was the
westernmost point of the known world. Even today
the island is largely untouched by tourism and
retains its "end-of-the-world" feel. The magnificent
mountain scenery compensates for the lack of
sandy beaches. Wild terrain, shrouded in mist and
often overgrown with dense pine forest, attracts
nature lovers. Some less accessible places can only
be reached on foot. Equally attractive is the
maritime nature reserve to the south, a paradise
for divers. The local cuisine revolves around fresh
fish, and the island is known for its delicious wines.

Locator Map

Giant junipers, twisted into fanciful shapes
by the wind, in El Sabinar

0 kilometres 2
0 miles 2

Sights at a Glance

1. Valverde
2. Frontera
3. Las Puntas
4. Sabinosa
5. El Sabinar
6. Santuario de Nuestra Señora
   de los Reyes
7. La Restinga
8. Isora
9. San Andrés
10. Puerto de la Estaca

Tiny Puerto de la Estaca – the island's only ferry harbour

For keys to symbols see back flap

Punta del
Guanche

Pozo de
las Calcosas

Echedo

Playa de Adentro

*Playa de
Agache*

Tesbabo

Mocanal

Tamaduste

Roques de Salmor

Guarazoca

*Playas del
Cantadal*

Jarales

VALVERDE ❶

LAS PUNTAS ❸

Mirador
de la Peña

Las Montañetas

HI1

*Playas del
Mulato*

Casas
de Guinea

Tiñor

La Caleta

**PUERTO
DE LA ESTACA** ❿

HI2

Playa de Tijeretas

❾ **SAN ANDRÉS**

La Cuesta

Punta de Tijimiraque

Tigaday

❷ **FRONTERA**

Mirador de
Jinama

Los Llanos

❽ **ISORA**

Los
Llanillos

La Torre

Mirador de
Isora

HI30

*Malpaso
1500 m*

HI1

△ Tenerife
1419 m

Mirador de
las Playas

Punta de Ajones

Roque de la Bonanza

*Mercadel
1251 m*

Las Casas

*Las
Playas*

Taibique

Parador del Hierro

Key

— Major road
═ Minor road
— Scenic route
△ Summit

El Río

Playa de Miguel

*del
rón*

Playa del Pozo

Punta del Miradero

Bahía de Naos

❼ **LA RESTINGA**

Getting There

El Hierro has air links with Tenerife, Gran Canaria and La Palma. A regular ferry service connects Puerto de la Estaca with Tenerife and La Gomera. In view of the scarcity of bus services and their limited range, it is necessary to hire a car when planning sightseeing. Ideally, cars should be booked before you arrive; most companies will meet you at the airport. The roads are in a reasonable state of repair, but some more remote places require an all-terrain vehicle.

Iglesia de la Concepción in Valverde

Pools in Pozo de las Calcosas near Valverde

❶ Valverde

🏘 4,870. 🚌 ℹ️ C/Dr. Quintero, 4, 922 550 302. 🎉 Fiesta de San Isidro (15 May), Bajada de la Virgen de los Reyes (every 4 years in Jul: 2017, 2021). 🌐 elhierro.travel

The full name of the island's capital is La Villa de Santa María de Valverde. Unlike the other island capitals, Valverde has no harbour. The small town is poised on the slope of an evergreen valley (hence the name) and is extremely quiet and often rather foggy.

The only noteworthy local historic sight is the **Iglesia Santa María de la Concepción**. Built in 1767 on the site of a former 16th-century chapel, this vast church was erected in thanksgiving for the repulse of a pirate attack. The belfry includes a large clock brought from Paris in 1886. The main feature of the interior is the Baroque altar. The town hall, standing opposite the church, took 30 years to build (1910–40) and is in the local style.

Environs
Tamaduste, 10 km (6 miles) to the northeast, is the islanders' favourite resort, and has a quiet cove with a pleasant beach.

Charco Manso, 8 km (5 miles) to the north, is a complex of natural pools set in volcanic rock. These are reached by a narrow road with hairpin bends. The sea here can be dangerous, and swimming is not advisable.

Pozo de las Calcosas, 8 km (5 miles) to the northwest, is a good place to swim and features pools similar to those of Charco Manso, and a number of black stone huts on the ocean shore, all reached by steep steps.

An unforgettable view over **El Golfo** bay is to be had from **Mirador de la Peña**, 8 km (5 miles) to the west. The restaurant here was built in 1988 following a design by César Manrique.

❷ Frontera

🏘 3,900. 🚌 🎉 Fiesta de la Virgen de la Candelaria (Aug).

Many of the inhabitants of the island's second largest town make their living by growing grapes. These are the source of Viña Frontera – wines famous throughout the archipelago.

The **Iglesia de la Candelaria**, standing on the outskirts of the town, was built in 1818 and occupies the entire square. The interior, covered with a wooden ceiling, features a striking, gilded altar. Standing above the church, on a hill of red volcanic ash, is a belfry that is visible from afar.

Environs
Tigaday, 1 km (half a mile) to the west, is a relatively large village and a great wine-producing centre. It is the starting point for the road to Las Puntas.

❸ Las Puntas

🎉 Fiesta de San Juan (24 Jun).

Standing on the old wharf, where until 1930 ships arrived bringing supplies, is the Hotel Puntagrande, which was once recognized as the world's smallest hotel. It began life in 1884 as a harbour building, until it was transformed into a hotel. It has four rooms, a bar and a restaurant. Although it is difficult to get a room here, it is still worth coming in order to admire the beautiful sunset and enjoy a swim in one of the rocky coves.

Another noteworthy local feature is the **Roques de Salmor**. These scenic rock formations rise from the sea, and are home to one of the island's most important bird colonies.

Environs
A little to the south, **Poblado de Guinea** is an old Norman settlement dating from the early 15th century. Along with Las Montañetas, it claims to be the oldest village on El Hierro. Today it houses the **Ecomuseo Poblado de Guinea** – a complex of former shepherds'

The famous Hotel Puntagrande in Las Puntas

huts that have been restored and kitted out with furniture from different periods. A small site known as **Lagartario**, above the museum, is used to provide natural breeding conditions for a rare species of lizard from Salmor, found only in El Hierro. The giant, 1.5-m (5-ft) lizards disappeared in the 1930s, and were believed to be entirely extinct, until some surviving sub-species were found in 1974. A project to save the endangered species from extinction commenced in 1975.

🏛 **Ecomuseo Poblado de Guinea**
Tel 922 555 056. **Open** 10am–6pm daily. 🅿

🏛 **Lagartario**
Tel 922 555 056. **Open** 10am–2pm, 4–6pm Tue–Sat, 11am–2pm Sun. 🅿

Pozo de la Salud, perched by the shore of El Golfo bay

❹ Sabinosa

🗻 270. 🚌 🎎 San Simón (end Oct).

Swamped with flowers, Sabinosa is pleasantly remote, with picturesque narrow streets. Poised high up on a slope, overlooking almost all of El Golfo bay, it is known for its "well of health" – **Pozo de la Salud** – which can be found by the sea below Sabinosa. The water, drawn from a well, is highly radioactive and is believed to be something of a cure-all for a number of ailments. The Balneario Pozo de la Salud, a hotel catering to the needs of health-seeking visitors, is the only one of its type in the Canary Islands.

Bajada De La Virgen De Los Reyes

In the early 18th century, during a period of drought, the Madonna was carried down from the Nuestra Señora de los Reyes sanctuary by villagers to Valverde. It rained thereafter, and ever since, a feast has been held every four years (2017, 2021) on the first or second Saturday in July. The statue of the Holy Mother follows the same route along unmade country lanes – the Camino de la Virgen – and is carried on a litter to Valverde. The ceremony, which begins at 5am and goes on till late, is accompanied by a week of merriment, with many villagers dressed in red and white costumes.

The "Descent of the Virgin"

Environs

Playa de Arenas Blancas, 6 km (4 miles) to the west, is a sandy beach, popular with tourists and locals alike.

Some 10 km (6 miles) to the west is **Playa de Verodal**. This small, scenic, windswept beach, with its rust-coloured volcanic sands, lies at the foot of a high cliff. Accessible via a bumpy, coarse-gravel road, it is generally considered to be the most beautiful beach on the island.

East of Sabinosa, a road leads through banana and pineapple plantations to **Los Llanillos**, a tiny village with a small chapel built of blocks of volcanic rock. Standing by the roadside is a workshop producing all shapes and sizes of birdcages. A little further along, the road reaches **Charco Azul**, where rocky coves with turquoise water tempt visitors to swim.

❺ El Sabinar

The name of this upland, swept by Atlantic winds and crossed by a gorge, derives from the local word *sabina* (juniper). It features a forest of white-trunked juniper trees that have bent and twisted into bizarre shapes by strong winds.

El Sabinar is reached by a road that starts as asphalt and later becomes a dirt track running among pastures and crossing cattle gates. It is just under 4 km (2 miles) from the sanctuary of **Nuestra Señora de los Reyes**, the patron saint of the island.

Environs

Mirador de Basco, 3 km (2 miles) to the north, offers a view (on sunny days) not only of El Golfo, but also of La Palma, La Gomera and Tenerife.

The island's symbol – a wind-twisted juniper tree in El Sabinar

Santuario de Nuestra Señora de los Reyes, surrounded by a low wall

❻ Santuario de Nuestra Señora de los Reyes

Set among wooded hills in the western part of the island, surrounded by a low wall, is the pilgrim sanctuary of the Holy Mother of the Kings (Magi) – the patron saint of El Hierro. Inside is a statue of the Madonna, kept on a silver litter. Every four years, in the course of a ceremonial procession known as the Bajada de la Virgen de los Reyes, the statue is carried to Valverde *(see p138)*.

Legend has it that a French ship was becalmed near the shores of the island, and the crew were only able to survive thanks to the help of El Hierro's inhabitants. Having no money to pay for food and water, the captain presented the islanders with a statue of the Virgin Mary. On the same day, 6 January 1577, the day of the Epiphany, a strong wind sent the ship on her way.

Environs
The **Faro de Orchilla** lighthouse is 7 km (4 miles) to the southwest. In AD 150, the Greek geographer Ptolemy declared this western end of the island to be the end of the world. In 1634, the zero meridian was drawn through this point and remained recognized as such until 1884, when it was moved to Greenwich. Even so, El Hierro still refers to itself as "Isla del Meridiano," and visitors can buy a decorated certificate confirming that they have crossed the zero meridian.

❼ La Restinga

🏠 550. 🚌 🎭 Fiesta de San Juan (24 Jun), Fiesta de la Virgen del Carmen (16 Jul).

La Restinga is a small fishing harbour and yacht marina, situated on the sunnier, southern end of the island. It is also one of the most popular resorts on El Hierro. There's a large hotel and a small apartment complex, and the coastal road – the Avenida Maritima – features a wide variety of shops, bars and restaurants. This is a good place to sit out and watch the world drift by.

In the centre is a small, black sand beach that is sheltered by the large harbour. Though generally rather quiet, La Restinga has plenty of facilities for water sports, including diving. The local waters around here have protected status and feature rich marine fauna and flora combined with under-water gullies and interesting rock formations to explore. Diving centres are open all year round and offer trips and night-time expeditions.

Environs
A short way to the northwest is **Bahía de Naos** – which is known principally as the place where Jean de Béthencourt landed in 1403.

Some 10 km (6 miles) to the northwest is **Cala del Tacorón** – a number of small coves carved into the volcanic shore of Mar de las Calmas. Here, swimmers find the clear waters and steps down to the sea particularly inviting.

Cueva Don Justo, 2 km (1 mile) to the north, within the Montaña de Irama massif, is a great attraction to potholers, with its 6-km (4-mile) labyrinth of under-ground volcanic tunnels.

Spectacular view from the Mirador de las Playas

❽ Isora

🏠 397. 🎭 Fiesta de San José (19 Mar).

Situated in the eastern part of the island, Isora is a picturesque assembly of several hamlets, and is famous for cheese production. It is well worth trying to arrive

Volcanic peaks around La Restinga

here at dawn to admire the magnificent sunrise. Another attraction is the famous *lucha canaria* contests, when feats of Canary-style wrestling take place at the local stadium.

Environs
About 1 km (half a mile) to the south, at the edge of the mountain range of El Risco de los Herrenos, is the **Mirador de Isora**, offering enchanting panoramic views over the ocean. A narrow footpath, some 4 km (2 miles) long, leads down to the coast.

About 3 km (2 miles) to the south is the **Mirador de las Playas** – a high viewpoint, set among Canary pines. The broad terrace provides magnificent panoramic views over Las Playas bay, from Roque de la Bonanza up to the parador.

El Pinar, 6 km (4 miles) to the south, is the collective name often used to describe two villages, **Las Casas** and **Taibique** – which has a main street featuring bars, restaurants, shops, a hotel and bank. The local Artesanía Cerámica sells ceramics and handmade jewellery. There is also a small church – **Iglesia de San Antonio Abad**.

Mist-shrouded fields around San Andrés

⑨ San Andrés

🗺 250. 🚌 🎉 Fiesta de la Apañada (1st Sun in Jun).

A heady 1,100 m (3,610 ft) above sea level, the prickly pear and fig trees of San Andrés are often shrouded in cold, damp mist for hours on end, and especially at night. This small agricultural town tends to be very hot in the summer, but winters are cold, and often battered with strong winds.

Its inhabitants live mainly off the land, cultivating crops and grazing sheep and goats. Despite the fertile soil, the unfavourable weather conditions cause many of them to leave this extremely rough and inhospitable terrain.

Environs
To the north, an asphalt road a little under 4 km (2 miles) long, which later becomes a footpath, leads to **Árbol Santo**, the holy Bimbache tree, known to locals as the *Garoé*. According to legend, water once flowed from the tree to give the island its entire supply (in fact the pine tree's needles had the ability to accumulate large quantities of water). The ancient tree was destroyed in 1949 by a hurricane; in its place grows a laurel tree, planted here in 1957.

Goat's cheese produced in San Andrés

Some 2 km (1 mile) to the southwest is the **Mirador de Jinama**. It is reached by road through fields divided by dry stone walls. In clear weather, the viewpoint provides a fine panorama over the bay of El Golfo.

⑩ Puerto de la Estaca

🗺 90. 🎉 San Telmo (14 Sep).

Until 1972, when the airport opened, this small harbour, cut off from the land by high volcanic cliffs, was the island's only link with the world. The name of the harbour, built in 1906, is derived from the word *estaca*, a type of wooden pile, to which fishermen tied their boats.

Environs
The **Roque de la Bonanza**, or "Rock of the Silent Ocean," is found in Las Playas bay. A bare basalt rock, it rises vertically from the sea a few steps from the shore, 9 km (6 miles) to the south of Puerto de la Estaca. It can be reached via a beautiful coastline road that is in the shadow of a steep volcanic slope. Take care: at one point the road passes through a single-lane tunnel with intermittently functioning traffic lights.

Some 2 km (1 mile) further south stands the **Parador del Hierro**. The most comfortable hotel on the island, it has an isolated waterfront location, with views of the cliff walls round the bay, and was built in the Castilian style in 1976. Its opening was delayed by five years, due to the slow building of the road that terminates here.

Roque de la Bonanza, or "Rock of the Silent Ocean," in Las Playas bay

LA PALMA

The Palmeros refer to La Palma as La Isla Bonita, "the Beautiful Island", or La Isla Verde, "the Green Island". Both nicknames are justified as the island is both pretty and strikingly lush. The rich vegetation of ferns and laurel forests, together with the fine domestic gardens, regarded as the best-kept in the archipelago, make this one of the greenest spots in the region.

The island's greenery is in large part thanks to the highest average annual rainfall in the Canary Islands. In spring and autumn, the sun stays behind the clouds for an average of 63 days and the plants enjoy excellent growing conditions.

The fifth largest island of the archipelago, La Palma is shaped like a Stone Age axe. It is claimed to be among the world's most mountainous islands, in terms of its height to area ratio (the island is 706 sq km/ 273 sq miles). The highest peak – Roque de los Muchachos – measures 2,426 m (7,959 ft). Like the rest of the archipelago, La Palma is a volcanic island, and its volcanoes cannot be regarded as truly extinct. The last eruption occurred in 1971 in the south of the island, where the black lava fields and reddish brown volcanic rocks contrast with the lush greenery of the remaining part of the island. Opinion is divided as to when the next eruption is likely to take place.

The island's population engages mainly in agriculture. An abundance of water ensures good crops of grapes, avocados, bananas and tobacco. The latter is used to make cigars that are considered by experts to be as good as the cigars produced in Cuba. La Palma is also known for its production of honey, and, as on many of the islands, fishing too plays an important part in the local economy. Mass tourism remains less of a feature here, due in part to the shortage of pleasant beaches along the island's craggy coastline, though there are resorts on the east and west coasts.

Glittering volcanic rocks, providing a fairytale-like spectacle of colour around Pico de la Cruz

◀ Colourful houses with traditional wooden balconies in Santa Cruz

Exploring La Palma

La Palma is excellent for walking trips and can cater for all tastes from a gentle stroll to a strenuous hike. Its varied landscapes, from the volcanic ash region of Fuencaliente to the lush, almost tropical forests of Los Tilos, fully compensate for the lack of great historic sights. Free of the bustle of the larger resort islands, there's ample opportunity for rest and relaxation, while the coastal waters of La Palma, rich in aquatic life, will attract divers. An excursion along the volcano trail, in the south of the island, is one of the highlights of a visit here, as is sampling the local wines and cuisine.

Colourful wooden balconies on the sea promenade at Santa Cruz de La Palma

0 kilometres   3
0 miles   3

Sights at a Glance

Getting There

La Palma has air links with Tenerife, Gran Canaria and El Hierro, as well as with some cities of mainland Spain. There are charter flights to and from several Western European airports. Planes touch down at the airport on the east coast, which connects to Santa Cruz de La Palma via a 13-km (8-mile) motorway. Ferries from Tenerife and La Gomera sail to Santa Cruz de La Palma harbour. Most of the island's towns and villages have bus transport. However, in order to explore the more remote parts of La Palma, you will have to hire a car.

Atlantic Ocean

Santa Cruz
de Tenerife

Las Palmas
de Gran Canaria

Locator Map

BARLOVENTO 5

Gallegos

LP1

Faro de
Punta Cumplida

La Cuesta

Roque
del Faro

Los Sauces

SAN ANDRÉS 4

Barranco del Agua

LOS TILOS 3

La Galga

Pico de la Cruz
2351 m

Playa de
Nogales

Puntallana

Punta
Salinas

Pico de la Nieve
2239 m

LP1

LP4

PARQUE NACIONAL DE
LA CALDERA DE
TABURIENTE

9

La
Cumbrecita

Barranco

LAS NIEVES 2

SANTA CRUZ 1
DE LA PALMA

Playa de Bajamar

Brena Alta

Playa Los Cancajos

Túnel de
la Cumbre

LP3

Miranda

San Antonio

La Rosa

MAZO 12

Cráter del Hoyo Negro
1797 m

La Sabina

Cueva de Belmaco

Malpaíses

13

LP2

Tigalate

Playa Arenas Blancas

Volcán Martín
1606 m

Monte
de Luna

Punta
del Porís

El Charco

as Indias

Las Caletas

11

FUENCALIENTE
DE LA PALMA

Punta Malpaís

Punta de
Fuencaliente

RUTA DE LOS VOLCANES

Astronomical observatory on top of the Roque de
los Muchachos

Key

— Major road

═ Minor road

━ Scenic route

- - Track

△ Summit

Bathing area in Charco Azul, near San Andrés

❶ Santa Cruz de La Palma

Situated on a bay known to the Guanches as Timibucar, Santa Cruz de La Palma has from its early days played a vital role in the economic and political life of Spain. During the 16th century, it was the third most important port in the entire Spanish empire, after Seville and Antwerp. It was also considered the best shipbuilding centre in the Canary Islands. The town's wealth attracted pirates, who plundered it on several occasions, including a particularly brutal raid in 1553 by Jean-Paul de Billancourt, otherwise known as "Pegleg". However, Santa Cruz de La Palma always managed to recover and today it is the capital of the island and an important communications centre.

Calle O'Daly, the main street of Santa Cruz's old town

Exploring Santa Cruz de La Palma

Poised on the slopes of a volcanic crater, this is one of the Canary Islands' loveliest towns. Its compact layout features many modern houses and a picturesque old town. The centre developed within a short space of time and consequently has a harmonious look to it.

But Santa Cruz de La Palma is more than a collection of colonial architectural relics. Numerous bars and restaurants along Avenida Marítima are popular with locals and tourists alike, and add to the town's atmosphere.

Statues of musicians in Calle O'Daly

🏛 Calle O'Daly

The main street, now turned into a pedestrian precinct, bears testimony to the town's former wealth and prestige. It was named after an Irish banana merchant who settled here. The street is lined on both sides with historic houses and residences. The most outstanding of these are the **Casa Principal de Salazar** (No. 22), which dates from the early 17th century and features distinctive wooden balconies, and the 19th-century **Casa Pinto** (No. 2).

🏛 Ermita de San Sebastián

Plaza de San Sebastián.

This small chapel, which is usually closed, is one of several in Santa Cruz; the others include the 16th-century **Ermita de Nuestra Señora de la Luz**, which stands in the picturesque Plaza de San Sebastián. Inside is a statue of St Catherine, which was brought here from Antwerp.

🏛 Plaza de España

At the very heart of Santa Cruz lies the Plaza de España. This triangular space, with its 16th-century fountain, is surrounded by historic buildings. The statue in the middle is of Manuel Díaz Hernández (1774–1863), a priest of the Salvador church who preached political liberalism in his sermons.

🏛 Iglesia de El Salvador

Plaza de España, 3. **Tel** 922 413 250.
Open 10am–8pm daily.

Built at the end of the 15th century, the church acquired its present shape in the second half of the 16th century. This is the most monumental example of the Canary Islands' Renaissance architecture. Its façade has a portal in the form of a triumphal arch (1503) – an allegory of Christ and his Church. The interior features a *Mudéjar* (Spanish-Moorish) coffered ceiling and sculptures by Fernando Estévez.

🏛 Casas Consistoriales

Plaza de España.

Casas Consistoriales, formerly the bishop's palace and now the town hall, was built in 1559–63. Its Renaissance façade, resting on columned arcades, is decorated with the bust of Philip II, carved in low relief, and the crests of La Palma and the Habsburgs. The inside walls are decorated with paintings by Mariano de Cassio, depicting island life.

🏛 Avenida Marítima

This is regarded as one of the Canary Islands' most beautiful and best-preserved shorelines. At its southern end stands a dragon tree (*see p19*), with curiously twisted branches. At the

The Iglesia de El Salvador in the Plaza de España

northern end of the shore stands the **Casas de los Balcones** – a row of picturesque old houses that have been wonderfully restored, with colourful elevations, featuring beautiful wooden balconies.

Main altar in the Iglesia de San Francisco

🔼 Iglesia de San Francisco

Plaza de San Francisco, 5. **Tel** 928 364 663. **Open** 9am–1pm & 6–8pm daily. 🅿️

In 1508, Franciscan monks accompanying Alonso Fernándo de Lugo in his conquest of the island began to build their abbey in Santa Cruz. The church, built in the 16th to 17th centuries, is one of the earliest examples of Renaissance architecture on La Palma. Outstanding features include the main altar and the coffered ceiling, as well as the richly painted decor. Today, the abbey houses the **Museo Insular** exhibiting local relics, along with Guanche skulls, stuffed animals and Spanish-school paintings.

🏛 Museo Naval

Plaza de la Alameda. **Open** 10am–3pm Mon–Fri (to 2pm Sat & Sun). 🅿️

Near Plaza de la Alameda stands a 1940 replica of

the *Santa María* – the tiny ship in which Christopher Columbus set off in 1492 to discover the New World. The inhabitants of Santa Cruz have named the ship *El Barco de la Virgen* – the Ship of the Holy Virgin. Inside is a modest maritime museum. The core of its collection consists of old charts, navigational instruments and a variety of ships' flags.

🔼 Castillo de Santa Catalina

Avenida Marítima.

This 16th-century castle is also known as Castillo Real. It was built as a defence against pirates who plundered ships

VISITORS' CHECKLIST

Practical Information
🗺 16,330. 🚍 🚍
✈ 13 km (8 miles) south.
ℹ Plaza de la Constitución, s/n, 922 412 106. 🚍 Sat, Sun. 🎭 Carnival (Jan/Feb), Fiesta de la Cruz (3 May), Bajada de la Virgen (Jun/Jul/Aug), every 5 years: 2020, 2025).

Transport
🚍🚍✈ 8 km.

as they left the port for the Americas with exports of goods such as sugar cane. In 1585, gunfire from the castle prevented Sir Francis Drake from taking over the island. The castle can be viewed only from the outside.

El Barco de la Virgen, a replica of Christopher Columbus's ship

---

Santa Cruz de La Palma

① Calle O'Daly
② Ermita de San Sebastián
③ Plaza de España
④ Iglesia de El Salvador
⑤ Casas Consistoriales
⑥ Avenida Marítima

0 metres   100
0 yards   100

Rich interior of Santuario de Las Nieves

❷ Las Nieves

🚌 📷 Bajada de la Virgen de las Nieves (Jun/Jul, every 5 years).

This village, lying among green hills above Santa Cruz de La Palma, is the main pilgrimage centre and the most important religious shrine on the island.

Standing in a picturesque spot is the **Santuario de la Virgen de las Nieves**. Its small church was built in 1657 on the site of the original chapel. It forms a historic complex together with the neighbouring buildings: the 17th-century **Pilgrim's House**, the early 18th-century **Parish House** and several houses that belonged to members of the local aristocracy.

The church is a typical example of colonial Canary architecture, with wooden balcony façades, whitewashed walls and a lovely *Mudéjar* (Spanish-Moorish) ceiling of Canary pine. The flickering candles, lit by the faithful, and the rich decor give the place its unique atmosphere. The gilded Baroque main altar is occupied by a 14th-century 82-cm (32-inch) high terracotta statue of the Madonna of the Snow, the island's patron saint, which was made in Flanders. Her image refers to her miraculous appearance during a freak August snowstorm in Rome. The side walls of the church are decorated with a row of *ex-voto* canvases. These votive pictures are in thanks for miracles performed by the patron saint, including saving a ship caught in a storm and answering the prayers of childless couples.

❸ Los Tilos

3 km (2 miles) west of San Andrés. ℹ️ Centro de Investigaciones e Interpretación de la Reserva de Biosfera "Los Tilos", 922 451 246. **Open** 9am–6:25pm daily (closed for 30 mins at noon).

The rocky, almost vertical sides of the Barranco del Agua ravine are overgrown with an evergreen rainforest, which includes moss-covered laurel trees – the island's largest concentration of the ancient *laurisilva* – plus lime, myrtle and ferns.

In 1983, Los Tilos was declared a biosphere reserve by UNESCO. A 3-km (2-mile) winding asphalt road, running along the bottom of the ravine, leads to the tourist centre, with its information point and restaurant.

The reserve area, measuring some 5 sq km (2 sq miles), has several marked walking trails. One leads to a viewpoint, the **Mirador de las Barandas**. A longer, more difficult (6-km/4-mile) trail with steep ascents leads in a southwesterly direction to **Caldera de Marcos y Cordero**, where determined tourists can admire the picturesque waterfalls.

❹ San Andrés

🗺️ 300. 🚌 📷 Fiesta de San Andrés (30 Nov).

This pretty seaside village, with cobbled streets and squares planted with flowers and palms, is filled with typical local houses.

At its centre stands the **Iglesia de San Andrés Apóstol**. Built as a fortified church in the 16th century and extended in the 17th century, this is one of the oldest churches in the Canary Islands. The interior features a Baroque main altar and *Mudéjar*-style coffered ceiling. Look out for the paintings of assorted human limbs on the wall, hung in thanks for the supposed healing powers of the church's patron saint.

San Andrés remains under joint administration with the larger town of **Los Sauces**, hence the combined name of San Andrés y Los Sauces. The environs of both towns are famous for the cultivation of bananas and sugar cane.

The most noteworthy building in Los Sauces is the **Iglesia Nuestra Señora de Montserrat**, the largest church on the island, which dates back to 1515. Its present Neo-Romanesque appearance is the result of refurbishment in 1960. Inside is a picture of the Madonna, attributed to the Dutch artist, Pieter Poubrus.

Environs

A short way to the south is **Charco Azul**, a tiny village set among banana tree plantations. High cliffs provide effective shelter for a natural tidal pool of a startling blue shade.

About 7 km (4 miles) to the south is **Puntallana**, home to the Iglesia San Juan Bautista. However, Puntallana owes most of its popularity to Playa de Nogales, a long, black sand beach backed by steep cliffs.

The Iglesia de San Andrés Apóstol

5 Barlovento

1,910. Fiesta de la Virgen del Rosario (2 Aug, every 2 years: 2017, 2019).

Besides the **Iglesia de Nuestra Señora**, with its altar of 1767 and some 16th to 18th-century Spanish sculptures, Barlovento's main claim to fame is its fiesta held every two years in August, when the villagers recreate bloody scenes from the Battle of Lepanto (1571).

Environs
The **Piscinas de Fajana**, 6 km (4 miles) to the northeast offers a rock pool topped up with cool water from the Atlantic. The nearby lighthouse at **Punta Cumplida** is the oldest on the island, dating from 1861.

Picturesque gullies crisscrossing the area around Barlovento

6 La Zarza

10 km (6 miles) west of Barlovento.

The archaeological site of La Zarza provides visible evidence of the Benahoares – the former inhabitants of La Palma – who left strange signs carved into the rock in several sites throughout the north of the island, including Roque Faro, Don Pedro and Juan Adalid. These carvings consist mostly of spirals, circles and linear figures, and have survived in their natural environment, though their meaning remains unknown.

Mysterious rock carvings in La Zarza

The information centre has a small museum illustrating the everyday life of the Benahoares. The exhibition includes a 20-minute video and shows how the ancient inhabitants of the island lived, and reveals their diet, medical practices and burial rites. The illuminated screens display images of erupting volcanoes, island scenery, its flora, fauna, and a map pointing out where the rock carvings were found.

When the carvings were discovered here in 1941, they became an archaeological sensation. Apart from the puzzling pictures, the ancient inhabitants of the island also left two Aztec-style carved images: one of a man, and an abstract figure of a woman with the head of an insect.

Parque Cultural La Zarza
Ctra. General del Norte, s/n. **Tel** 922 695 005. **Open** winter: 11am–5pm; summer: 11am–7pm.

7 Tazacorte

4,800. Fiesta de San Miguel (29 Sep).

In 1492, Alonso Fernández de Lugo commenced the conquest of the island from Tazacorte. Today, the skyline of this small town, surrounded by banana plantations, is dominated by the **Iglesia de San Miguel Arcángel**. The church, built in the 16th century, was extended in 1992 and given a magnificent, abstract stained-glass window.

In the **Museo del Plátano**, visitors can learn about the export of bananas, the most important source of economy in La Palma. Next door, at the **Museo del Mojo**, there is even more about this Canarian specialty (see p165).

Environs
Just 12 km (7 miles) north is **Mirador del Time**, which offers a fine view over Los Llanos de Aridane, Tazacorte, the mountains and the ocean.

Museo del Plátano
Camino de San Antonio.
Tel 922 480 151. **Open** 10am–1:30pm & 4pm–6pm Mon–Fri, 10am–1pm Sat.

Museo del Mojo
Camino de San Antonio. **Tel** 922 480 803. **Closed** for renovation.

Banana plantations growing almost in the centre of Tazacorte

❽ Los Llanos de Aridane

🏙 20,000. **Tel** 922 402 583. 🚌
🎉 Fiesta de los Remedios (2 Jul, every 2 years: 2018, 2020).

La Palma's second town is a modern affair, with the exception of the **Plaza de España**. This charming square, with laurel trees casting a pleasant shade over café tables, is a venue for concerts.

One side of the square is occupied by the **town hall**. Opposite it stands the **Iglesia de Nuestra Señora de los Remedios**. This white 16th-century church is built in the Canarian colonial style. Its Baroque main altar features a 16th-century Dutch statue of its patron saint. In the Museo Arqueológico Benahoarita, you can learn more about the indigenous people of La Palma.

Environs
About 3 km (2 miles) to the east is **El Paso**, a small town famous for its handmade cigars. Its main feature is the old quarter, with traditional Canary-style buildings surrounding the chapel of **Nuestra Señora de Bonanza**. Next to the chapel stands a modern church with Neo-Gothic furnishings, dedicated to the same saint.

A short way south of El Paso is the **Parque Paraíso de las Aves** – a combination of botanical garden and miniature zoo, housing exotic birds from many corners of the world.

❾ Parque Nacional de la Caldera de Taburiente

See pp152–3.

❿ Puerto Naos

🏙 900. 🚌

A small, quiet resort, Puerto Naos was once a fishing village, but now features an ever-increasing number of low-built apartment complexes. Its main tourist attraction is the guaranteed

The wide boulevard leading to Plaza de España in Los Llanos de Aridane

good weather, with some 3,300 annual hours of sunshine.

Set in a beautifully restored mansion in Las Manchas, the Wine Museum provides information on the production of different varieties of wine, and visitors can even taste some of them. Also worth seeing is the mosaic-decorated Plaza de la Glorieta by Luis Morera.

Environs
Charco Verde, about 2 km (1 mile) to the south, is a scenic beach, which is sheltered from the waves, and ideal for families.

⓫ Fuencaliente de La Palma

🏙 1,750. 🚌 ℹ️ Plaza Minerva, s/n, 922 444 003. 🎉 La Vendimia (Aug), San Martín (Nov).

The name of this place derives from *fuente caliente*, meaning "hot spring," although the spring has long since been swallowed up by a series of volcanic eruptions. Set amid vineyards, the small

town is best known for its sweet, heavy wine and is the home of the oldest and largest winery on the island, established in 1948. Evidence of the town's past can be seen in the parish church of **San Antonio Abad** (1730).

Environs
A little over 10 km (6 miles) to the south is **Punta Fuencaliente**, La Palma's southernmost point. Here there are two lighthouses and the salt extraction plant of Salinas Teneguía with its numerous brine pools.

⓬ Mazo

🏙 4,900. 🚌 ⛴ Sat, Sun.
🎉 Corpus Christi (May–Jun).

Mazo is famous for its hand-made cigars *(puros)*. Tourists also shop here for handicrafts including woven baskets and lacework.

The **Escuela Insular de Artesanía** has these for sale and holds demonstrations of how they are made. Other sights include the **Cerámica el Molino**, known for its production of replica Guanche vessels, and the **Museo de Corpus**, which exhibits decorations for the feast of Corpus Christi.

A Madonna from Mazo's San Blás

The **Iglesia de San Blás** (1512) looks out towards Tenerife and was extended in the 19th century. It features a beautiful Baroque altar.

Environs
Just 4 km (2 miles) to the south is the **Parque Arqueológico de Belmaco**, a cave with original Guanche inscriptions.

San Antonio volcano near Fuencaliente de La Palma

⑬ Ruta de los Volcanes

A somewhat arduous trail leads along the Cumbre Vieja mountain ridge, from Refugio del Pilar (alt. 1,450 m/4,757 ft) towards Fuencaliente. The hike, which should take a fit walker some 6 to 7 hours, is an unforgettable experience. Winding round steep volcanic rims, the path leads past striking geological formations and provides magnificent views of the eastern and western coasts of the island.

① Refugio del Pilar
This ridge, with a walkers' shelter, is a popular picnic spot. It can be reached by car and is a good starting point for hikes.

⑥ Fuencaliente
From here the trail continues further south, towards the nearby volcanoes of San Antonio (last eruption in 1677) and Teneguía (last eruption in 1971).

② Montaña de los Charcos
A powerful eruption of this volcano took place in 1712, when a vast flow of lava swamped much of the southwestern part of the island.

⑤ Volcán Martín
The eruption of the volcano in 1646 destroyed the former springs (believed to be a cure for leprosy) that gave the nearby town its name.

③ Cráter del Hoyo Negro
The trail runs along the edge of the San Juan volcano, which last erupted in 1949. The crater, with its rubble of solidified lava, is a reminder of how relatively recent the eruption was.

④ Cráter del Duraznero
This large crater was left after the eruption of San Juan, Duraznero and Hoyo Negro volcanoes in 1949. To the left of it stands the peak of Nambroque.

Refugio del Pilar ①
② Montaña de los Charcos
Cráter del ③ Hoyo Negro
④ Cráter del Duraznero
Parque Natural de Cumbre Vieja
Los Llanos de Aridane
Santa Cruz de la Palma
El Charco
LP2
Volcán Martín ⑤
LP2
Las Indias
⑥ Fuencaliente

Tips for Walkers

Length: 19 km (12 miles).
Stopping-off points:
Fuencaliente is a good place to halt for a meal.
Note: Don't stray from the marked trail, and be sure to carry a supply of drinking water.

0 km   1
0 miles   1

Key

▬ Main trail
▬ Scenic route
= Other road
••• Footpath

❾ Parque Nacional de la Caldera de Taburiente

La Caldera de Taburiente, a massive crater formed in the course of several powerful volcanic eruptions, is a natural fortress and served as a refuge for the last Benahoares when the Spanish invaded in the 15th century. Some of its walls reach up to 2,000 m (6,560 ft). Awarded national park status in 1954, the crater has many walking trails (some walks require a very good head for heights!). No roads run right through the park, and walkers should make sure they take with them enough water and a snack.

Roque de los Muchachos
Six telescopes have been placed along the steep, mountain road around Roque de los Muchachos, which passes through scrubland.

Observatorio del Roque de los Muchachos
Consisting of several observatories on the slopes of the Roque de los Muchachos, this constitutes the European Northern Observatory along with the Teide Observatory in Tenerife.

Key

— Major road
— Other road
— Footpath
— Park boundary
-·- Seasonal river

Garafía
Instituto de Astrofísica
Fuer Nuev 2351 n
Roque de los Muchachos 2426 m
Hoyo Verde
Roque Palmero 2306 m
Roqu del H
Morro Pinos Gachos 2179 m
Zona de Acampada
Somada Alta 1926 m
Roque Idafe
Lomo de las Chozas
La Cumbrecita
Barranco de las Angustias
Pico Bejenado 1845 m
Tazacorte

Astronomical Observatory

Thanks to their clear skies, the Canary Islands, and La Palma in particular, are regarded as one of the best places for conducting observations of the cosmos. The International Astrophysical Observatory near Roque de los Muchachos was opened in 1985, in the presence of King Juan Carlos and many European heads of state. Gran Telescopio Canarias (GTC) is the world's largest reflecting telescope, with an effective mirror opening of 10.40 m, and was inaugurated in 2009. Plans for a visitor centre are underway but guided tours can be booked for the summer months (Jun–Oct). These are booked out well in advance so organize as soon as possible (www.iac.es).

The Herschel telescope inside the observatory

Mirador de los Andenes
These bare rocks, eroded by wind and moisture over thousands of years, have been shaped into curious natural works of art.

Pico de la Cruz
This is one of the park's highest peaks. A challenging 4–5 hour walking trail, connecting Pico de las Nieves with Roque de los Muchachos, leads over the peak through some breathtaking scenery.

VISITORS' CHECKLIST

Practical Information
Carretera General de Padrón 47, El Paso.
Tel 922 922 280.
Open 9am–6pm daily.
w magrama.gob.es

Transport
The Observatory and viewpoints at Los Brecitos and La Cumbrecita can be reached by car.

irador de
s Andenes

Pico de
la Cruz
2351 m

Pico Piedra
Llana
2321 m

Pinar de
Mantigua

Pico de
la Nieve
2239 m

Santa Cruz
de la Palma

Pico de
la Sabina
2118 m

Punta de
los Roques
2087 m

Trail to Roque de los Muchachos
The trail, running along the highest peaks of Caldera de Taburiente, provides a view over the stunningly steep walls of the crater, shrouded with dense fog.

0 kilometres | 1

0 miles | 1

Oviejas
1845 m

Besucherzentrum,
↓ El Paso

Lomo de las Chozas
A short and easy trail leads through Canary pines from La Cumbrecita westwards, to Lomo de las Chozas, where the views are at their best at sunrise and sunset.

La Cumbrecita
A good asphalt road leads to La Cumbrecita, which has an information point. This is a good viewpoint from which to see the park.

TRAVELLERS'
NEEDS

WHERE TO STAY

The Canary Islands are among the world's most frequently visited places and have a sophisticated and highly organised tourist industry. However, this can lead to accommodation prices being high, particularly on the larger islands, such as Tenerife and Gran Canaria. It can be especially difficult to find cheap places to stay during high season.

The smaller, less-frequented islands, such as El Hierro and La Gomera, offer lower prices, but do not have many hotels, and affordable *casas rurales* have become more widespread. Usually in country properties full of charm and character, they provide much more varied and individual alternatives to conventional hotels.

Bright, airy rooms at Gran Hotel Bahía del Duque Resort in Costa Adeje, Tenerife *(see p160)*

Hotels

This is the most pricey form of accommodation on the Canary Islands. Many hotels belong to chains, such as Riu, NH Hotels, TRYP or the Spanish groups (Meliá Hotels, H10 Hotels and Paradores) and are block-booked by package-tour operators.

The hotels in large town centres cater mainly to business visitors. Popular coastal resorts have huge hotel complexes, aimed squarely at the tourist market. These are generally close to the beach and surrounded by lush gardens. Most afford fabulous views of the sea and the verdant landscape.

Complexes vie with each other to offer guests maximum fun, day and night. Many have tennis courts, mini-golf courts and gyms. It is advisable to check in advance whether these facilities are included in the price, or are charged for separately.

Paradors

Paradors are government-run hotels predominantly located in scenic areas, either on the coast or near a national park. They are distinguished by excellent service and are reputable. There are five paradors in the Canary Islands: Parador de La Palma, Parador de El Hierro, Parador de La Gomera, Parador de Cañadas del Teide and Parador de Cruz de Tejeda.

Apartments

The most popular form of accommodation on the islands, apartments can be situated within hotel buildings or as separate blocks or complexes. The quality varies, but most include a lounge, fully equipped kitchen, bathroom and one or two rooms. Most can accommodate between two and six people, but it is sometimes possible to combine two apartments into one. Apartments are especially suitable for families with young children.

Apartments are generally better value than staying in a hotel, though many require you to stay at least three to five nights; sometimes a week is the minimum.

Some apartments form part of a complex and provide similar facilities to those offered by hotels. Most of these have a swimming pool and a small playing field or tennis courts.

Casas Rurales

Rural houses *(casas rurales)* are generally converted farms or village houses and are suitable for those seeking quiet, out-of-the-way places. Most are located far from the traditional resorts, in small towns and villages. Some have limited access to public transport, so it is wise to check whether you will need to hire a car in advance. *Casas rurales* offer a degree of authenticity and individuality. Rooms and communal spaces

Pool of the Hacienda del Buen Suceso, Arucas, Gran Canaria *(see p156)*

◀ The Moorish style Haima Blue Bar at H10 Sentido White Suites, Lanzarote are often full of character and furnished with local handicraft items. They are a perfect choice for those who appreciate a personal touch. However, *casas rurales* are not necessarily a cheap option, nor can they offer the same variety of facilities as the large hotel complexes, although for some, this is part of their charm.

Camp Sites

Most islands have at least one or two basic camp sites and some glamping options. Before travelling, it is wise to find out about the situation on a particular island. Just turning up and pitching your tent on the beach is generally forbidden.

Booking

Most of the islands' hotel rooms and apartments are booked by travel agents and tour operators in advance. They then re-sell the holidays, including flights and half-board options. Such holidays do not suit everyone but are the cheapest way to visit the Canary Islands. It is obviously possible to make a booking without a travel agent. It is best to do so well in advance, although it is sometimes possible to find something at short notice.

Hotels and *pensions* can be booked over the telephone, or online. Some places, particularly smaller hotels and *casas rurales*, may require a deposit. When booking, bear in mind peak tourist times and festivals, especially when going to Gran Canaria or Tenerife.

Prices

Hotel prices depend on the season and the island. The dates when prices change are determined by individual hoteliers, so it is worth finding out in advance what tariffs apply at particular times. Tariffs will obviously be higher during popular holidays and carnivals. It should be understood that hotels quote their prices in various ways. Some are per night in a twin room; others are per

The beautiful outdoor pool at Finca Arminda in Mazo, on La Palma *(see p161)*

person per night. It is best to check this while booking.

The price is subject to 7 per cent IGIC tax, which is generally included in the quote. Prices quoted by apartments, guesthouses and *casas rurales* do not usually include breakfast.

Most hotels accept credit cards. Guesthouses and *casas rurales* usually prefer to be paid in cash. However, some cottages and smaller hotels work with companies like Gran Canaria Natural (www.grancanariafincas.com) to facilitate credit-card bookings.

Recommended Hotels

The accommodation options listed in this guide have been selected across a wide price range for their excellent facilities and unique appeal. They have been divided into a number of categories.

Value options predominantly list low-budget hotels that keep holiday costs down. **Apartments** offer self-catering facilities, while **B&B** options provide charming rooms with a hearty breakfast.

There are a variety of **family-friendly** options, which frequently provide entertainment for kids, while **resorts** cater to those looking for ease and maximum relaxation.

Casas rurales are hotels off-the-beaten track, and fall under **rural retreats**, while **boutique** hotels are generally small with high-end design elements. **Historic** options promise a characterful stay in a building of note, while **luxury** options promise excellent food and service in beautiful surroundings.

For the best of the best, look out for the entries labelled DK Choice. These establishments have been highlighted because they are outstanding in some way – a stunning location, notable architecture, exceptional facilities or a combination of these. Whatever the reason, a DK Choice will provide an especially memorable stay.

DIRECTORY

Hotels

- W hotelsearch.com
- W spain.info
- W turismodecanarias.com

Paradors

- W parador.es

Casas Rurales

- W ecoturismocanarias.com
- W pueblos-espana.org
- W toprural.com

Camp Sites

- W campingsonline.com
- W glampinghub.com

The stunning San Roque in Garachico, Tenerife's first boutique hotel *(see p162)*

Where to Stay

Gran Canaria

AGAETE: Finca Las Longueras Hotel Rural   €€
Historic
Carretera del Valle, 35480
Tel *928 898 145*
🆆 laslongueras.com
This hotel, set in an idyllic 19th-century building, has great views, spacious rooms and friendly staff.

AGÜIMES: Casa de los Camellos   €
Value
Calle el Progreso 12, 35260
Tel *928 785 003*
🆆 hotelruralcasadeloscamellos.com
This old inn, located in the historic city centre, has been renovated with style, while maintaining its original features.

ARUCAS: Hacienda del Buen Suceso   €€
Historic
Carretera de Arucas a Bañaderos, km 1, 35400
Tel *928 622 945*
🆆 haciendabuensuceso.com
This *hacienda*, tastefully converted into a hotel, features a heated outdoor pool and fitness centre.

CRUZ DE TEJEDA: El Refugio   €
Boutique
Calle de Cruz de Tejeda, 35328
Tel *928 666 513*
🆆 hotelruralelrefugio.com
Stay at this welcoming retreat with a rustic decor, set in a 19th-century country home.

FATAGA: Molino de Agua de Fataga   €
Historic
Carretera General, km 31, 35108
Tel *928 071 084*
🆆 elmolinodeagua.com
This country hotel has an old water mill, a vegetable garden and small farm. Rustic rooms.

LAS PALMAS: Hotel Parque   €€
Value
Calle Muelle de las Palmas 2, 35003
Tel *928 368 000*
🆆 hotelenlaspalmas.es
A modern hotel right by the pier and close to the city centre. Popular with business travellers.

LAS PALMAS: Reina Isabel   €€
Luxury
Calle Alfredo L. Jones 40, 35008
Tel *928 260 100*
🆆 bullhotels.com
The location, right on Las Canteras Beach, is a big draw for this upscale hotel with old-fashioned charm. An on-site fitness centre and spa.

DK Choice

LAS PALMAS: Santa Catalina   €€€
Historic
Calle León y Castillo 227, 35005
Tel *928 243 040*
🆆 hotelsantacatalina.com
Built in British colonial style, this hotel, surrounded by sub-tropical gardens, exudes an atmosphere of luxury. Past guests include Winston Churchill and Agatha Christie. It has its own casino, plus a free gym and spa.

MELONERAS: Lopesan Costa Meloneras Resort   €€€
Calle Mar Mediterráneo 1, 35100
Tel *928 128 100*
🆆 lopesanhr.com
Unwind at this resort set in idyllic gardens between the sea and the golf course. Free shuttle service to the course.

PLAYA DEL INGLÉS: Bungalows Doña Rosa   €
Apartments
Avda. de Alemania 23, 35100
Tel *928 760 250*
🆆 drosa.com
These well-equipped, peaceful bungalows are located close to the beach, with shops nearby.

PLAYA DEL INGLÉS: IFA Catarina   €€
Family-Friendly
Avenida de Tirajana 1, 35100
Tel *928 762 812*
🆆 lopesan.com
This child-friendly, beachfront hotel has an extensive sports

and entertainment programme, as well as a baby-sitting service.

PUERTO RICO: Marina Suites   €€
Family-Friendly
Calle Juan Díaz Rodríguez 10, 35130
Tel *902 996 093*
🆆 marinasuitesgrancanaria.com
These modern suites, with a children's playground and clubhouse, are ideal for families. Exclusive harbourside location.

SAN AGUSTIN: Dunas Don Gregory Resort   €€
Avenida las Dalias 11, 35100
Tel *928 773 877*
🆆 hotelesdunas.com
This splendid hotel offers affordable four-star luxury right on the beach. There is live music at the piano bar every night, plus a fitness centre and outdoor pool.

VEGA DE SAN MATEO: Las Calas   €
Rural Retreat
Calle Arenal 36, 35320
Tel *928 661 436*
🆆 hotelrurallascalas.com
Escape to the tranquillity of this historic manor house, set among tropical gardens and fruit trees.

Fuerteventura

ANTIGUA: Agroturismo La Gayría   €
Rural Retreat
C/Inmaculada 9, Lugar de Abajo, 35629
Tel *928 164 991*
🆆 agroturismolagayria.com/en
This complex of rural houses offers a peaceful getaway in a natural setting. There are barbecue facilities, as well as horse-riding, a telescope and free tastings of the house wine and olive oil.

CALETA DE FUSTE: Castillo Playa   €
Apartments
C/Pitera 8, 35610
Tel *928 163 210*
🆆 castilloplaya.es
A complex of 80 fully equipped apartments set around a pool with a bar and sun terrace. There is also a sauna and children's playground.

The ornate interior of the Hacienda del Buen Suceso, Arucas

The beautiful pool, overlooking the beachfront, at Tindaya, Costa Calma

DK Choice

CALETA DE FUSTE:
Elba Palace Golf   €€
Luxury
Fuerteventura Golf Club, 35610
Tel *928 163 922*
🆆 hoteleselba.com
Experience pure luxury with a
round of golf. Rooms are
sumptuously furnished and
offer stunning sea views while
the restaurant is one of the best
on the island. Adults only.

CORRALEJO:
Atlantis Dunapark   €€
Value
Calle La Red 1, 35660
Tel *928 536 151*
🆆 atlantisdunapark.com
The large, beautiful rooms are
complemented by the lovely gar-
dens, plus a pool, gym and sauna.
Only for guests over 16 years.

CORRALEJO:
Riu Palace Tres Islas   €€
Resort
Avenida Grandes Playas, 35660
Tel *928 535 700*
🆆 riu.com
The spacious rooms here have
balconies and sea views, plus
pools, Jacuzzi and spa. The fitness
centre is free to guests.

COSTA CALMA:
Tindaya   €€
Luxury
Calle Punta del Roquito, s/n, 35627
Tel *928 547 020*
🆆 hotelh10tindaya.com
Tindaya has well-equipped rooms
and facilities such as a spa and
sauna, plus access to the beach.

COSTA CALMA: VIK Suite
Hotel Risco del Gato   €€
Apartments
Calle Sicasumbre 2, 35627
Tel *928 547 175*
🆆 vikhotels.com
These luxurious yet inexpensive
bungalows, with pools, a sauna
and a spa, are good value.

PÁJARA: Casa Isaítas   €
B&B
Guize 7, 35626
Tel *928 161 402*
🆆 casaisaitas.com
This B&B has been painstakingly
restored, transforming what were
once ruins into a peaceful retreat.

PÁJARA: Faro Jandía   €€
Family-Friendly
Avenida del Saladar 17, 35626
Tel *928 545 035*
🆆 murhotels.com
Stay in large, well-equipped rooms
and suites. Pool, spa, tennis courts
and mini-golf on-site as well.

VILLAVERDE: Mahoh   €
B&B
Sitio de Juan Bello, 35660
Tel *928 868 050*
🆆 mahoh.com
This old country house with rustic
rooms also has a pool, library and
stables. Buffet breakfast included.

Lanzarote

ARRECIFE: Miramar   €
Value
Avenida Coll 2, 35500
Tel *928 812 600*
🆆 hmiramar.com
This hotel is nestled between
the beach and the old town and
has spacious and cheerful rooms.

DK Choice

COSTA TEGUISE:
Meliá Salinas   €€€
Luxury
Avenida Islas Canarias, s/n, 35509
Tel *928 590 040*
🆆 melia.com
Meliá Salinas promises a
memorable stay, with its
exclusive beach location and
lush tropical gardens. Fresh,
modern decor runs throughout, while the restaurants serve
haute cuisine. Recommended
for adults only.

PLAYA BLANCA: Hesperia
Playa Dorada   €€
Resort
Urb. Costa Papagayo, 35570
Tel *928 517 120*
🆆 nh-hotels.com
Located on the stunning Costa
del Papagayo, this hotel has com-
fortable rooms and several pools
to choose from.

PLAYA BLANCA: H10 Sentido
White Suites   €€€
Boutique
Calle Janubio 1, 35580
Tel *928 517 037*
🆆 h10hotels.com
Built in the Moorish style, this
establishment has several pools
and a beauty centre. Adults only.

PUERTO DEL CARMEN:
Nautilus Lanzarote   €
Apartments
C/Gramillo 5, 35510
Tel *928 514 400*
🆆 nautilus-lanzarote.com
Stay in a peaceful setting in
modern, sustainable apartments.
Many works of art are on display
throughout, adding to the charm.

PUERTO DEL CARMEN:
Pensión Magec   €
Value
Calle Hierro 11, 35510
Tel *928 515 120*
🆆 pensionmagec.com
A cost-effective alternative to
the pricier hotels on the beach,
with simple rooms and a
communal kitchen.

PUERTO DEL CARMEN:
Los Fariones   €€
Value
Calle Roque del Este 1, 35510
Tel *928 510 175*
🆆 farioneshotels.com
This hotel, surrounded by tropical
gardens on the beach, offers
large, bright rooms.

PUERTO DEL CARMEN:
VIK Hotel San Antonio   €€
Family-Friendly
Avenida de las Playas 84, 35510
Tel *928 514 200*
🆆 vikhotels.com
A beachfront hotel that offers
all the amenities, plus a games
room and bike rental. Ideal
choice for families.

SAN BARTOLOMÉ: Finca
de la Florida   €€
Rural Retreat
El Parral 1, 35550
Tel *928 521 124*
🆆 hotelfincalaflorida.com
A short drive from the beach, this
old country house, surrounded by
vineyards, offers a tranquil refuge.

For more information on types of hotels *see pp156–7*

Tenerife

COSTA ADEJE:
H10 Gran Tinerfe　　€€
Luxury
Avenida Rafael Puig Lluvina 13, 38660
Tel *922 791 200*
W h10hotels.com
This hotel features avant-garde
rooms, plus a Jacuzzi and three
pools. Not suitable for children.

COSTA ADEJE: Gran Hotel
Bahía del Duque Resort　　€€€
Luxury
Avenida de Bruselas, s/n, 38660
Tel *922 746 900*
W bahia-duque.com
Style, grandeur and good service
are guaranteed at this hotel, with
pools, waterfalls and gardens.

COSTA ADEJE: Jardín Tropical　€€€
Family-Friendly
Calle Gran Bretaña, 38660
Tel *922 746 000*
W jardin-tropical.com
The hotel has Arabian-inspired
architecture, plus tropical
gardens and a golf course.

GARACHICO: San Roque　　€€
Boutique
Esteban de Ponte 32, 38450
Tel *922 133 435*
This hotel in an 18th-century
estate combines the contemp-
orary with the historic.

DK Choice

GUÍA DE ISORA:
The Ritz-Carlton, Abama　€€€
Luxury
Carretera General, km 9, 38687
Tel *922 126 000*
W ritzcarlton.com
This Moorish-style, luxury hotel
is spectacularly located on a
promontory, hiding between
greenery and the sea. There is
a 72-par golf course and an
excellent spa.

LA CALETA:
Costa Adeje Palace　　€€€
Resort
Playa La Enramada, 38679
Tel *922 714 171*
W h10hotels.com
A chic beachfront hotel with a
range of facilites, including a shut-
tle service to Playa de las Américas.

LA CALETA: Hotel
Sheraton La Caleta　　€€€
Resort
La Enramada 9, 38670
Tel *922 162 000*
W starwoodhotels.com
Set among lush gardens, and

overlooking the sea, this hotel
has a large spa and several pools.

LA LAGUNA: Costa Salada　€€
Rural Retreat
Camino La Costa, s/n, Finca Oasis,
Valle Guerra, 38270
Tel *922 690 000*
W costasalada.com
A country hotel on a small *finca*
far from all hustle and bustle, the
rooms here come with antique
furniture and a private terrace.

LA OROTAVA: Hotel Rural
La Orotava　　€
Historic
Calle Carrera del Escultor
Estévez 17, 38300
Tel *922 322 793*
W hotelruralorotava.es
With a touch of old Tenerife, this
16th century house has
individually designed rooms.

LA OROTAVA: Parador
de Cañadas del Teide　　€€€
Historic
Las Cañadas del Teide, s/n, 38300
Tel *922 38 64 15*
W parador.es
This mansion has a fabulous
location at the foot of Teide, with
views of the Montaña Blanca.

LOS CRISTIANOS: Sensimar
Arona Gran Hotel & Spa　€€
Resort
Avenida Juan Carlos I 38, 38660
Tel *922 750 678*
W springhoteles.com
In a beautiful location overlook-
ing the old harbour and the city,
this hotel has spacious rooms.

PLAYA DE LAS AMÉRICAS:
Bitácora　　€€
Family-Friendly
Calle California 1, 38660
Tel *922 791 540*
W hotelbitacora.com
A haven for children, complete
with water slides, a playground
and plenty of activities.

PLAYA DE LAS AMÉRICAS:
Mediterranean Palace　　€€
Resort
Avenida de Las Américas, 38660
Tel *922 757 545*
W marenostrumresort.com
Offering superb views of the sea
and Teide, this hotel has over 500
rooms, set around a huge pool.

PUERTO DE LA CRUZ: Tigaiga　€€
Value
Parque Taoro 28, 38400
Tel *922 383 500*
W tigaiga.com
Enjoy a tranquil stay at this
hotel set amid botanical gardens,
with a great view of Teide.
Well-appointed, spacious rooms.

SANTA CRUZ:
Iberostar Mencey　　€€
Historic
Calle Dr. José Naveiras 38, 38004
Tel *922 609 900*
W grandhotelmencey.com
The history of Santa Cruz is still
alive in this classic hotel full of
grandeur. Three restaurants, a
spa and a fitness centre on-site.

SANTA CRUZ: Taburiente　　€€
Value
Calle Dr. José Naveiras 24a, 38001
Tel *922 276 000*
W hoteltaburiente.com
This centrally located hotel offers
modern elegance and a touch
of old-fashioned class. Rooftop
pool, sauna and fitness room.

La Gomera

HERMIGUA: Ibo Alfaro　　€
Historic
Barrio Ibo Alfaro, 38820
Tel *922 880 168*
W hotel-gomera.com
This country house is framed by
charming gardens and has taste-
fully decorated rooms throughout.
The sun terrace has great views.

The majestic Gran Hotel Bahía del Duque Resort, Costa Adeje

PLAYA DE SANTIAGO:
Jardín Tecina €€
Family-Friendly
Lomada de Tecina, s/n, 38811
Tel *922 145 850*
w jardin-tecina.com
This comfy hotel is perched high
above the cliffs affording stunning
views. Facilities include mini-golf,
racquetball and tennis courts.

SAN SEBASTIÁN:
Apartamentos Quintero €
Apartments
Plaza de las Américas 6, 38800
Tel *922 141 744*
w apartamentosquintero.com
These basic but well-equipped
apartments are located just a
short walk away from the beach.

DK Choice

SAN SEBASTIÁN:
Parador de la Gomera €€
Rural Retreat
Lomo de la Horca, s/n, 38800
Tel *922 871 100*
w parador.es
Magnificent ocean views, with
the island of Tenerife and Mount
Tiede on the horizon, are alone
worth a visit. The parador is
built in the style of a traditional
country house, with Castilian
and maritime decor. Lush
gardens with subtropical plants.

VALLE GRAN REY: Gran Rey €
Eco
Avenida Marítima 1, 38870
Tel *922 805 859*
w hotelgranrey.es
This hotel, near the beach, has
been designed in marble, wood
and stone. Rooftop pool.

VALLEHERMOSO:
Hotel Rural Tamahuche €
Eco
Calle la Hoya 20, 38840
Tel *922 801 176*
w hoteltamahuche.com
An old, restored Canarian
house in a unique location,
with comfortable rooms and
traditional-home cooking.

El Hierro

EL PINAR: Casas Rurales
Los Almendreros €
Apartments
C/Los Almendreros 6, 38916
Tel *608 225 664*
w losalmendreros.com
A peaceful complex of three fully-
equipped stone houses, each
with a private garden and terrace.
Minimum three-night stay.

Cosy salon in the Parador de Cañadas del Teide, La Orotava *(see p160)*

FRONTERA: Ida Inés €
Value
Belgara Alta 2, 38911
Tel *922 559 445*
w hotelidaines.com
A small hotel in the El Golfo valley,
with cosy rooms and sea views.
Five minutes from the beach.

LAS PUNTAS: Balneario
Pozo de la Salud €
Rural Retreat
Sabinosa, s/n, 38912
Tel *922 559 561*
Pamper yourself in the spa and
relax by the pool at this stylish
hotel on the northwestern coast.

DK Choice

VALVERDE: Parador
de El Hierro €€
Rural Retreat
Las Playas 15, 38910
Tel *922 558 036*
w parador.es
Crouching amid the rocks
between the volcano and the
ocean, this colonial-style hotel
enjoys a location that is out of
this world. Built in a colonial style.

La Palma

BARLOVENTO: La Palma
Romántica €
Value
Las Llanadas, s/n, 38726
Tel *922 186 221*
w hotellapalmaromantica.com
An inviting place set in an ancient
laurel forest, with views of the
mountains and the Atlantic. The
restaurant serves local cuisine.

BREÑA BAJA: Las Olas €
Apartments
Calle Salinas 42, 38712
Tel *922 433 015*
w hotellasolas.es
This beautiful complex has
elegant apartments right on the
beach. Bike rental available.

BREÑA BAJA: Hacienda
San Jorge €€
Apartments
Playa de los Cancajos 22, 38712
Tel *922 181 066*
w hsanjorge.com
Built in the traditional style, the
fully equipped apartments in this
charming complex offer comfort
and relaxation. Mini-market on site.

BREÑA BAJA:
Parador de la Palma €€
Rural Retreat
Carretera El Zumacal, s/n, 38712
Tel *922 435 828*
w parador.es
Enjoy views over the coast of
Santa Cruz from the rooms and
pool area of this modern hotel,
built in typical Canarian style.

DK Choice

MAZO: Finca Arminda €€
Historic
Lodero 181, 38730
Tel *922 440 411*
w fincaarminda.es
This small, old *finca* on the
slopes of Mazo, surrounded by
banana plantations, has only
five rooms. The ambience and
atmosphere are as unique as
the guest service.

PUERTO NAOS: Sol La Palma €
Resort
Carretera Punta del Pozo, s/n, 38769
Tel *922 408 000*
w melia.es
This self-sufficient, family-friendly
resort has all the amenities, from
a gym room to a supermarket.

TAZACORTE: Hotel Hacienda
de Abajo €€
Boutique
Calle Miguel de Unamuno 11, 38770
Tel *922 406 000*
w hotelhaciendadeabajo.com
With its superb location, this
17th-century restored manor
house offers a sumptuous
retreat, though only for adults.

For more information on types of hotels *see pp156–7*

WHERE TO EAT AND DRINK

The Canary Islands offer a good selection of restaurants able to satisfy the most discerning palates. Traditional Canarian cuisine is in plentiful supply, as are dishes from other regions of Spain. In addition, a wide range of international cuisines, including German, French, Italian, Chinese, Middle Eastern and Indian, can be easily found. Many restaurants offer fusion menus, and chefs create sophisticated dishes by experimenting with a range of local ingredients and various culinary traditions. A number of these restaurants are highly regarded and very popular. The majority of Canary Island restaurants, however, are actually small bars near beaches and tourist centres.

A modest restaurant in one of El Golfo's quiet streets

Places to Eat

The islands offer countless bars and restaurants, with diverse menus. The majority of restaurants open for lunch and dinner. Tourists and locals alike enjoy going to restaurants, which accounts for the variety on offer, including *marisquerías* (seafood restaurant) and *cervecerías* (pubs).

There is no dress code in restaurants, apart from a few exclusive places that require evening dress. Apart from in the fast-food bars close to the beaches, swimwear is not acceptable in bars and restaurants.

There are also fast-food chains, local and foreign, including McDonald's, TelePizza, Slow Boat (Chinese) and Little Italy (pizza and pasta), as well as cafés serving English-style breakfasts, and fish and chips. For authentic Canarian cuisine, visitors should head inland, where the majority of traditional Canarian restaurants can be found.

Canarian Cuisine

The islands' cuisine is a relatively simple one. Ingredients include fish, meat, rice, vegetables, potatoes and tropical fruit.

The most popular meats are goat and lamb, although beef is also favoured. Typical species of fish include *dorada* (sea bass) and *pez espada* (swordfish). Canarian dishes are easy and quick to prepare. Most types of fish and meat are fried or roasted. They are usually served with the local *mojo* sauces, made of olive oil, seasoning and herbs.

Local bars serve basic *raciones* (portions), including *tortilla de papa* (omelette with potatoes), *jamón Serrano* (Spanish ham), *queso* (cheese) and many others.

Lunch with a view at El Mirador, Tenerife *(see p173)*

Also popular are the so-called *platos combinados* – inexpensive combinations of basic dishes, including chips, fried egg and cutlet. These are large helpings and usually reasonably priced.

Also available are "single pot" courses. These consist mainly of potatoes and pulses, along with any combination of meat, fish and vegetables.

One should not forget *gofio*. This roasted sweetcorn flour can be added to everything: soups, stews, desserts and even ice cream!

Opening Hours

As with the rest of Spain, mealtimes on the Canary Islands are fairly irregular. Lunchtime *(la comida)* is usually between 1pm and 3pm, but restaurants that cater principally for locals tend to have unusually late meal times. Regardless of the hour, however, having ordered a meal you are generally allowed to finish it in peace. Outside traditional mealtimes, it is always possible to eat in bars, which offer a wide variety of food. Beachside restaurants are good for snacks any time of day.

Dinner *(cena)* starts late, at about 9pm. It is served in all restaurants until 11pm or midnight. After this, it is generally only possible to buy sandwiches, kebabs or hot dogs in small bars. Dinner in Spain is usually a hot meal. Like lunch, it may include two courses. At dinnertime, restaurants offer only meals *à la carte*. Bars usually serve

Dining room of El Patio de Lajares in El Cotillo, Fuerteventura *(see p171)*

tapas or *raciones*. When eating in a group, it is fun to order a selection of tapas and sample a little bit of each dish.

Spanish breakfast *(desayuno)* tends to be a light affair and usually consists only of coffee with milk and a sweet bun. An alternative is toast with ham and cheese. Many bars offer a set breakfast, generally including coffee, fresh orange juice and a snack. If you want a bowl of breakfast cereal or a fry-up, you should head for a hotel-restaurant.

Booking

The large number of restaurants on the islands means that there should be no problem with finding a table. Nevertheless, it is worth booking in advance to avoid disappointment, particularly when you fancy a specific restaurant.

Vegetarians

All restaurants offer some vegetarian dishes, but the concept of a strictly meatless or fishless diet is not always understood in the Canaries. It is wise to check before ordering whether vegetarian dishes contain meat stocks or ham.

Prices

Restaurant prices can vary. In exclusive establishments a full meal, including wine, may cost up to €50 per head. In other, provincial restaurants, the same meal could cost around €15. During lunch hours many restaurants offer, besides *à la carte* dishes, an inexpensive and tasty *menú del día* (menu of the day).

Beautifully prepared starters at Franchipani, El Paso, La Palma *(see p175)*

Such menus always include a selection of starters, main courses and desserts, as well as bread and often beverages (wine, beer or soft drinks). The average price of such a meal is from €4 to €10.

Some more upmarket restaurants also offer "tasting" menus. The dishes from these menus are much more expensive, since they include all of the specialities recommended by the chef.

Paying

Almost all restaurants accept credit cards to pay *la cuenta* (the bill). Even bars are willing to accept this form of payment, if it is more than a certain amount. Be prepared to pay in cash in smaller restaurants not oriented towards tourists. If in doubt, ask before ordering. Most restaurants accept chip-and-PIN cards; those that don't may request an additional form of ID, such as a passport.

Tipping

Tipping is expected in restaurants with table service. The general rule is to leave around 10 per cent of the total bill. Tipping in small cafés and bars is rare.

Recommended Restaurants

The restaurants listed in this guide have been carefully selected for their excellent value, good food, delightful ambience and stunning location. Diners can choose from a wide range of eateries, including traditional Canarian restaurants and tapas bars serving typical regional fare, bistros offering a selection of tasting menus and steakhouses specialising in a variety of meats.

Establishments labelled DK Choice have been chosen because they are exceptional in some way. They may offer superb cuisine, creative menus, outstanding service or a combination of these.

Lunch right on the Playa de las Canteras, Gran Canaria

The Flavours of the Canary Islands

The fruits and vegetables that grow in the sub-tropical Canarian climate, and the fish caught in local waters, have led to a cuisine very different from that of the Iberian peninsula. Culinary traditions from Guanche inhabitants survive in local staples such as *gofio* (maiz meal). Over the centuries, Spanish, Portuguese and North African influences have been incorporated into the local cuisine, but the underlying theme is always one of simplicity and a reliance on fresh local produce. There are all kinds of unusual delicacies, from sweet-fleshed parrot-fish to succulent fruits.

Maiz (corn)

Appetizers

Tapas are popular throughout Spain and can, of course, be found in the Canary Islands. There are countless variants of the small dishes (*see pp166–7*), comprising meat, cheese, seafood, olives and vegetables.

Traditional Canarian appetizers are *papas arrugadas* – wrinkly potatoes that are boiled in water, seasoned with a lot of sea salt, until the water has evaporated. This process leaves behind a beautiful salt crust on the bowl. They go best with a *mojo rojo* or *mojo verde*, both of which are traditional, cold sauces. On almost every menu you will also find *pulpo a la gallega*, which is squid seasoned with paprika and salt. Equally appetizing are *jamón* (ham) and *chorizo* (paprika salami). A traditional dish popular with locals is *gofio escaldado*. Here the gofio is mashed with a fish or meat broth. Last, but not least, a s*opa de pescado* is always a good starter. A variant is *tinerfeña* with sea bass.

Main Courses

The Atlantic provides a wide variety of seafood. Among well-known favourites, some of the rare specialties that you can discover on the menu include wreck-fish, dentex, bream and parrotfish. These delicacies can be served either baked in a salt crust, fried or dried. One specialty is *vieja sancochada* (boiled sea bream).

Besides seafood, Canarians like to eat hearty dishes of pork, kid, chicken and beef,

Mangoes · Bananas · Pineapple · Papaya · Dates · Guavas

Typical fresh fruits from the Canary Islands

Traditional Dishes

Even the Greeks called the Canaries "the Fortunate Islands", and they are certainly blessed in terms of the freshness and abundance of the local produce. Whatever you choose to eat, you can be sure of encountering a bowl of the ubiquitous *mojo* sauce. This aromatic Canarian creation accompanies almost every dish, and appears in countless versions: the main ones are red *picón*, which is spiced up with pepper and paprika, and green *verde*, with parsley and coriander. The Canarian staple *gofio* (roasted maiz meal) is served for breakfast and used in local dishes such as *gofio de almendras*, a rich almond dessert. The islands are also known for delicious pastries including the honey-drizzled *bienmesabes* (meaning "tastes good to me"), and traditional cheeses accompanies almost every dish".

Roasted, salted almonds

Papas arrugadas
Wrinkled potatoes with a sea-salt crust and a traditional red *mojo* sauce.

cooked according to traditional Guanche recipes. Also popular are stews, such as *ropa vieja* (beef stew), which roughly translates as "old clothes"; there is also *puchero canario* (a hearty stew with vegetables and chickpeas). *Conejo en salmorejo* (marinated and sautéed rabbit) is another typical dish, as is *morcilla* (Canarian black pudding), which gets its unique sweet taste from the added raisins, almonds and cinnamon. Another culinary delight is *carne de cabra compuesta* (goat stew). Generally speaking, meat dishes are well seasoned with garlic marinade, oregano, thyme, bay leaves, salt and pepper, and flavoured with wine or rum. One seasonal delicacy is *lapas* (limpets), served during the summer months, and usually grilled *(a la plancha)*.

Desserts

Fruits in great abundance can always be found fresh on the table: bananas, mangoes or papayas. But fruit is also part of the many desserts served at the end of every meal. Try *cabello*

de ángel (dough patties with candied pumpkin filling), *tortitas de plátano* (fried banana patties) or sherbet with *bienmesabe*, which is translated as "it tastes good to me". These dishes include the traditional Canarian almond cream, a refinement found in many desserts. Almonds are also an ingredient in *gofio de almendras* (*gofio* with almonds).

For dessert, there is often a choice between flan and *frangollo*, a popular Canarian dish. Popular with the young and old alike are *rapaduras*, small, sweet cones of *gofio* with sugarcane syrup, and sprinkled with almonds, cinnamon and lemon. Not to be missed are the biscuits and meringues from Moya, which are very sweet and traditionally baked. Less sweet, but spicy and aromatic, are local cheeses, which conlude every good meal. The wide variety and high quality of goats' and

Piscolabis: small snacks eaten between meals

sheep's cheese offer something for every taste. The average annual consumption of cheese in the Canary Islands is almost 10 kg (22 lb) per capita. Not only is this the highest in Spain, but it also means that local cheese is a highly valued product for the Canarians.

SEA FOOD DISHES

Parrotfish
Vieja a la plancha – parrotfish, fried in olive oil and seasoned simply with salt and lemon, is a light delicacy even in hot weather.

Dentex
Sama en escabeche – freshly caught dentex in a spicy sauce, plus a few *papas arrugadas* and fresh salad with olive oil.

Wreckfish
Cherne al cilantro – wreckfish with coriander, a traditional Canarian dish.

Logo of the Canarian banana plantations

Sopa de pescado tinerfeña
Fish soup, with sea bass and potatoes, seasoned with saffron and cumin.

Pez espada
Grilled swordfish, seasoned with lemon and oregano – a popular dish in the Canaries.

Frangollo
This dessert is flavoured with almonds, cinnamon, and raisins, each island making it a different way.

Choosing Tapas

Tapas, sometimes called *pinchos*, are small snacks that originated in Andalusia in the 19th century to accompany sherry. Stemming from a bartender's practice of covering a glass with a saucer or *tapa* (cover) to keep out flies, the custom progressed to a chunk of cheese or bread being used, and then to a few olives being placed on a platter to accompany a drink. Once free of charge, tapas are usually paid for nowadays, and a selection makes a delicious light meal. Choose from a range of appetizing varieties, from cold meats to elaborately prepared hot dishes of meat, seafood or vegetables.

Mixed green olives

Patatas bravas are piquant fried potatoes with a spicy red sauce.

Albóndigas (meatballs) are a hearty *tapa*, often served with a spicy tomato sauce.

Almendras fritas are fried, salted almonds.

Banderillas are canapés skewered on toothpicks.

Calamares fritos are squid rings and tentacles that have been dusted with flour before being deep-fried in olive oil. They are usually served garnished with a piece of lemon.

Jamón serrano is salt-cured ham dried in mountain (*serrano*) air.

On the Tapas Bar

Almejas Clams

Berberechos Cockles

Berenjenas al horno Roasted aubergines (eggplants)

Boquerones Anchovies

Boquerones al natural Fresh anchovies in garlic and olive oil

Buñuelos de bacalao Salted cod fritters

Butifarra Catalonian sausage

Calabacín rebozado Battered and fried courgettes (zucchini)

Calamares a la romana Fried squid rings

Callos Tripe

Caracoles Snails

Champiñones al ajillo Mushrooms fried in white wine with garlic

Chistorra Spicy sausage

Chopitos Cuttlefish fried in batter

Chorizo al vino Chorizo sausage cooked in red wine

Chorizo diablo Chorizo served flamed with brandy

Costillas Spare ribs

Criadillas Bulls' testicles

Croquetas Croquettes of ham, cod, chicken or mushrooms

Empanada Pastry filled with tomato, onion and meat or fish

Ensaladilla rusa Potatoes, carrots, red peppers, peas, olives, hard-boiled egg, tuna and mayonnaise

Gambas al pil pil Spicy, garlicky fried king prawns (shrimp)

Longaniza roja Spicy red pork sausage from Aragón; *Longaniza blanca* is paler and less spicy

Magro Pork in a paprika and tomato sauce

Tapas Bars

Even a small village will have at least one bar where the locals go to enjoy drinks, tapas and conversation with friends. On Sundays and holidays, favourite places are packed with whole families enjoying the fare. In larger towns it is customary to move from bar to bar, sampling the specialities in each. A *tapa* is a single serving, whereas a *ración* is similar to a main. Tapas are usually eaten standing or perching on a stool at the bar rather than sitting at a table, for which a surcharge is usually made.

Diners at a busy tapas bar

Chorizo, a popular sausage flavoured with paprika and garlic, may be eaten cold or fried and served hot.

Salpicón de mariscos is a cold salad of assorted fresh seafood in a zesty vinaigrette.

Gambas a la plancha are simple but flavourful grilled prawns (shrimp).

Tortilla española is the ubiquitous Spanish omelette of onion and potato bound with egg.

Queso Manchego is a sheep's-milk cheese from La Mancha.

Pollo al ajillo consists of small pieces of chicken (often wings) sautéed and then simmered in a garlic sauce.

Manitas de cerdo Pig's trotters

Mejillones Mussels

Morcilla Black (blood) pudding

Muslitos del mar Crab-meat croquettes, on a claw skewer

Navajas Grilled razor-shells

Orejas de cerdo Pig's ears

Pa amb tomàquet Bread rubbed with olive oil and tomatoes (Catalan)

Pan de ajo Garlic bread

Patatas a lo pobre Potato chunks sautéed with onions and red and green peppers

Patatas alioli Potato chunks in a garlic mayonnaise

Pescadito frito Small fried fish

Pimientos de padrón Small green peppers, which are occasionally hot

Pimientos rellenos Stuffed peppers

Pinchos morunos Pork skewers

Pisto Thick ratatouille of diced tomato, onion and courgette

Pulpitos Baby octopus

Rabo de toro Oxtail

Revueltos Scrambled eggs with vegetables, meat or fish

Sepia a la plancha Grilled cuttlefish

Sesos Brains, usually lamb or calf

Surtido Ibérico Assortment of cold cuts/charcuterie

Tabla de quesos A range of Spanish cheeses

Tortilla riojana Ham, sausage and red pepper omelette

Tostas Bread with various toppings such as tuna or Brie

Verduras a la plancha Grilled vegetables

What to Drink in the Canary Islands

The Canary Islands have a number of surprises in store on the drinks menu – mineral water sourced in the volcanic rocks of Firgas, coffee originating in Europe's last coffee-growing areas in Agaete, freshly squeezed fruit juices, red wines and white wines from grapes that have ripened in Lanzarote, El Hierro or Fuerteventura, plus Canary beers and liqueurs made from rum and honey. An excellent choice should be available whether you are in a bar, on the beach, in the club, enjoying lunch, or at sunset.

Rum was produced in the Canaries even before it was made in Cuba

Wine

The year-round mild climate and volcanic soil of the Canary Islands allows local grapes to develop, producing fine wines with unique aromas. More than 30 different grape varieties are nurtured, and they yield both red and white wines with different characters and bouquets. The extensive cultivation (the vines mostly lie on the ground) does not, however, produce large quantities of fruits. The best-known Canary wine today is Malvasia, which was for many years viewed as a rare, fine wine intended for the royal houses of Europe.

Negro   Yaiza   Malvasía   Los Berraziales

Beer

In spite of the excellent local wines, beer is a popular drink with locals. In addition to countless imports there are several Canarian beers – traditional brands include Tropical and Dorada, while Viva Beer is winning an increasing number of devotees. It has been brewed in Gran Canaria since 1999, and is made in accordance with German purity laws. Its ingredients include German hops and malt as well as the best mountain spring water from Santa Lucía.

Tropical

Cruzcampo   Mahou

Rum and Liqueur

Rum production and the sugar industry were prevalent in the Canary Islands even before they took off in the Caribbean. It was Christopher Columbus who exported sugar cane and, with it, the art of making rum from Gran Canaria to San Salvador. In Arucas (see p56), you can visit a rum factory, where the famous Arehucas rum is still being produced. Rum is also the basis for the famous honey-rum liqueur of the islands, the sweet-tasting *Ron Miel*.

Artemi   Cuarenta y tres   Ron Miel Cocal

Juices, Shakes and Smoothies

The variety of local fresh fruits makes the Canary Islands a paradise for top-quality, healthy and refreshing juices, non-alcoholic cocktails and shakes. An ideal summer drink popular throughout Spain is *horchata de chufa*, which can be served frozen (as *granizada*) or runny (*liquida*). This tigernut milk is rich in minerals and vitamins, and is very refreshing.

Ice Shake

Milkshake

Freshly squeezed orange juice

Horchata de chufa

Non-alcoholic cocktail

Mineral Water

This is readily available throughout the Canary Islands. *Aguas minerales de Firgas*, from the small town of Firgas in the north of Gran Canaria, is well known throughout the islands, and there is hardly a bar or restaurant that does not have this excellent mineral water on the table.

Vichy Catalan

Lanjaron

Cocktails and Long Drinks

Local rum and fresh fruit juices are the basic ingredients of many cocktails and long drinks. Of course, *Sangria*, well-known throughout Spain, is also enjoyed in the Canary Islands. One spot recommended to all those who enjoy both culture and cocktails is the Ábaco in Puerto de la Cruz in Tenerife. This museum turns into a cocktail bar at night (www.abacotenerife.com).

Sangria

Caipirinha

Cuba Libre und Planter's Punch

Coffee

Café solo (espresso), *café cortado* (coffee with condensed milk), *café con leche* (coffee with fresh milk) and *café carajillo* (black coffee with brandy, rum or Licor 43) are all popular coffees enjoyed by the islanders.
One speciality in Tenerife is *barraquito*. Drunk from a glass, the coffee has three layers – condensed milk at the bottom, followed by espresso with a shot of Licor 43, and, in the uppermost layer, frothed milk sprinkled with cinnamon. It is sweet and delicious.

Chocolate with churros

Café con leche

Where to Eat and Drink

Gran Canaria

AGAETE: La Palmita €€
Canarian
Carretera de Las Nieves, s/n, 35480
Tel *928 898 704*
La Palmita serves typical Canarian dishes made with fresh fish. *Sama a la espalda* (grilled dentex) and the vegetable stew of the day are recommended.

AGAETE: Ragu €€
Italian
Avda. de las Poetas 10, Puerto de las Nieves, 35840
Tel *605 453 965*   **Closed** *Mon & Tue; Fri lunch*
Overlooking the harbour, this friendly restaurant offers a variety of fresh fish and seafood options, as well as pasta dishes. There's also a good selection of local wines.

AGÜIMES: La Farola €€€
Seafood
C/Alcalá Galiano 3, 35118
Tel *928 180 410*   **Closed** *Sun & Mon dinner*
Not far from the airport, this restaurant specializes in delicious, simply prepared seafood. Don't miss the baked saltfish.

ARUCAS: Casa Brito €€€
Steakhouse
Pasaje de Ter 17, 35400
Tel *928 622 323*   **Closed** *Sun dinner; Mon & Tue*
The focus here is Argentinean meat, although there are also some tempting fish dishes, such as the *lomo de cherne en salsa de cilantro con langostinos* (Atlantic wreckfish in coriander sauce with prawns).

LAS PALMAS: Asturias €€
Spanish
C/Capitán Lucena 6, 35468
Tel *928 274 219*
As the name suggests, dishes from Asturias, in north-west Spain, are served here. Portions are hearty, with a heavy emphasis on meat and bean stews, plus fish, seafood, ham and chorizo.

LAS PALMAS: Kamakura €€
Japanese
C/Galileo Galilei 4, 35010
Tel *928 222 670*   **Closed** *Sun; Mon lunch*
Dishes at this charming restaurant are prepared in front of diners. Specialities include *tempura* (lightly battered, fried seafood and vegetables), fish tartar and *sashimi* (slices of raw fish).

LAS PALMAS: Kitchen Lovers €€
Mediterranean
Paseo de las Canteras 16, 35008
Tel *928 987 610*
Everything here is a must-try, from the expertly prepared lamb and seafood dishes to the heavenly desserts. Lovely seaside views add to the ambience.

LAS PALMAS: La Chacalote €€€
Seafood
C/Proa 3, 35016
Tel *928 312 140*
The fresh seafood and friendly service here attracts a loyal clientele. The baked fish in a salt crust is a speciality.

DK Choice

LAS PALMAS: El Churrasco Restaurante Grill €€€
Steakhouse
C/Olof Palme 33, 35100
Tel *928 272 077*
An upscale Argentinean-style grill, El Churrasco offers a wide variety of meats, although there is an excellent selection of vegetables and salads as well. The top-quality Aberdeen Angus beef, imported directly from Argentina, is a highlight. The sumptuous food is paired with equally attentive service. Reservations are recommended.

LAS PALMAS: Clandestino €€€
Canarian
C/Dr. Miguel Rosas 8, 35007
Tel *928 229 603*
This restaurant in the harbour area offers tempting meat dishes with an exotic touch. The kitchen specializes in creative variants of Canarian dishes. Try their *menú del día* or three-course meal of the day.

Rustic dining area at the popular Novillo Precoz, Las Palmas

LAS PALMAS: Deliciosa Marta €€€
Mediterranean
C/Pérez Galdos 23, 35002
Tel *928 370 882*   **Closed** *Sat & Sun*
Imaginative dishes are paired with a great ambience at this elegant restaurant with lovely outdoor seating.

LAS PALMAS: La Dolce Vita €€€
Italian
C/Agustín Millares Torres 5, 35001
Tel *928 310 463*   **Closed** *Sun*
Vintage film posters and a menu of Italian staples, including pizza and pasta, give this restaurant a rustic charm.

LAS PALMAS: Mestizo Tasca €€€
Fusion
C/Portugal 79, 35010
Tel *828 014 344*   **Closed** *Tue dinner; Wed*
Choose between a variety of cuisines with international influences at this casual, unassuming restaurant. Try the *volovanes de bacalao y crujiente de Parmesano al suave curry* (cod vol-au-vents with crispy Parmesan and a touch of curry).

LAS PALMAS: Novillo Precoz €€€
Steakhouse
C/Portugal 4, 35010
Tel *928 221 659*
This restaurant has established itself as an institution with the locals for its steaks and grilled meat. The fillet steak cooked on a wooded grill is a must-try.

LAS PALMAS: Restaurante La Marinera €€€
Seafood
C/Alonso Ojeda, s/n, 35007
Tel *928 468 802*
Top-notch food and a glorious view over Las Canteras beach make this restaurant one of the best in the city.

LAS PALMAS: Rías Bajas €€€
Seafood
C/Simón Bolívar 3, 35007
Tel *928 271 316*
This Galician restaurant in the heart of the entertainment district is one of the best in town, serving excellent seafood.

MASPALOMAS: El Salsete €€
Canarian
C/Segundo Delgado 4–5, 35100
Tel *928 778 255* **Closed** *Sun*
This restaurant offers
contemporary variations of
traditional Canarian dishes. The
decor is quaint and intimate.

MOGÁN: Acaymo €€
Canarian
C/Los Pasitos 23, 35140
Tel *928 569 263*
One of the most popular places
on the island, Acaymo gives a crea-
tive twist to local cuisine, offering
great fish dishes and tapas.

PLAYA DEL INGLÉS:
Las Cumbres €€
Canarian
Avda. de Tirajana 11, 35100
Tel *928 760 941* **Closed** *Tue lunch*
Rustic elements adorn this beach-
restaurant, which serves traditional
Canarian dishes. The succulent lamb
dishes are popular with locals,
while the seafood is excellent too.

PLAYA DEL INGLÉS:
El Portalón €€€
Spanish
Avda. de Tirajana 27, 35100
Tel *928 771 622*
Sit at one of the pleasant outdoor
terraces of this restaurant in
Hotel Sol Barbacán. The speciality
is traditional Basque cuisine.
The wine list is good as well.

PUERTO DE MOGÁN:
N'Enoteca €€
Italian
*Urb. de Puerto de Mogán, Local
380/381, 35140*
Tel *673 478 886* **Closed** *lunch*
Simple and authentic Italian
cooking is paired with friendly
and attentive service here. The
harbour views are breathtaking.

PUERTO DE MOGÁN:
Qué Tal by Stena €€€
International
*Urb. de Puerto de Mogán, Local 101,
35138*
Tel *928 565 534* **Closed** *lunch*
This chic restaurant on the
harbour offers a selection of
set lunching menus, each one
more enticing than the other.
Reservations are necessary, and
all guests are seated at 8pm.

SAN AGUSTÍN: Anno Domini €€€
French/Italian
CC San Agustín, Local 82–85, 35100
Tel *928 762 915* **Closed** *lunch*
Owner and chef Jacques Truyol
maintains the elegant flair of this
impeccable French-Italian restaurant. Don't miss the snails, prepared in the Burgundien style, and

The bright and welcoming interior at Casa Santa María, Betancuria

the *tournedos Rossini* (French steak)
with one of the excellent wines.

SANTA BRÍGIDA: Satautey €€€
Canarian
*C/Real de Coello 2, Monte
Lentiscal, 35310*
Tel *928 478 421*
Satautey is part of Hotel Escuela
Santa Brígida, where students of
the hotel management school
prepare Canarian appetizers.

VEGA DE SAN MATEO:
Restaurante La Raiz del Verol €€
Spanish
Calle el Retiro 33, 35320
Tel *928 661 757*
This charming restaurant offers
lovely views of the valley and has
a good selection of local cuisine,
with a focus on meat.

Fuerteventura

**BETANCURIA: Bodegón
Don Carmelo** €€
Spanish
C/Alcalde Carmelo Silvera 4, 35637
Tel *928 878 391*
Find tasty tapas and regional
dishes at reasonable prices at this
cosy restaurant. Outdoor seating
is available as well.

DK Choice

BETANCURIA:
Casa Santa María €€€
Canarian
Plaza de Maria 1, 35637
Tel *928 878 036* **Closed** *dinner;
Sun*
Located in a 17th-century farm-
house near the Iglesia de Santa
María, this restaurant has a
garden and wine bar. Try the
house speciality, roast kid goat
in rosemary sauce, or the king
prawns in a saffron sauce.

**CORRALEJO: Cofradia
de Pescadores** €€
Seafood
Muelle Chico 5, s/n, 35660
Tel *928 867 773*
Enjoy the lively atmosphere and
amazing ocean views at this
casual beach-restaurant. Fresh
fish at reasonable prices.

**CORRALEJO: Infusion
Restaurante** €€
International
C/Crucero Baleares 21, 35660
Tel *633 551 354* **Closed** *Thu dinner;
Sat & Sun lunch*
Located behind the main
beach, this bistro is run by
British expats. The menu
includes classic dishes, with a
number that are gluten-free.

CORRALEJO: La Marquesina €€€
Seafood
Muelle Chico, s/n, 35660
Tel *928 535 435*
This family-friendly restaurant
offers internationally oriented
cuisine with plenty of fresh fish
and seafood. The warm interior
complements the view outside.

**EL COTILLO: El Patio
de Lajares** €€€
German
C/La Cerca 9, La Oliva, 35650
Tel *650 134 030* **Closed** *Mon & Tue*
Enjoy traditional German cuisine
with a generous serving of
Spanish sunshine at this hotel-
restaurant. Views of an elegant
Canarian garden adds to
the charm.

PÁJARA: Restaurante Laja €€
Seafood
*Avda. Tomas Grau Gurrea, s/n,
Morro Jable, 35625*
Tel *928 542 054* **Closed** *Sat & Sun*
This lively restaurant serves
excellent fish dishes. The vege-
tarian options include goat's
cheese and *pimientos de padrón*.

For more information on types of restaurants *see pp162–3*

PUERTO DEL ROSARIO:
Mesón A Roda €
Spanish
C/Beethoven 1, 35600
Tel *928 877 826*
The traditional Galician and
tapas menu in this friendly
restaurant transports guests to
the Spanish mainland.

PUERTO DEL ROSARIO:
Casa Pon €€
Seafood
Casino Puertito de los Molinos, 35600
Tel *654 931 181*
This beach-restaurant offers a
good introduction to the local
cuisine. The seafood meals change
daily, depending on the catch.

Maritime decor in the dining room of Casa Brígida, Playa Blanca

Lanzarote

ARRECIFE: Altamar €€€
Mediterranean
*Arrecife Gran Hotel, Parque
Islas Canarias, 35500*
Tel *928 800 000* **Closed** *lunch*
Located in the Arrecife Gran
Hotel, this restaurant serves
international dishes with a
Mediterranean focus.

ARRECIFE: Restaurante
Que Muac €€€
Fusion
*C/Castillo de San José, Ctra. de
Puerto Nao, 35500*
Tel *928 812 321* **Closed** *Sun & Mon;
Tue–Thu dinner*
Housed in a castle, this high-end
restaurant is a treat for art lovers,
with its fusion delicacies and
magnificent harbour views.

COSTA TEGUISE: Chu-Lin €€
Chinese
Avda. del Jablillo 8, 35508
Tel *928 592 011*
This Chinese restaurant in the
heart of Costa Teguise serves
Far Eastern delicacies, which are
among the best on the island.

COSTA TEGUISE: Restaurante
Grill La Vaca Loca €€
Steakhouse
*Avda. de las Islas Canarias 2, Local 2,
35508*
Tel *928 945 418* **Closed** *Thu*
The main focus at this
meat-lover's paradise is the
grilled meat, accompanied with
home-made Chimichurri sauce.

COSTA TEGUISE: Restaurante
El Navarro €€€
Fusion
Avda. de Mar 13, 35508
Tel *928 592 145* **Closed** *lunch*
A first-rate dining experience,
with an inventive and exciting

menu and excellent service.
The setting is relaxed and
comfortable. Book ahead.

DK Choice

MÁCHER: La Tegala €€€
Canarian
Carretera de Tías a Yaiza 60, 35572
Tel *928 524 524* **Closed** *Sun;
Mon lunch*
The Michelin-starred La Tegala
caters to those who are
prepared to dig a little deeper
into their pockets for Canarian
cuisine of the utmost quality.
The panoramic views of the
coast and nearby Fuerteventura
are terrific.

NAZARET: Lagomar €€€
Mediterranean
C/Los Loros 2, 35509
Tel *928 845 665* **Closed** *Mon lunch*
Lagomar is located in a villa
designed by César Manrique and
set inside a quarry, creating a
magical atmosphere reminiscent
of *The Arabian Nights.*

PLAYA BLANCA:
Casa Brígida €€€
Seafood
*Puerto Deportivo Marina Rubicón,
35570*
Tel *928 518 946*
Savour high-quality, modern
variations of traditional fish
and seafood dishes along with
excellent views of the harbour.

PLAYA BLANCA: La Cocina
de Colacho €€€
Mediterranean
C/Velázquez 15, 35570
Tel *928 519 691* **Closed** *lunch;
Fri–Sun*
Art meets food in this chic restaurant that has a permanent
exhibition of paintings and photographs. The geometric design and
attractive decor complements
the Mediterranean cuisine, cooked
with Canarian influences.

PUERTO DEL CARMEN:
El Asador €€
Steakhouse
Avda. Varadero, s/n, 35510
Tel *928 515 821* **Closed** *lunch*
A key selling point of this restau-
rant, with its original Spanish
carvery, is that it operates the
only wood stove on the island.

PUERTO DEL CARMEN:
La Cañada €€€
Canarian
C/César Manrique 3, 35510
Tel *928 510 415*
The elegant La Cañada is known
for impeccable local cuisine,
prepared with ingredients
selected by the family owners.

PUERTO DEL CARMEN:
Lani's Café Restaurant €€€
Mediterranean
Avda. de las Playas 26, 35510
Tel *928 596 068*
Spectacular ocean views set the
tone for the magnificent cuisine
on offer here. Good selection of
Canarian wines, along with a
variety of cocktails.

YAIZA: La Casona de Yaiza €€€
Canarian
C/El Rincón 11, 35570
Tel *928 836 262* **Closed** *Tue–
Sun lunch*
This bodega belongs to the
boutique hotel of the same name,
and has long been regarded as
the best restaurant in Lanzarote.
The chef combines Canarian and
Mediterranean traditions.

Tenerife

ADEJE: Restaurante Oasis €€
Canarian
C/Grande 5, 38670
Tel *922 780 827*
Restaurante Oasis is not the most
elegant establishment, but its
fried chicken, made from a secret
recipe, is exceptional.

ARONA:
Oliver's with a Twist €€
British
C/Hermano Pedro de Béthencourt, Edif. Cerromar, 38650
Tel *680 693 977*   **Closed** *lunch; Sun & Mon*
A cosy, family-run restaurant offering tantalizing British staples and top-notch service. With just 11 tables and reservations often running into months, advance booking is a must.

BUENA VISTA: El Burgado €€
Seafood
Avda. El Rincón, s/n, 38480
Tel *922 127 831*
The view over the Atlantic Ocean is one of many plus points at El Burgado, which offers a wide selection of fresh fish and paella. One of the best places to enjoy the sunset views.

EL SAUZAL:
Casa Del Vino La Baranda €€€
Canarian
C/San Simon 49, 38360
Tel *922 563 886*   **Closed** *Mon*
Housed in a museum about wine production on the island, this restaurant focuses on modern Canarian dishes.

GUÍA DE ISORA: El Mirador €€€
Seafood
Carretera General del Sur, km 9, 38687
Tel *922 126 000*
Visitors to the restaurant at The Ritz-Carlton, Abama *(see p160)*, are guaranteed to eat well. The imaginative dishes are prepared with fresh ingredients. The seafood is especially popular.

LA CALETA:
Restaurante La Vieja €€€
Seafood
Edif. Terrazas de La Caleta I, 38679
Tel *922 711 548*
Perhaps the best seafood restaurant in the fishing village of La Caleta, La Vieja has a maritime interior including a brightly coloured fishing boat that is used as a bar. On the terrace looking out at the sea, the eponymous fish, *vieja*, is served, along with other seafood.

LA CALETA:
Rosso Sul Mare €€€
Italian
Avda. de las Gaviotas 4, 38679
Tel *922 782 374*
Enjoy delightful food such as *risotto azafrán y frutos del mar* (saffron risotto with seafood) at this chic restaurant overlooking the bay of La Caleta. Service is quick and efficient.

LA MATANZA: Casa Juan €€
Spanish/German
C/Acentejo 77, 38370
Tel *922 577 012*   **Closed** *Mon & Tue*
This family-run establishment dishes out a mixture of Spanish and German meals. You can eat outside their lovely garden. There is also an outdoor playground for children.

LOS ABRIGOS: Los Roques €€€
Mediterranean
C/Marina 16, 38618
Tel *922 749 401*   **Closed** *Sun dinner; Mon*
Mediterranean cuisine enriched with Moroccan and Asian ingredients lines the menu here. The food is excellent, the wine list impressive. Stunning terrace views of the harbour.

LOS CRISTIANOS:
The Surrey Arms €€
British
Paloma Beach, 38660
Tel *922 449 217*
This pub-like restaurant will transport you to the UK. All the standard British staples are served at teatime, and the Sunday roast should not be missed.

LOS CRISTIANOS:
Casa Tagoro €€€
Mediterranean
C/Valle de Menéndez 28, 38650
Tel *922 660 833*   **Closed** *Mon; Tue–Sat lunch*
Marvel at the delicious meals prepared by the owner-chef at this exquisite, Michelin-starred restaurant in Granadilla.

LOS REALEJOS: La Finca €€€
Seafood
C/El Monturio 12, 38418
Tel *922 362 143*   **Closed** *Sun; Mon–Wed lunch*
This award-winning restaurant is famous both for its tapas and its imaginative mains. Housed in an historic building, it has a dining room with a nautical decor.

PLAYA DE LA ARENA:
Casa Pancho €€
Canarian
C/Playa de la Arena, 38683
Canarian
Tel *922 861 323*   **Closed** *Mon*
The terrace here offers what is probably the island's most beautiful view over the sea. The restaurant specializes in Canarian and Spanish cuisine. The seafood and the desserts are delicious.

PLAYA DE LAS AMÉRICAS:
Bianco €€
Italian
CC Safari 5, 38660
Tel *922 788 697*   **Closed** *Sun lunch*
Bianco serves a wide range of pizza and pasta, and a number of vegetarian options.

PUERTO DE LA CRUZ:
El Magnolia €€
Spanish/International
Avda. Marqués de Villanueva del Prado, 38400
Tel *922 385 614*   **Closed** *Jun*
Dine on international cuisine with a Catalan twist at this relaxed restaurant. Specialities include the Spanish custard dessert, *crema catalana*.

PUERTO DE LA CRUZ: El Patio del
Puerto de la Cruz €€€
Fusion
Plaza Benito Pérez Galdos 8, 38400
Tel *922 376 096*   **Closed** *Mon & Tue*
This place does modern tapas, such as deep-fried goats' cheese with macadamia nut and pumpkin chutney. The desserts are to die for. Great for a leisurely lunch.

PUERTO DE LA CRUZ: Régulo €€€
Canarian
C/Pérez Zamora 16, 38400
Tel *922 384 506*   **Closed** *Sun; Mon lunch*
Local fish and lamb are among the specialities at Régulo. Try the fig mousse for dessert. Request a table on their lovely patio.

Outdoor seating at Bianco in Playa de las Américas

For more information on types of restaurants *see pp162–3*

El Laurel, Hotel Jardín Tecina's award-winning restaurant in Playa de Santiago

SAN JUAN DE LA RAMBLA: Las Aguas €€
Seafood
C/La Destila 20, 38420
Tel *922 360 428* **Closed** *Sun; Mon & Tue dinner*
Las Aguas attracts plenty of regulars with its exquisite rice and seafood dishes, plus breathtaking views from its location just off the seashore.

SANTA CRUZ: Casa Africa – Bar Playa €€
Canarian
Roque de las Bodegas 3, Taganana, 38130
Tel *922 590 100* **Closed** *dinner*
This unpretentious beachfront spot features well-prepared local cuisine, with an emphasis on fresh fish and seafood. The *pulpo frito* (fried octopus) is a must-try.

SANTA CRUZ: Cortxo Gastrobar €€
Spanish
Plaza Ireneo 5, 38002
Tel *922 151 695* **Closed** *Sun; Mon lunch*
Tucked away in a quiet courtyard, this place has modern decor that complements the cuisine. Great tapas and excellent service.

SANTA CRUZ: La Hierbita €€
Canarian
C/El Clavel 19, 38003
Tel *922 244 617*
This popular restaurant is housed in an old mansion built in the Canarian style. The traditional dishes and the wine list draw in both locals and tourists.

SANTA CRUZ: El Líbano €€
Lebanese
C/Santiago Cuadrado 36, 38006
Tel *922 285 914*
Popular with locals, this restaurant serves authentic cuisine, including expertly prepared kebabs. Located in a small side street.

SANTA CRUZ: Cofradía de Pescadores €€€
Seafood
Playa de Teresitas, 38129
Tel *922 549 024*
End the day here with seafood and a chilled bottle of white wine. The setting is simple and unpretentious, much like the food.

SANTA CRUZ: El Coto de Antonio €€€
Canarian
C/Perdón 13, 38006
Tel *922 272 105*
This excellent restaurant is popular with those on business and with celebrities for its old-world charm. High-quality food and service is guaranteed, which explains the price. The roasted kid and home-made desserts stand out.

SANTA CRUZ: Los Menceyes €€€
Canarian
C/Dr. José Naveiras 38, 38001
Tel *922 609 900* **Closed** *lunch*
The art of cooking in the restaurant at the luxurious Iberostar Mencey (*see p160*) matches the classically elegant interior. For a sensational experience, try one of the chef's tasting menus.

SANTA CRUZ: La Mesa Noche €€€
Mediterranean
C/Aguere 2, 38005
Tel *922 882 429* **Closed** *Sun–Thu dinner*
This popular eatery serves tasty, well-prepared food in a pleasant setting. They also have a good selection of regional wines.

SANTA CRUZ: Mesón Castellano €€€
Spanish
C/Callao Lima 4, 38003
Tel *922 271 074* **Closed** *Sun dinner*
Choose from among Castilian meat and fish choices at this cellar restaurant. Several dishes have a sausage base.

DK Choice
SANTA CRUZ: Restaurante Sagrario €€€
Mediterranean
C/Dr. Guigou 37, 38001
Tel *922 102 788* **Closed** *Sun dinner*
This establishment represents Mediterranean fine dining at its best. Expect abundant portions, organic ingredients of the highest quality, special attention to detail and excellent service. There is also a large selection of local wines – ask for recommendations.

TACORONTE: Los Limoneros €€€
International
Ctra. General del Norte 447, 38340
Tel *922 636 637* **Closed** *Sun*
Set in an charming old Canarian house, the menu at Los Limoneros offers a selection of international dishes. Impeccable service and exquisite decor.

La Gomera

AGULO: La Vieja Escuela €€
Canarian
C/Poeta Trujillo Armas 2, 38830
Tel *922 146 004* **Closed** *Sun*
The old village school is home to this simple bar-restaurant. It serves regional dishes, seafood, goat and *almogrote*, a savoury pie made of smoked cheese, tomatoes and pepper.

HERMIGUA: El Silbo €€€
Canarian
Carretera General 102, 38820
Tel *922 880 304* **Closed** *Mon–Wed dinner*
This indigenous restaurant on the beach offers simple, classical Canarian dishes.

PLAYA DE SANTIAGO: El Laurel €€€
Canarian
Lomada de Tecina, s/n, 38811
Tel *922 145 850*
The decor of the award-winning restaurant in the hotel Jardín Tecina (*see p161*) features starched tablecloths, rustic stone walls and wooden ceiling beams.

SAN SEBASTIÁN: Cuatro Caminos €€
Canarian
C/Ruiz de Padrón 36, 38800
Tel *922 141 260* **Closed** *Sun*
Discover indigenous Canarian cuisine in this small dining room on the veranda of a typical Canarian house. There are grills, soups,

stews and Castilian specialities such as *cochinillo* (suckling pig), all at reasonable prices.

DK Choice

SAN SEBASTIÁN:
El Charcón €€€
Seafood
Playa de la Cueva, 38800
Tel *922 141 898* **Closed** *Sun*
Innovative dishes, exquisitely prepared and beautifully presented, compete with stunning ocean views at one of the best eating establishments on the island. Finish with one of their spectacular desserts.

SAN SEBASTIÁN: La Forastera €€€
Fusion
C/Real 15, 38800
Tel *636 771 218*
This simple eatery serves big portions of home-made tapas and vegetarian choices. Outdoor seating only. Book in advance.

SAN SEBASTIÁN: Restaurante
Especia €€€
Canarian
Cerro de la Horca, s/n, 38800
Tel *922 871 100*
This elegant restaurant is located in Parador de la Gomera *(see p161)*. The focus is on local cuisine, especially seafood. Try the watercress stew.

VALLE GRAN REY: Mango €€
Canarian
Paseo de las Palmeras 2, 38870
Tel *928 805 961*
The cuisine here draws on the agricultural tradition of the region. Fresh salads, tapas and smoothies feature on the menu.

El Hierro

FRONTERA:
Guachinche Frontera €€
Canarian
Carretera la Cumbre, Plaza Candelaria, 38911
Tel *922 555 111* **Closed** *Mon*
Set in a converted farm building, this unassuming restaurant serves huge portions of delicious, home-cooked food. The menu changes daily.

FRONTERA:
El Pollo Asado €€
Canarian
C/Las Lajas 4b, 38911
Tel *922 555 051*
This reasonably priced bar-restaurant offers simple tapas; the signature dish is fried chicken.

LA RESTINGA: Casa Juan €€
Canarian
C/Juan Gutiérrez Monteverde 23, 38915
Tel *922 557 102* **Closed** *Wed*
The simple decor goes well with the native cuisine. The emphasis is on fresh fish and seafood brought in from the docks.

VALVERDE: El Mirador
de la Peña €€
Canarian
Mirador de la Peña, Guarazoca, 38900
Tel *922 550 300*
This house, built into a rock, was designed by César Manrique. On offer are traditional dishes such as *lenguado con salsa de almendras* (sole with almond sauce).

DK Choice

VALVERDE: Parador
del Hierro €€
Canarian/Spanish
Las Playas, s/n, 38900
Tel *922 558 036*
The magnificent location, on a hill, and the elegant atmosphere make this the perfect place for special occasions. Fine selection of Spanish wines available.

La Palma

BARLOVENTO: La Palma
Romántica €€
Canarian/International
Ctra. General Las Llanadas, s/n, 38726
Tel *922 186 221*
Located in the hotel La Palma Romántica *(see p161)*, this elegant restaurant, surrounded by beautiful gardens, serves a diverse range of local and international dishes.

BREÑA ALTA: La Fontana €€
Italian
C/Los Cancajos, 38712
Tel *922 434 729* **Closed** *Mon*

Papas arrugadas con mojo, or wrinkled potatoes with a pepper sauce

Choose from classics such as pizzas, pastas and risottos at this beach-restaurant. Excellent wine selection. Good value for money.

EL PASO: Franchipani €€€
International
Ctra. General Empalma Dos Pinos 57, 38750
Tel *922 402 305* **Closed** *Wed*
The ingredients are organically grown at this cheerful restaurant. The recommended wine is world-class.

LOS LLANOS DE ARIDANE:
San Petronio €€
Italian
Cno. Pino de Santiago 40, 38760
Tel *922 462 403* **Closed** *Sun; Mon dinner; Jun*
This restaurant is not easy to find, but it's worth the search. Italian classics feature on the menu, plus some international dishes.

SANTA CRUZ: La Bodeguita
del Medio €€
Canarian
Calle Álvarez de Ábreu 58, 38700
Tel *922 415 912* **Closed** *Sun*
This lively bar-restaurant is popular with both locals and tourists. Depending on your appetite, you can order tapas or a full meal. The menu includes various simple Canarian specialities.

SANTA CRUZ: Restaurante
Parrilla Los Braseros €€
Steakhouse
C/Mirca los Alamos 51, 38700
Tel *922 414 360* **Closed** *Sun–Thu dinner*
Relish the excellent selection of meat and stews, prepared to perfection, along with stunning views of the sea. Gluten-free options available.

SANTA CRUZ: Chipi-Chipi €€€
Canarian
C/Juan Mayor 42, 38713
Tel *922 411 024* **Closed** *Sun & Wed*
This reasonably priced restaurant specializes in grilled meats and local dishes such as chickpea soup and roasted cheese with *mojo verde (see p164)*.

DK Choice

TAZACORTE: Playa Mont €€€
Seafood
Calle del Puerto, s/n, 38770
Tel *922 480 443* **Closed** *Wed dinner; Thu*
This award-winning terrace restaurant is located directly behind the black sandy beach in Tazacorte. Lovely, fresh seafood and great wine selection.

For more information on types of restaurants *see pp162–3*

SHOPPING IN THE CANARY ISLANDS

As with Spain's other regions, the Canary Islands boast their own culinary specialities. Many tourists buy local delicacies including goat's cheese, rum, wine and the delicious *mojo* (ready-made sauce). Potted plants are also popular presents from the islands. These may even include small banana trees, palms and dragon trees. Other souvenirs, such as handicraft products, embroidery and lace, leather goods and pottery, are likewise snapped up as mementos. Some visitors notice a price difference – a remnant of the days when the islands were a duty-free zone. Other products such as alcohol, cigarettes, perfumes, sunglasses and the majority of electronic equipment are generally cheaper than in mainland Europe and are among the most easily purchased items in the Canary Islands.

Entrance to the shopping centre at Playa de las Américas, Tenerife

Where to Buy

There are many shopping centres in large towns and around resorts. They offer almost every essential food product and manufactured item, and are less imposing than the megastores you find in mainland Spain and elsewhere. They often include bars and restaurants.

Apart from the large department stores, the resorts have many small shops, offering souvenirs, clothes and cosmetics. They can be found along the main streets and seafront boulevards. There are many electronics shops too. Fixed prices are not set in stone on the islands, and it is well worth haggling. Just as numerous as the electronics stores are the *artesanía* shops, selling souvenirs and handicraft items. Here, too, haggling over the price is almost expected. The local shops in smaller towns and villages are worth checking out, particularly when you are shopping for food, as they may sell products that do not reach larger towns.

Those wishing to buy local handicraft products can also try buying directly from local artists, typically at lower prices than at seaside shops.

Opening Hours

Large shopping centres in big towns are generally open from 9am until 9pm Monday to Saturday. Some of the smaller ones may close for the siesta, i.e. between 2pm and 5pm, and then stay open for another few hours. Many shops, particularly food stores in tourist centres, are open until late at night.

Most smaller shops and boutiques do not have such regular opening hours and may close without warning. After-noon closing hours are also often not fixed. In small towns and villages, where the pace of life is slower, siesta breaks are longer, and shops may close earlier than in larger towns.

How to Pay

Most shops accept major credit cards. The most popular are Visa and MasterCard. When shopping in small provincial shops and bazaars, you should bear in mind that credit cards may not be accepted. When venturing outside large towns, it is best to carry a certain amount of cash.

Markets and Bazaars

Markets and bazaars are an inherent feature of life on the Canary Islands. Markets are held at regular intervals in small towns and generally serve the local population. The articles on offer include food and items of everyday use for at home and on the farm. Prices are usually low. The olives and varieties of cheese are exceptionally tasty, and good value.

African carvings on sale at a market in Teguise

Bazaars are set up in larger towns, typically with tourists in mind. They sell mainly handicraft products and island souvenirs. Prices are relatively high, but you can always haggle. A number of the bigger towns also have flea markets once a week, and these can be good places to pick up a curiosity.

In Gran Canaria and Lanzarote, the bazaar vendors usually include African traders. They sell goods that really have nothing to do with the islands, but are attractive and eye-catching nevertheless.

Art and Handicrafts

Among the most popular island handicraft products is the Canarian knife (*cuchillo canario*). It is not advisable to purchase these, however, as increased airport security means you may not be able to take them home.

The most popular product made of wood is undoubtedly the *timple* – a kind of ukulele. It is also worth taking a look at other wooden products such as small boxes, bowls and smoking pipes. Wooden castanets are an especially popular souvenir. Wickerwork is also worth seeking out. Traditional woven baskets and other knick-knacks are on sale virtually everywhere.

Ceramic items for sale are often based on traditional Guanche designs. They include statuettes, beads and countless vessels, including bowls, pots, jugs and vases. They are often decorated in traditional geometric patterns, typical of the first inhabitants of the islands.

Popular among textiles are embroidery, woollen hand-woven cloths and lace. Many shops offer textile products such as tablecloths, shawls and napkins, which can also be found in bazaars. Some shops have their own workshops, where you can see the products being made. Visitors interested in ethnography can buy the traditional folk costume.

Canarian craftsmanship, in the style of the Guanches

A jar of palm honey

Food and Drink

Goat's cheese is one of the traditional Canarian food items. The best known are *majorero*, from Fuerteventura, and *queso herreño*, from El Hierro. In small villages you can often buy locally made cheese. Here, preference is given to neighbours, with tourists only being offered the surplus.

Popular among alcoholic beverages are rum and its honeyed version – *ron miel* – as well as sweet Malvasía. Other wines have not gained such recognition with the Spaniards, although the locals are very keen on wines made on Tenerife and Lanzarote.

Another speciality is *gomerón* from La Gomera. It is made by combining palm juice with a grappa-like spirit. Many tourists like to take home Canarian sauces – *mojos*. There are several types and they can be found in every supermarket.

The Canary Islands are also famous for the production of *puros palmeros* – cigars from La Palma. Although not as well known as the Havana cigars, they are nevertheless valued for their flavour and are even purchased for the royal court in Madrid. Offering a wide variety of goods at moderate prices, supermarkets are often the best place to buy food.

Another popular gift item is flowers, especially *estrelitsia*, the bird-of-paradise plant. You can buy them ready-packed, from a flower shop or at the airport.

Cosmetics

There are several large aloe vera plantations on the Canary Islands and medicinal aloe vera creams can be purchased in shops throughout the Canaries. In addition to this natural product, branded-cosmetics are inexpensive here.

Triana, the main shopping street in Las Palmas

ENTERTAINMENT IN THE CANARY ISLANDS

The Canary Islands offer seemingly endless forms of entertainment to tempt tourists. There are plenty of demonstrations of traditional skill on offer, from Spanish and local dancing, to the old custom of *lucha canaria* – Canarian wrestling. Typical modern attractions, including bars, nightclubs, casinos, cinemas, theatres and concerts, are likewise much in evidence. A wide variety of holiday entertainment is also available. The islands feature many small parks and botanical gardens, with tropical plants and wild animals. A trip in a glass-bottomed boat to see the marine fauna, including dolphins and whales, is a memorable experience, while the many water parks, with their slides and splash pools, will have children squealing with delight.

Imperial penguins at Loro Parque in Puerto de la Cruz on Tenerife.

Information

Details of cultural events and concerts may often be found in the local press, which advertises them some days in advance. Keep your eyes peeled for street posters too. Other good sources of information are hotel reception foyers and tourist information centres.

Nightlife

There is a vast selection of nightclubs across the Canaries. Clubs, pubs, bars, karaoke bars and casinos tempt visitors with their neon signs, drinks deals and music. The resort areas on the islands have severe night-time noise-level restrictions in place, but this has done little or nothing to curb the number of pubs, clubs and bars.

There is a basic difference between bars and pubs on the islands. Bars *(tabernas)* are open all day, serving mostly beer and wine, as well as snacks. This is often the first stop before the evening "ruta", where you can have a drink and a quiet conversation. They close around 1am.

Beer halls *(cervecerías)*, or pubs on the other hand, provide more typical evening entertainment. They also serve alcohol but this rarely includes wine; beer is the real draw. The music is loud, and those wishing to dance can do so.

Nightclubs open late and close around 5am. They become crowded around 1am, or later, when other bars and pubs close.

Daytime Entertainment

During the daytime, entertainment includes glass-bottomed boat and submarine trips. There are also dolphin and whale-watching trips (prices usually include lunch on board).

For the benefit of younger guests, the islands have developed numerous water parks with merry-go-rounds, slides and swimming pools. Gardens such as Palmitos Park *(see p63)* and Loro Parque *(see pp116–17)* will fascinate the young and old alike with many species of animals, reptiles and birds. Another fun way to spend the day is to take one of the numerous safaris over wilderness areas, on camel-back or by jeep.

Theatre and Cinema

Only the large towns have cinemas, theatres and concert halls. New films are shown close to their general release,

Restaurant at Cruz de Tejeda on Gran Canaria

Ornate interior of the Teatro Guimera in Santa Cruz de Tenerife

but films are usually dubbed (except in a few cinemas). For films in English, look for the symbols VO (*versión original*), or VOS (*versión original subtitulada*), meaning 'subtitled.' Keep in mind that if the film isn't of English origin, it will be played in the original language.

Music and Concerts

Lovers of classical music can visit the concert halls in Las Palmas de Gran Canaria and Santa Cruz de Tenerife. The biggest music event in the Canaries is the **Festival de Música de Canarias**, a festival of classical music held in January and February. The main venues are the **Auditorio Alfredo Kraus** (Las Palmas de Gran Canaria) and the **Auditorio de Tenerife** (Santa Cruz de Tenerife), but from 2017 there will be venues on all the islands. On Gran Canaria, the Teatro Guimerá hosts the annual **Alfredo Kraus Opera Festival** in honour of the famous Canarian tenor, who was born in Las Palmas.

Fans of jazz music will certainly enjoy the **Festival Internacional Canarias Jazz & Más**. It is organised every year, generally in July, with concerts held on Gran Canaria, Lanzarote and Tenerife.

Hotels, and particularly resorts, often organise their own shows of flamenco dancing, as well as Spanish and local folk dances. These performances are very popular with guests, and are included in the cost of a stay.

Festivals

The best-known event on the Canary Islands is the carnival, held in Feb/Mar. The biggest and liveliest one, held in Santa Cruz de Tenerife, is often compared to the famous Rio de Janeiro.

The tri-continental theatre festival in Agüimes on Gran Canaria, **Festival de Sur – Encuentro Internacional Tres Continentes**, is the only one of its kind in Spain. Held in September, it attracts a wide range of theatre groups from Europe, Latin America and Africa.

The **Festival Internacional de Cine Las Palmas de Gran Canaria** (Las Palmas Film Festival), held in March, showcases international films, with special emphasis on European, African and Latin American movies.

CajaCanarias foundation sponsors the annual **Otoño Cultural** in Santa Cruz de Tenerife. The festival, held in October and November, features music concerts, exhibitions and children's activities.

MASDANZA is an international and dance event held on Gran Canaria. **MUECA** is a street arts festival that takes place annually in early May, in Puerto de la Cruz (El Hierro).

Fiestas

The focus of most fiestas is the processions in which religious statues are carried, but they may also include fancy-dress parades. Fiestas can easily last several days, during which time town life comes to a virtual halt.

DIRECTORY

Theatres

Teatro Cine Victor
Avda. de la Asuncion, 1, Santa Cruz de Tenerife. **Tel** 922 287 585.
🅦 cinevictor.es

Teatro Guimerá
Pl. Isla de la Madera, s/n. Santa Cruz de Tenerife. **Tel** 922 609 407.
🅦 teatroguimera.es

Teatro Pérez Galdós
Plaza de Stagno, Las Palmas de Gran Canaria. **Tel** 928 433 334.
🅦 teatroperezgaldos.es

Concert Halls

Auditorio Alfredo Kraus
Avda. Principe de Asturias, s/n. Las Palmas de Gran Canaria. **Tel** 928 491 770. 🅦 auditorio-teatrolaspalmasgc.com

Auditorio Insular de Puerto del Rosario
C/Ramiro de Maeztu, Puerto del Rosario. **Tel** 928 532 186.

Auditorio de Tenerife
Avda. de la Constitución, 1, Santa Cruz de Tenerife. **Tel** 922 568 600.
🅦 auditoriodetenerife.com

Sala "Teobaldo Power"
C/Cantos Canarios, 1, La Orotava. **Tel** 922 330 224.

Festivals

🅦 cajacanarias.com
🅦 canariasjazz.com
🅦 festivaldecanarias.com
🅦 festivaldelsur.com
🅦 festivalmueca.com
🅦 lpafilmfestival.com
🅦 masdanza.com
🅦 operalaspalmas.org

Carnival is celebrated in great style in the Canary Islands

OUTDOOR ACTIVITIES

Because of their superb climate, the Canary Islands are an excellent place for all types of sport. Visitors seeking to combine lounging on the beach with something more active can come here at any time of the year, sure to find professional help and guidance. The most popular are, of course, water sports. Pozo Izquierdo on Gran Canaria is one of the world's best beaches for windsurfing. The coastal waters are considered some of the most attractive diving sites. Tenerife and the remaining islands offer excellent conditions for paragliding and hang-gliding. Anyone interested in golf, tennis, horse riding, hiking or cycling will also find plenty of opportunities to indulge in their favourite pastimes.

Hiking

The islands, with their pleasant climate, diverse landscape and numerous national parks and nature reserves, present many opportunities for hikers. Tourist offices on all the islands can offer advice as to the best walking trails. The national park areas, including Teide on Tenerife, are particularly attractive and feature many marked trails, but walkers should bear in mind the obligatory rules and restrictions. Walking trips around the islands are often the best method of exploring. The routes are not too difficult or arduous, though most footpaths are rocky.

Many routes lead over high ground along mountain ridges. Temperatures here can be low, even in the summer, when the sun's rays still do not generate much heat. You should always make sure to bring warm clothing and do not forget to pack sunscreen, water and something to eat.

Windsurfer off Fuerteventura

Jogging

There are excellent conditions for running on the Canaries. Seaside promenades and sandy beaches, such as the ones on Fuerteventura, are ideal places for burning off the calories. In the rugged central regions of the islands, small villages offer less favourable conditions for jogging. The best times to take a run are mornings and evenings, when temperatures are lower and the crowds thinner.

Racquet Sports

Good-quality tennis courts, some of them floodlit, can be found in the grounds of many hotels and apartments. These can often be hired out, even if you are not a resident. Instructors and equipment hire are easy to organise. More information about holidays combined with tennis lessons can be obtained from the Real Federación Española de Tenis. Those longing for a game of squash will also find appropriate facilities, mainly within the hotel complexes.

In Spain, the racquet sport 'padel' (a mix of tennis and squash) has surpassed tennis in popularity, and the abundance of padel courts is a testament to this rapidly spreading European trend.

Valle Gran Rey beach, La Gomera

Horse Riding

There are several riding centres on the islands, offering facilities for beginners as well as for advanced riders. In the main, however, the islands do not offer attractive riding opportunities. The rocky and uneven terrain and the hard surfaces mean that there is a lack of routes suitable for galloping. The latter can only be enjoyed on some sandy beaches.

Among the most interesting trips on horseback are those offered by riding schools such as the one run by the **Real Club de Golf** in Gran Canaria.

All horse-riding outings, whether carried out individually or in groups, are always supervised by the owner of the stable or an instructor who knows the area well.

Hikers on Gran Canaria

Cyclists by Castillo Santa Barbara, near Teguise, Lanzarote

Cycling

The mountainous character of the islands creates excellent conditions for riding mountain bikes or racers. On steep, winding roads you can often encounter groups of cyclists whizzing past. However, given the nature of the terrain on the islands, great care must be taken when cycling. Be wary, too, of traffic.

More ambitious cyclists can undertake a guided tour. These usually lead over areas of wilderness and require a lot of stamina. The best places for this type of adventure are the national parks. There are many agents offering such tours. They organise transport for cyclists and their equipment to the starting point and collect them at the end. Some firms also include a picnic lunch in the price of the outing.

Bicycles are an excellent means of transport around the islands. Many tourists use touring bikes to reach distant beaches, for shopping trips or just to escape from the crowds.

Fishing

The Canary Islands' waters were once packed with different varieties of fish that attracted anglers, but due to depleted stocks there are now more restrictions in place. Almost every island offers sea trips combined with marlin fishing. One of the best places for trying to catch this fish are the waters around La Graciosa, off the north coast of Lanzarote.

Tourists can hire a boat or join an organised expedition. Fishing equipment is generally provided by the organiser.

Sailing

Almost every large coastal town or village has a marina. These ports have been important calls for transatlantic sailors since the time of Columbus, and are still visited by yachts from all over Europe. Modern marinas have facilities for yacht repair. Food supplies are available in local shops, while the many harbour restaurants tempt hungry sailors. In smaller places, yacht harbours are usually combined with fishing harbours.

Conditions for sailing are favourable the whole year through, and you can charter a yacht or catamaran for a day or longer, provided you have the relevant qualifications.

Everybody has the chance to learn the basic skills of sailing in the Canary Islands. All islands have sailing centres, offering short sailing courses for all ages. A more leisurely option is a cruise, which can last a day or longer. Many of the cruises offer food, and even drink, as part of the price.

Naturism

Naturism is "officially" legal on all of Spain's beaches, including the Canary Islands' sandy swathes, though discretion is advised when stripping off completely in the more populated family resorts.

Yachts moored in Puerto de Mogán harbour

Some beaches are more popular with nudists, such as La Tejita to the south-east of Tenerife, and Playa Guasimeta near Arrecife airport in Lanzarote. In Gran Canaria, the Maspalomas dunes provide plenty of privacy for naturists. All these beaches may also be used by non-nudists.

For those seeking more than nude sunbathing, Lanzarote and Gran Canaria both offer "clothing-optional" resorts.

Fishing at Puerto de las Nieves, Gran Canaria

Hang-gliding and Paragliding

Hang-gliding and paragliding offer unforgettable ways to see the islands. The large islands, such as Gran Canaria and Tenerife, have particularly favourable weather for this type of activity.

Many centres offer hang-gliding courses. They are held in the island's interior regions, which feature the best lifting currents. When the weather is right, it is possible to fly over an entire island by hang-glider. Those wanting a less risky taste of gliding can try their hand at parasailing behind a motorboat.

Water Motorsports

Motorboat races and other similar events are a rare sight on the islands, although not unheard of. Many people take the opportunity to try jet-ski rides. Equally popular are water-skiing and bumping along in rubber rafts towed by a speeding boat.

Diving

Snorkelling and scuba diving are both well catered for on the islands and provide the opportunity to see rays, barracuda, turtles and a variety of tropical fish. You might even see a shark! There are many diving centres (*centros de buceo*) where you can hire equipment, go for a test dive with an instructor or join courses, for all levels of proficiency. In order to go scuba diving in Spain, you must have a proper diving certificate. The recognised ones include PADI, CUC, CMAS/FEDAS and SSI.

Parasail towed by a motorboat near Los Gigantes cliffs

Certificates holders can join underwater expeditions. Diving around Famara, on Lanzarote, or La Restinga on El Hierro, provides an unforgettable experience. Underwater spearfishing is permitted only to snorkellers.

Windsurfing

Hitching yourself to a windsurfing board is one of the islands' most popular sports. The strong winds, combined with the sunshine, create excellent conditions for this sport.

There are several schools that can teach you how to do it. They also rent sailboards to stronger swimmers.

Advanced windsurfers (or *windsurfistas*, as they are known to the locals) should definitely try the beaches at El Medano on Tenerife, Playa de Sotavento on Fuerteventura and Pozo Izquierdo on Gran Canaria. These also play host to a number of international windsurfing events.

It should be remembered that along beaches where international events take place, the conditions can be treacherous. Winds are strong and variable,

and the waves are big. The winds are particularly strong from April until the end of summer, while, in the winter months, the Atlantic waves are bigger and more dangerous to inexperienced windsurfers.

Surfing

You will find surfers or boogie boarders on practically all Canary Island beaches. There are surfing schools on the larger islands, plus a number of hire shops in places that have particularly favourable sea conditions, such as Gran Canaria's Canteras Beach. Surfing is popular with locals, but it can be extremely dangerous, and you should exercise caution, particularly around the northern shores, where waves are stronger than they seem from the shore. Another hazard is the rocky seabed. Check whether the beach is safe beforehand.

Windsurfer off the coast of Fuerteventura

Whale and Dolphin Watching

There are some 20 whale and dolphin species in the waters surrounding the Canary Islands. Observation trips are becoming more and more popular with visitors; tours operate year-round, although the best chance of a sighting is between the months of March and May. These whale and dolphin safaris are offered predominantly in Tenerife.

Diving is one of the most popular island sports

DIRECTORY

Horse Riding

Centro Hípico del Sur
Camino Los Migueles 82,
Buzanada, Tenerife.
Tel 922 720 643.
W **centrohipicodel
sur.com**

Lanzarote a Caballo
Ctra – Arrecife – Yaiza,
km 17. **Tel** 928 830 038.
W **lanzarotea
caballo.com**

Mamio Verde
C/Los Olivos 39,
La Orotava, Tenerife.
Tel 653 736 704.
W **mamioverde.com**

**Real Club de Golf
de Las Palmas**
Ctra. de Bandama, Santa
Brigida. **Tel** 928 350 104.
W **realclubde
golfdelaspalmas.com**

**Sociedad Hípica
Miranda**
Lugar Caserío Miranda
s/n, Breña Alta, La Palma.
Tel 922 437 696.

Cycling

Bike 'n' Fun
C/Calvo Sotelo 20,
Los Llanos de Aridane,
La Palma. **Tel** 922 401 927.
W **bikenfun.de**

Cycle Gran Canaria
PO Box 416, Maspalomas.
Tel 617 799 924.
W **cyclegran
canaria.com**

Fishing

Carp Gran Canaria
Tel 637 939 680.
W **carpgrancanaria.com**

Sailing

**Club de Mar
de Radazul**
Avda. Colón s/n, Radazul –
El Rosario, Tenerife.
Tel 922 680 908.
W **clubmradazul.com**

**Real Club Náutico
de Gran Canaria**
C/León y Castillo 308, Las
Palmas de Gran Canaria.
Tel 928 234 566.
W **rcngc.com**

Naturism

Charco Natural
(Naturist bungalow
complex), C/Montaña
Redonda s/n, Lanzarote.
Tel 928 529 595.
W **charconatural.com**

**Federación Española
de Naturismo**
(Nudist beach listings).
W **naturismo.org**

Magnolias Natura
(Naturist bungalow com-
plex) Avda. T.O. Tjaereborg
s/n, Maspalomas, Gran
Canaria. **Tel** 928 770 122.
W **magnoliasnatura.com**

**Monte Marina
Apartments**
(Naturist apartment
complex), Volcán de
Vayoyo 8, Esquinzo,
Jandía, Fuerteventura.
Tel 928 544 052.
W **montemarina
playa.com**

Hang-gliding and Paragliding

**Club Guelillas
del Hierro**
C/Dr. Quintero 23,
Valverde. **Tel** 922 551 824.
W **clubguelillas.com**

**Escuela Parapente
Palmasur**
C/La Cruz 2, Los Que-
mados. **Tel** 609 647 103.

Ibrafly Parapente
C/San Vicente 35, Santa
Cruz de Tenerife. **Tel** 609
546 192. W **ibrafly.net**

Skydive Gran Canaria
Aeródromo El Berriel,
Ctra. General del Sur, km
43.5, San Bartolomé de
Tirajana, Gran Canaria.
Tel 928 157 325.
W **skydivegran
canaria.net**

Diving

Atlantik Diving Center
Hotel Puerto de Mogán,
Gran Canaria. **Tel** 689 352
049. W **grancanariadive
resort.com**

Blue Explorers Tenerife
C/10 de Agosto.
Tel 655 573 098.
W **blue-explorers.com**

Buceo Sub
H10 Costa Salinas, Los
Cancajos, La Palma. **Tel**
922 181 113. W **4dive.org**

**Centro de Buceo
El Hierro**
C/El Rancho, 12, La
Restinga. **Tel** 922 55 70 23.
W **centrodebuceo
elhierro.com**

**Dive Academy
Gran Canaria**
Club Amigos del Atlántico,
C/La Lajilla s/n, Gran
Canaria. **Tel** 928 736 196.
W **diveacademy-
grancanaria.com**

Dive Center Corralejo
C/Nuestra Señora del
Pino 22, Corralejo,
Fuerteventura.
Tel 928 535 906.
W **divecenter
corralejo.com**

Rubicon Diving
Puerto Deportivo Marina
Rubicón, Local 77b, Playa
Blanca, Lanzarote.
Tel 928 349 346.
W **rubicondiving.com**

Windsurfing

**Centro Insular de
Deportes Marítimos
de Tenerife**
Ctra. a San Andrés, 38150.
Tel 922 597 525.
W **deportestenerife.com**

**Flag Beach
Windsurf Centre**
Apto de Correos 285,
Corralejo, Fuerteventura.
Tel 609 029 804.
W **flagbeach.com**

René Egli
Hotel Meliá Los Gorriones,
Sotavento, Tenerife.
Tel 928 547 483.
W **rene-egli.com**

**Windsurfing Club
Las Cucharas**
CC Las Maretas 2, C/Marajo,
Lanzarote. **Tel** 928 590 731.
W **lanzarotewind
surf.com**

Surfing

**Costa Noroeste
Lanzarote**
Avda. El Marinero, 11,
Caleta de Famara,
Lanzarote. **Tel** 928 528 597.
W **costanoroeste.com**

K16 Surf School
C/México, Playa de las
Américas, Arona, Tenerife.
Tel 928 788 779.
W **k16surf.com**

**Pro Surfing
Company**
Ave. de Moya, 6, Playa del
Inglés, Gran Canaria.
Tel 628 104 025.
W **prsurfing.com**

Rapa Nui Surfschool
C/Punta de los Molinillos,
s/n, Costa Calma, Pájara,
Fuerteventura. **Tel** 928
549 140. W **rapanui-
surfschool.com**

Réne Egli
Hotel Meliá Los Gorriones,
Sotavento, Tenerife.
Tel 928 547 483.
W **rene-egli.com**

**WaterSports
Fuerteventura**
Tarajalejo, Costa Calma,
Fuerteventura. **Tel** 928
875 110. W **watersports-
fuerteventura.com**

**Windsurfing Club
Las Cucharas**
CC Las Maretas, 2, Calle
Marajo, Costa Tequise,
Lanzarote. **Tel** 928 590
731. W **lanzarote
windsurf.com**

Whale and Dolphin Watching

**Mar de Ons
Tenerife**
Rincón del Puerto Los
Cristianos 6, Arona,
Tenerife. **Tel** 922 751 576.
W **mardeons-
tenerife.com**

**Neptuno Sea
Company**
Calle Colón, s/n, Puerto
Colón, Adeje, Tenerife.
Tel 922 798 044.
W **barcostenerife.com**

Nostramo, S.A.
CC Ocean Center,
Local Playa de las
Americas 15, Tenerife.
Tel 922 750 085.
W **tenerifedolphin.com**

Ocean Explorer
Marina Los Gigantes,
Pontoon 4, Los Gigantes,
Tenerife. **Tel** 687 395 856.
W **ocean-explorer.net**

Esmeralda Beach, Fuerteventura ▶

Golfing in the Canary Islands

Famously known for attracting neon-seeking party-goers, the Canary Islands have become a Mecca for a different breed of clubber. It is clear that the lucrative golf market in the Canaries has been a target for the region's local tourist authorities, keen to grab a slice of the Algarve's visiting golf fraternity. There are more than 20 large golf courses, divided between five of the seven islands. Lured by a sub-tropical climate, ocean-side fairways and award-winning designs, golfers of all abilities and from all over Europe come to lap up the greens and the year-round sunshine.

Spectacular view of the Atlantic at Buenavista golf course, Tenerife

General Information

All of the Canary Islands' golf courses are open to the public. Some offer facilities for non-golfing companions, such as swimming pools, tennis courts and restaurants. All have driving ranges, pro-shops and buggy rentals. Golf packages are offered at dozens of hotels and resorts, and these usually include discounts on green fees and tee-time booking facilities. Green fees vary, with October through to April being the peak season, and May to September affording lower rates. A "bono" discount is available at many courses, if a number of rounds are booked at once.

PGA Spanish Open golf at Abama Golf, Tenerife

Tenerife

With nine courses, Tenerife is golf central in the Canaries. There are courses for every level, from an easy par-27, to the more challenging championship fairways of the 27-hole **Golf del Sur**. Several legs of the PGA Spanish Open have been held on the island's courses over the years, with **Abama Golf** being the newest venue to join **Golf Costa Adeje** as championship hosts. Also in the south is **Golf Las Américas**, a green jewel located between the resorts of Las Americas and Los Cristianos. The legendary golfer Seve Ballesteros designed **Buenavista Golf**, which is the most environmentally friendly course on the island, boasting a minimal negative impact on the environment. Although it is the second-oldest golf club in Spain, the **Real Club de Golf de Tenerife** still exudes a distinctly British air.

Gran Canaria

The seven courses of Gran Canaria offer an array of backdrops, from the smooth sandy dunes looming over the fairways of **Maspalomas Golf** to the craggy volcanic scenery

surrounding the **Real Club de Golf de Las Palmas**. Inaugurated in 1891, the latter stakes a claim as being the first golf club in Spain, although it moved to a different site in 1956. Another club in the north, **El Cortijo Club de Campo** has been the venue for several international championships including the Canaries Open of Spain. **Las Palmeras Golf** is an 18-hole par-3 course located close to the city centre, with a spa, gym, swimming pool, nursery and restaurant on site. The neat, trimmed greenery of **Salobre Golf** stands in stark contrast to the wild moonscape edging its fairways. This demanding 18-hole course is set amongst volcanic cones and cacti-studded brushland. A similar landscape of lakes and volcanic mountains surrounds the 9-hole course at **Anfi Tauro Golf**. **Meloneras Golf** near Maspalomas, meanwhile, is unique on Gran Canaria, as it's the only course where several holes can be played right beside the sea.

Real Club de Golf de Las Palmas on Gran Canaria

Lanzarote

Although golf has been played in Lanzarote for around three decades, the choice is still limited to two golf courses, **Lanzarote Golf**, near Puerto del Carmen, and **Costa Teguise Golf**. The latter was designed by British landscape architect John Harris. This 18-hole par-72 course runs along the side of an old volcano with stunning views of the ocean. In addition to the dramatic scenery, the course also has all the amenities you would expect from a top-class club, including buggies, pro-shop, clubhouse, golf school and restaurant. Due to the dry nature of the island's climate, providing the necessary resources has always been a challenge. However, the introduction of desalination plants has made it possible to provide the moisture necessary to grow the premium-quality grass that is vital for playing top-level golf. Elsewhere, the Hesperia Playa Dorada is home to the only pitch-and-putt course on the island.

Players enjoy sea views from Tecina golf course, La Gomera

Fuerteventura

It is no surprise to find that the relatively flat topography of Fuerteventura is a feature on the island's three golf courses. Only the 17th and 18th holes are elevated on **Fuerteventura Golf Club**, near Caleta de Fuste, but this does not detract from its demanding nature. Three lakes and a handful of dog-legs usually add a few unwanted numbers to the scorecard. Covering

more than 1.5 km (0.6 sq miles), it is the largest expanse of green on the whole island. In 2004 it was also the home of the Spanish Open. The par-70 **Salinas de Antigua** is equally level, but it is pock-marked with an array of low-lying volcanic cones. The 18-hole Playitas golf course is suitable for all handicaps.

La Gomera

La Gomera is famed more for its walking than for its sports facilities. Now, thanks to a combination of the two, the

island has an outstanding course that draws plenty of enthusiasts from Tenerife, a 45-minute ferry ride away. **Tecina Golf** is an outstanding course. Perched on a cliff, overlooking the Atlantic Ocean, this challenging 18-hole course has great views. Lush, tropical vegetation lines the fairways, tall palm trees stretch from the bright green baize into the sky, and greens seem to balance precariously above the waves below. The stunning design is by Donald Steel, the architect behind the New St Andrews course in Scotland.

DIRECTORY

Tenerife

Abama Golf
Ctra. Gral TF-47, km 9.
Playa San Juan.
Tel 922 126 300.
w abamahotel
resort.com

Amarilla Golf
Urb. Amarilla Golf, San
Miguel de Abona.
Tel 922 730 319.
w amarillagolf.es

Buenavista Golf
C/ Vista La Monja s/n,
Buenavista del Norte.
Tel 922 129 034.
w buena vistagolf.es

Golf Costa Adeje
Finca de los Olivos s/n,
Adeje. **Tel** 922 710 000.
w golfcostaadeje.com

Golf del Sur
Urb. Golf del Sur, San
Miguel de Abona. **Tel** 922
738 170. **w** golfdelsur.net

Golf las Américas
C/ Landa Golf 22, Playa de
las Américas, Tenerife.
Tel 922 752 005.
w golflasamericas.com

**Real Club de Golf
de Tenerife**
C/ Campo de Golf 1,
Tacoronte. **Tel** 922 636
607. **w** rcgt.es

Gran Canaria

Anfi Tauro Golf
Valle de Tauro s/n, Mogán.
Tel 928 560 462.
w anfi.es

**El Cortijo Club
de Campo**
Autopista GC-1, km 6.4,
Telde. **Tel** 928 711 111.
w elcortijo.es

Las Palmeras Golf
Avda. Doctor Alfonso
Chiscano Diaz s/n, Las
Palmas. **Tel** 928 220 044.
w laspalmerasgolf.es

Maspalomas Golf
Avda. Touroperador
Neckermann s/n,
Maspalomas. **Tel** 928 762
581. **w** maspalomas
golf.net

**Real Club de Golf
de Las Palmas**
Ctra. de Bandama. Santa
Brigida. **Tel** 928 350 104.
w realclubde
golfdelaspalmas.com

Salobre Golf
Autopista GC-1, km 53,
Maspalomas. **Tel** 928 943
000. **w** salobregolf
resort.com

Lanzarote

Costa Teguise Golf
Avda. de Golf s/n, Costa
Teguise. **Tel** 928 590 512.
w lanzarote-golf.com

Lanzarote Golf
Ctra. del Puerto de Carmen
s/n, Tias. **Tel** 928 514 050.
w lanzarotegolfresort.
com

Fuerteventura

**Fuerteventura
Golf Club**
Ctra. De Jandía,
km 11, Antigua.
Tel 928 160 034.
w fuerteventura
golfclub.com

**Golf Club Salinas
de Antigua**
Ctra. Jandía
km 12, Antigua.
Tel 928 877 272.
w salinasgolf.com

Jandía Golf
Barranco Vinamar
s/n. Pájara.
Tel 928 871 979.
w jandiagolf.com

La Gomera

Tecina Golf
Lomada de Tecina s/n,
San Sebastián de
La Gomera.
Tel 922 145 950.
w tecinagolf.com

SURVIVAL
GUIDE

PRACTICAL INFORMATION

The Canary Islands' warm climate means that the tourist season here lasts the whole year. The huge investment in the tourist infrastructure means that the islands are readily prepared to receive multitudes of visitors and have extensive hotel and catering facilities, plus numerous attractions and things to do. Frequent charter flights to the islands plus a very well-developed information service, particularly on the internet, make planning a holiday here a reasonably straightforward business. Those intending to visit can easily find all the necessary information and organise any hotel bookings in advance. This is important since, particularly in summer and winter, the islands can get extremely crowded (although no longer so busy that you can't find accommodation without booking in advance).

When to Visit

The holiday season lasts practically all year round on the Canary Islands. Thanks to the magnificent weather here, the beaches can be used from January to December. The islands are particularly popular with visitors during winter months.

The second most popular season is summer, especially July and August, when the islands are packed, and early spring is also very busy. Late autumn has fewer visitors.

The islands are not only attractive for their sunshine and beaches. One local event that attracts crowds of tourists is the carnival in February. Visitors from Spain, and further afield, come mainly to Santa Cruz de Tenerife or Las Palmas de Gran Canaria to join the carnival celebrations. Fiestas, including the Bajada de la Virgen de las Nieves in Santa Cruz de La Palma, provide another reason to visit the islands.

Visas

Regulations covering admission to the Canary Islands are exactly the same as for the rest of Spain. Nationals of all the European Union member states do not require a visa to enter the islands for tourist visits of up to 90 days. Other non-EU countries including Australia, Canada, Israel, Japan, New Zealand and the USA are likewise not required to obtain a visa before entry. When in doubt, contact the Spanish Embassy or seek advice from a travel agent. Anyone who does require a visa must apply in person at the consulate in their own country.

Travel Safety Advice

Visitors can get up-to-date travel safety information from the **Foreign and Commonwealth Office** in the UK, the **State Department** in the US and the **Department of Foreign Affairs and Trade** in Australia.

The Canary Islands are served by many cruise ships

Customs Regulations

When Spain joined the EU, the Canary Islands lost their status as a duty-free zone. For customs purposes, however, the islands are still not considered to be part of the EU, and there are detailed regulations as to the amount of goods permitted for export. For UK citizens, they include 200 cigarettes or 50 cigars, two litres of wine and one litre of alcohol over 22 per cent or two litres of sparkling wine.

In addition, visitors are allowed 250 ml of eau de toilette and up to €162 worth of souvenirs. Tobacco and alcohol allowances apply.

Specific cases may be referred to the *Departamento de Aduanas e Impuestos Especiales* (Customs and Excise Department) in Madrid. Travel agents and tour operators can provide further information. Travellers should consult their home country's regulations and be sure to save proof-of-purchase for all goods obtained.

Colourful fruit and vegetables grown in the Canary Islands

◀ Winding roads leading to Pico del Teide, Tenerife

Traditional musicians are central to many Canarian fiestas

Language

The official language of the Canary Islands is Spanish. Local accents differ from those of mainland Spain, but apart from this and a few words particular to the islands, there are no major differences.

It is possible to communicate in various foreign languages in all the tourist resorts, where you could get by without any Spanish at all. The second language is German, but most people also speak English. Information signs and restaurant menus are generally multi-lingual and are a combination of Spanish, German and English.

Communication problems may arise while away from the major tourist centres. Here most people speak only Spanish, though the younger population may be able to understand German or English.

Information packs promoting tourism

Tourist Information

Tourist information on the Canary Islands is a well-oiled machine. Bigger towns and tourist centres have an *oficina de turismo* (tourist information office). These provide information about the locality, accommodation (including staying on a farmstead or in a restored rural house), events and tourist attractions.

Tourist information offices can also provide visitors with free information packs and maps and can offer advice regarding the best walking routes, nearby historic sights and a variety of day trips.

The information packs are an excellent point of reference. They are illustrated with colour photographs and issued in several languages.

Outside Spain, there are plenty of Spanish information offices, which are usually attached to the embassies, where you can obtain all the necessary information prior to visiting the islands.

The Internet is another free source of information, but often official sites are not updated as often as they should be. Every island and many individual regions have their own websites that are nevertheless worth visiting. The Spanish Tourism Institute – *Turespaña* – has its own site (www.tourspain.es), which provides information about hotels, camping sites and tourist attractions throughout Spain. Various travel agents, hotels, restaurants, car-hire firms and other establishments also advertise their services on the Internet. Their pages generally include many photographs, which can be helpful when choosing a hotel.

DIRECTORY

Travel Safety Advice

Australia
w dfat.gov.au
w smarttraveller.gov.au

UK
w gov.uk/foreign-travel-advice

US
w travel.state.gov

Customs Regulations

Australia
w border.gov.au

UK
w gov.uk

US
w cbp.gov

Tourist Information

UK
6th Floor, 64 North Row, London W1K 7DE. **Tel** 020 7317 2020.
w spain.info

Gran Canaria
Avda. España, Playa del Inglés.
Tel 928 771 550.
w grancanaria.com
w ecoturismocanarias.com

Fuerteventura
C/Almirante Lallermand, 1, 35600 Puerto del Rosario. **Tel** 928 530 844. w visitfuerteventura.es

Lanzarote
C/Triana 38, Arrecife. **Tel** 928 811 762. w turismolanzarote.com

Tenerife
Plaza de España, s/n, 38003 Santa Cruz de Tenerife. **Tel** 922 281 287.
w webtenerife.com

La Gomera
C/Real, 32, 38800 San Sebastián de La Gomera. **Tel** 922 141 512.
w lagomera.travel

El Hierro
C/Dr Quintero, 4, Valverde. **Tel** 922 550 302. w elhierro.travel

La Palma
Plaza de la Constitución, s/n, 38700 Santa Cruz de La Palma.
Tel 922 412 106.
w visitlapalma.es
w la-palma-turismo-rural.de

Useful Websites

w hellocanaryislands.com
w lanzaroteinformation.com
w mydestinationtenerife.com
w elmejorclimadelmundo.com

Admiring the spectacular dunes of Maspalomas

Young People and Students

Holders of the International Student Identity Card (ISIC) and the Euro under-30 card are entitled to many benefits when visiting the Canary Islands. They can get discounts on ferry travel, entrance charges to museums and galleries, and tickets to many other tourist attractions. Many travel agents also offer cheaper flights to holders of these cards.

Under-30 cards can be obtained on Tenerife or Gran Canaria with a passport. To get an ISIC card you will need to provide proof that you are a full-time student.

Children

The Canary Islands are geared up for family holidays and, as in most of Europe, children are welcome almost everywhere. The beaches provide a safe playground all year round. The numerous water parks and the zoos, with exciting rides and shows, are a big draw and are aimed, to a large extent, squarely at kids.

Many travel agents specialise in arranging family holidays. They provide all-day childcare, giving parents a chance to take a well-earned rest. They also organise competitions, games and trips for their younger guests.

There is no problem dining out with young children. Children's portions, high-chairs, activity packs and outside seating are the norm rather than the exception in most restaurants.

Facilities for the Disabled

The islands are not particularly hospitable to disabled people. The majority of restaurants and hotels are not adapted to serve guests who use wheelchairs. Moving around some of the towns is also very difficult, and taking part in events or going on organised trips is practically impossible.

When planning a visit to the islands, a disabled tourist should check the travel conditions and hotel facilities with their travel agent. The organization that

Parking for the disabled sign

helps disabled people to plan their holiday on the Canary Islands is the Confederación Española de Personas con Discapacidad Física y Orgánica (COCEMFE) – the Spanish Association for the Disabled. There are also special guides published. Another helpful agency is Viajes 2000.

Sightseeing Tours

A wide range of sightseeing tours is available throughout the islands. Most tour providers and travel agents offer a variety of types. These may include desert safaris by jeep or on the back of a camel, fishing trips, organized walks, submarine cruises, trips in glass-bottomed boats, and visits to one of the islands' parks, including Palmitos Park or Loro Parque. People tend to see only one or two islands when they visit the Canaries, but there are day trips to small islands, such as the Isla de Los Lobos, close to Fuerteventura.

Those not wishing to join a trip organized by a hotel or travel agent can find many other alternatives. Hotel reception desks and tourist offices carry a range of colourful leaflets with relevant information. The tours are mainly reasonably priced day trips though some can last overnight or even longer. Most of them start after breakfast, and the price includes lunch on board a boat or in a friendly restaurant catering for groups of tourists. Visitors living away from the large towns are offered trips to city nightclubs. Shows, dancing and karaoke are the most common features of these forms of evening entertainment.

Time

The Canary Islands are on GMT, the same as the UK and Ireland, and an hour behind mainland Spain.

Fun slides for children at Aqualand

OFICINA DE TURISMO

Tourist information office sign

In summer, to make better use of the sunshine, the clocks go an hour forward. The change over takes place on the last Sunday in March. The clocks are put back again on the last Sunday in October.

Electrical Equipment

The mains voltage on the islands is generally 220 V. A readily available three-tier standard travel converter will enable you to use foreign equipment. Mains sockets require round-pin plugs.

Road sign for visitors to Parque Nacional de Garajonay

Religion

Like the rest of Spain, the Canary Islands are largely Roman Catholic. Religion plays an important role in community life. All religious festivals are lavishly celebrated, and many fiestas are of religious origin. Most of the islands' churches are Roman Catholic. Their opening hours differ; some are open only during services.

There are also churches of other denominations. Services are held in various languages, and their times change frequently. Hotel reception desks and tourist information centres can usually provide details. You will find a multi-denominational church – Templo Ecuménico – on Gran Canaria, in Playa del Inglés. A similar one is located in Puerto de la Cruz, on Tenerife.

Opening Hours

Most monuments and museums are open from Tuesday to Sunday. The hours are generally from 10am to 2pm. They close for the siesta and reopen from 5pm to 8pm. They usually close for public holidays and fiestas, similar to all offices. The hours for museums in smaller towns are more unpredictable, and it is best to phone ahead. Outside of the major tourist resorts, shops close on Sundays. Church opening hours also vary. The best time to visit is during the morning or evening services.

Theme parks and gardens are generally open seven days a week, but even these close for public holidays.

Water

Tap water on the Canary Islands is suitable for drinking, although it is usually heavily treated and can upset the stomach if you are not used to it. It is generally recommended that you drink bottled water and use tap water for cooking. The Canaries' sea breeze can be deceptive – you should remember to drink a lot of liquid to prevent dehydration.

Shops offer a large variety of bottled water, mainly from local wells. Particularly good are the different types of sparkling water, including those from Firgas and Teror on Gran Canaria.

Sign for Gran Canaria's botanical garden

Personal Security and Health

Visitors to the Canary Islands can generally feel safe. Thefts do occur in the most crowded places and even in hotels, but they can be minimized by taking sensible precautions. Credit cards and money are best hidden away or carried in a belt. Never leave anything visible in your car when you park it. It is also advisable to avoid carrying excessive amounts of cash. When in need, you can always ask a policeman for help. Basic medical help and advice is usually provided by a pharmacist. Holders of valid medical insurance can receive treatment in public hospitals and clinics.

Information board at Amadores beach on Gran Canaria

Personal Property

Before going away it is necessary to make sure you have adequate holiday insurance in order to protect you financially from the loss or theft of your property.

Even so, it is advisable to take common-sense precautions against loss or theft in the first place. Avoid carrying a lot of cash, and, if you have two credit cards, do not carry them together. Particular care should be exercised in crowded places, such as airports or bus stations, as well as inside tourist attractions, which are always full of people. Patrolling policemen often remind visitors about the need to be careful. There are also cases of tourists falling victim to theft when drunk. Never leave a bag or handbag unattended and do not put down a purse or wallet on the tabletop in a café. The moment you discover a loss or theft, report it to the local police station. The police will give you a *denuncia* (written statement), which you will need to make an insurance claim. If you have your passport lost or stolen, report it to your consulate.

Spanish Police

In the Canary Islands, as in the rest of Spain, there are essentially three types of police. The *Policía Nacional* (state police), the *Policía Municipal*, also known as the *Policía Local* (local police), and the *Guardia Civil* (National Guard).

The *Policía Nacional* wear blue uniforms and drive white cars with navy-blue doors. They operate in towns with a population of more than 30,000.

The uniform of the *Policía Local* varies depending on the locality. Their officers are mostly encountered in small towns, and patrol the streets of crowded tourist resorts; they have a separate branch for traffic.

The *Guardia Civil* wear green uniforms and generally drive white-and-green four-wheel-drive vehicles. They mainly patrol the open roads.

The islands' police are friendly towards tourists. They are, however, very firm with those who commit traffic offences. All three services will direct you to the relevant authority in the event of an incident requiring further help.

Uniform of the Guardia Civil

Local police four-wheel-drive car, a common sight on the islands

Sunshine

Though it is, of course, one of the attractions, the sun should be taken seriously in the Canary Islands. The archipelago lies in the tropical zone, where the sun is much stronger than in the rest of Spain. Always use high-factor sun cream to avoid burning. Many people tend to forget that these creams do not remain active throughout the entire day and should be reapplied every few hours.

When going to the beach, try to avoid the hottest hours of the day. Between 1pm and 4pm it is best not to stay in direct sun for too long. The sun is also strong in the mountains, above the clouds. The somewhat cooler air makes it feel less hot, but the results can be just as unpleasant. When sitting out in the sun you should remember to wear a hat, to help prevent sunstroke.

Outdoor Hazards

Another potential problem on the islands, besides the sunshine, is the ocean. Many people do not realize the strength of the ocean waves.

In order to avoid any unpleasant surprises, you should always swim where there are lifeguards. Always take note of warning signs. The currents can be particularly powerful around the Canary Islands. If you cannot see plenty of other people swimming in the water, then the chances are that it may not be safe. Never bathe where there are surfers or windsurfers. These are a potential hazard, especially when beginners come too close to the shore. Surfers and divers using unguarded beaches should be aware of the rocky ocean bottom. A violent wave can sometimes throw a person against the rocks, causing serious injuries.

When diving near the shore, it is always advisable to have another person with you for protection. The marine fauna do not present a danger to swimmers, although jellyfish can inflict a painful sting.

Medical Care

Both national and private healthcare is available in Spain. Visitors from EU countries are entitled to free national health treatment. They must, however, remember to travel with a certified copy of a European Health Insurance card (EHIC). These can be obtained in the UK before you travel by filling in an application form on either the EHIC website or at a post office. Please note that Spanish healthcare does not cover all expenses, such as the cost of dental treatment. Visitors from outside the EU should always carry valid insurance.

In case of illness, you should report to the nearest hospital or clinic. At night, you should contact the emergency service (*Urgencias*) and in case of an accident call for a Red Cross ambulance (*Cruz Roja*).

Ambulance in Las Palmas de Gran Canaria

Pharmacies

Pharmacists can offer help and advice. In some cases, they can also prescribe medicines. If you have a non-urgent medical problem the *farmacia* is a good place to start. Most pharmacists will speak English. They are open during the same hours as other shops and carry a green cross sign, often with the word *farmacia*. Details about those open at night and on public holidays can be found in the windows of all pharmacies.

Illuminated Spanish pharmacy sign

Fire Hazards

The high temperatures on the islands make them very dry. This should be remembered, particularly when travelling by car. At woodland camp sites and picnic spots, great care must be taken to prevent fire. When leaving, check carefully the remains of any bonfires and pick up glass, particularly empty bottles, which can cause fires. It goes without saying that you should be especially careful with cigarettes.

Outdoors

Visitors touring the islands may see signs written only in Spanish, as well as warning and information notices.

Coto de caza means a hunting ground. *Camino particular* means a driveway, while *privado* informs you that the area is private property.

Hiking routes are generally well signposted but can still test the most experienced hiker. When setting off, take the right equipment and plenty of water. Tell someone where you are going and when you intend to return.

DIRECTORY

Emergency Numbers

Ambulance
Tel 112.

Fire Brigade
Tel 080 (Gran Canaria).
Tel 112 (Tenerife).

Guardia Civil
Tel 062.

Police, ambulance, fire brigade
Tel 112.

Policía Municipal
Tel 092.

Policía Nacional.
Tel 091.

Sea Rescue
Tel 900 202 202.

Information on Medical Care

W nhs.uk1
W fefarcan.org
Tel 928 917 323 (Las Palmas).
Tel 922 204 310 (Tenerife).

Sign warning of the risk of forest fires

Banking and Currency

As the Canary Islands are a territory of Spain, the euro is the currency in circulation and so visitors from the Eurozone do not need to change money prior to visiting. Those from other countries will, however, find it quick and easy to change money in banks and hotels. Furthermore, credit and debit cards are widely accepted across the Canaries in most hotels, restaurants and large stores.

Changing Money

All major currencies can be exchanged without any problems in bureaux de change or banks. It is advisable to take your passport along with you, just in case you're asked to produce it.

Bureaux de change charge higher rates than banks, but even banks charge a few per cent commission. Depending on the bank, you can draw up to €300 on major credit cards at a cash machine.

In smaller towns and on islands, such as El Hierro, you may have problems exchanging money.

Logo of la Caixa

When travelling to some of the more remote places, you should carry enough cash to see you through.

Cajas de Ahorro (savings banks) can also exchange money. They are open from 8:30am to 2pm on weekdays and also on Thursday afternoons from 4:30pm to 7:45pm. Most banks are open from 8:30am to 2pm on weekdays, and until 1pm on Saturdays, although specific opening times do depend upon the branch. Banks are closed on public holidays and during island fiestas.

The most common banks on the islands are La Caixa, Bankia, Santander Central Hispano and BBVA.

One of the many signs for an automatic cash machine

Credit cards are widely used in the Canary Islands

ATMs

It is usually easy enough to find an ATM (automatic teller machine) on the islands. Machines can be found on almost every street corner in larger towns and cities. Some charge a commission on withdrawals with cards issued by other banks. If you want to avoid this, you should find out if any Spanish bank has an agreement with your own bank before travelling. Most ATMs provide instructions for cash withdrawal in several languages.

Almost all machines also accept credit cards as a means of withdrawing cash. The fees for credit card withdrawals vary from bank to bank and also depend on the level of the amount (the fee is usually around €5).

If your credit or debit card has been lost or stolen, you should immediately call the relevant emergency number to block the card.

Credit and Debit Cards

Credit cards (*tarjetas de crédito*) are generally accepted, particularly in the tourist resorts, where every effort is made to make life easy for visitors. The most widely accepted card in Spain is **Visa**, but **MasterCard** and **American Express** are also generally accepted. In less-frequented places, such as small shops and local bars,

it is sometimes necessary to pay in cash, and it is always worth carrying some cash to pay for small items. When you pay with a card, cashiers will often ask for ID. Your card might be swiped, or you will be asked to punch in your PIN number. Contactless payment (via NFC) is now accepted in many establishments in Spain, but for transactions over €20, PIN verification is mandatory.

Traveller's Cheques

The use of traveller's cheques (*cheques de viaje*) is declining in the Canary Islands, and it is not always easy to find places to cash the cheques. They can now only be exchanged at some major banks and hotels. Most restaurants and shops do not accept traveller's cheques, as either cash or credit and debit cards are the more preferable mode of payment.

DIRECTORY

Banks

La Caixa
Avda. Franchy Roca Esq. Ps. S. Artiles, 35007 Las Palmas de Gran Canaria.
Tel 928 687 470.

C/Virgen del Rosario, 5, 35600 Puerto del Rosario.
Tel 928 874 000.

C/León y Castillo, 15, 35500 Arrecife.
Tel 928 816 050.

Pl. Patriotismo, 1, 38002 Santa Cruz de Tenerife.
Tel 922 471 014.
w lacaixa.es

Lost or Stolen Credit Cards

American Express
Tel 902 375 637.

Diners Club
Tel 900 801 331.

MasterCard
Tel 900 971 231.

Visa
Tel 900 991 124.

The Euro

The euro (€) is the common currency of the European Union (EU). It went into general circulation on 1 January 2002, initially for 12 participating countries. Spain was one of those 12 countries adopting the euro, and its original currency, the peseta, was phased out by March 2002. EU members using the euro as sole official currency are known as the Eurozone. Euro notes are identical throughout the Eurozone countries, each including designs of architectural structures and monuments. The coins, however, have one side identical (the value side) and one side with an image unique to each country. Both notes and coins are exchangeable in each of the participating euro countries.

Bank Notes

Euro bank notes have seven denominations. The 5-euro note (grey in colour) is the smallest, followed by the 10-euro note (pink), 20-euro note (blue), 50-euro note (orange), 100-euro note (green), 200-euro note (yellow) and 500-euro note (purple). All notes show the stars of the European Union.

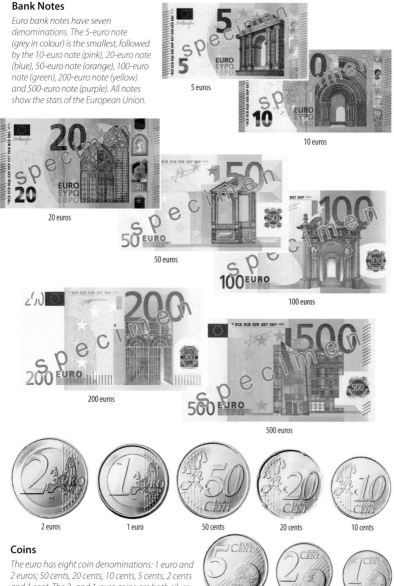

5 euros

10 euros

20 euros

50 euros

100 euros

200 euros

500 euros

2 euros

1 euro

50 cents

20 cents

10 cents

Coins

The euro has eight coin denominations: 1 euro and 2 euros; 50 cents, 20 cents, 10 cents, 5 cents, 2 cents and 1 cent. The 2- and 1-euro coins are both silver and gold in colour. The 50-, 20- and 10-cent coins are gold. The 5-, 2- and 1-cent coins are bronze.

5 cents

2 cents

1 cent

Communications and Media

Most public telephones, although not as common as they once were, are served by the Spanish company Telefónica. The mobile phone network covers practically the whole of the Canary Islands. The Spanish postal system is not among the best, so it is advisable to use e-mail when exchanging messages with Spanish firms. The *correos* (post offices) are recognizable by their blue or white crown on a yellow background. Stamps are available at all post offices, but also in *estancos* (tobacconists). Visitors can stay up-to-date with local news and tourism by following official social media posts.

Telephone area codes

- Country code for Spain: 0034.
- Always dial the entire number including the area code. The code numbers of the islands are: Tenerife, El Hierro, La Palma and La Gomera: 922; Gran Canaria, Lanzarote and Fuerteventura: 928.
- For international calls, dial 00, then the country code, the local code (omitting the first 0) and the number of the person you are calling.
- Country codes: UK 44, US 1, Australia 61.
- National information and connections: 11888.
- International information: 11825.

Public Telephones

Public telephone kiosks (*cabinas telefónicas*) and public telephones in bars are difficult to find. If you do locate a pay phone, there are two types on the island: card-and coin-operated, and card-operated (which do not accept coins). Some phones are equipped with multi-lingual electronic displays.

Phonecards are convenient and can be purchased at newsstands and *estancos* (tobacconists). There are two types of telephone cards. One has a magnetic strip with an encoded value, the other has a PIN number that is entered before a connection is made.

When dialling a number you should remember that in Spain the area code is a permanent part of the number, which consists of nine digits in total. For Tenerife and its dependent islands, El Hierro, La Palma and La Gomera the area code is 922. For Gran Canaria province and islands, Lanzarote and Fuerteventura, the number is 928. Calls between islands of the same province are

charged at the same rate as long-distance calls within the island. Other calls are charged at the inter-provincial rate. When calling Spain from abroad you should dial 34, followed by the subscriber's number, including the area code. When calling a mobile phone number, you should dial the country code followed by the subscriber's number.

International calls are cheapest at night (after 8pm) and on Sunday. A call from a public telephone box costs 35 per cent more than one made from a private phone. Visitors should note that using public telephones is always cheaper than making calls from a hotel.

Mobile Phones

There are several mobile operators in Spain – Movistar (which belongs to Telefónica), Vodafone, Orange and Yoigo. Signal coverage is generally good across the islands, though

Logo of Movistar, the mobile phone brand of Telefónica

it might prove patchy in more rural areas. Since roaming charges were capped for EU member states, and are set to be abolished by 2017, it is much cheaper for

visitors from the EU to use mobile phones abroad. Those from non-EU countries who anticipate using the phone a great deal while away might find it easier to purchase a cheap pay-as-you-go phone.

You can also buy a Spanish SIM card for your current phone. Check your phone before travelling to ensure that it is unlocked, so that you can change to a local carrier.

Internet

Many cities on the larger islands offer Wi-Fi hotspots, as do an increasing number of cafés, hotels and apartments. Some hotels and B&Bs offer Wi-Fi access, which can be either included in the room cost or incur a small usage fee. If you are looking to use a computer rather than a phone or tablet, there are several Internet cafés, also known as Cibercafés, on the Canaries.

Postal Service

The local post offices are generally open between 8:30am and 1:30pm, while the ones located inside El Corte Inglés stores are usually open from 10am to 9:30pm.

The main post office in San Cristóbal de La Laguna, Tenerife

Postage stamps can be bought at post office desks or any of the kiosks displaying the word *timbre*. Letters should be posted in yellow post boxes, marked *correos*. The Spanish *correos* (post office) is the only institution authorised to handle mail, so it is not recommended that you leave your letters in shops or hotels, which sometimes offer this service.

The postal system works at its own pace. You should therefore not be surprised if a letter or postcard takes a week or more to reach its destination.

Postal charges depend on where the item is being sent and fall into bands that include the EU, the rest of Europe, the USA and the rest of the world. Post offices also accept telegrams, registered mail and parcels. The international courier **DHL Express** can be found in Telde (Gran Canaria) and La Laguna (Tenerife). Spanish express company **MRW** also provides services on the islands.

Addresses

In Spanish addresses, the house number follows the name of the street, and the floor is added with a dash. Thus, 4–2°

Some popular daily newspapers in the Canary Islands

means: house number four, second floor. All postcodes have five digits, the first two being the province number.

Newspapers and Magazines

Alongside the national Spanish newspapers and magazines, each island has a local newspaper, which can be found both in print and online. These local papers contain relevant information for current listings, such as festivals and other cultural events. There are also Spanish-speaking publications that are geared towards the archipelago, such as Canarias7. For news in English, visit www. island connections.eu, www. thecanarynews.com or www. canarianweekly.com (also publishes a weekly paper copy).

Logo of the TV channel TV3

In many major cities, national newspapers from the rest of Europe are also available. Usually, however, you should expect to pay more for foreign papers, and they are usually a day old.

Radio and Television

Radio is quite popular in the Canary Islands, and can frequently be heard in shops and restaurants. There are many local radio stations that broadcast both Spanish and international music daily. For radio in English, tune into Holiday FM (Lanzarote 98.2 / 105.5 FM; Tenerife 99.0FM; Gran Canaria 101.8 FM), broadcast from London.

The Canary Island's public television station is Televisión Canaria. Many hotels also offer television with satellite reception, so visitors can watch English-language programmes. All major Spanish radio and television programmes are also available.

Logo of Televisión Canaria

DIRECTORY

Post Offices

Gran Canaria
C/Primero de Mayo 62,
Las Palmas de Gran Canaria.
Tel 928 371 822.
W correos.es

Fuerteventura
C/Canalejas 2,
Puerto del Rosario.
Tel 928 850 412.

Lanzarote
Avda. La Marina 8,
Arrecife.
Tel 928 800 673.

Tenerife
Plaza de España 2,
Santa Cruz de Tenerife.
Tel 922 533 629.

La Gomera
C/El Medio 60,
San Sebastián de La Gomera.
Tel 922 871 081.

El Hierro
C/Correo 3,
Valverde.
Tel 922 550 291.

La Palma
Plaza de la Constitución 2,
Santa Cruz de La Palma.
Tel 922 411 702.

Courier

DHL Express
C/José María Millares Sall, 46,
35230 Telde, Gran Canaria.
Tel 928 136 077.

P.I. El Mayorazgo, Parcela nº 34,
38108 La Laguna, Tenerife.
Tel 922 235 360.
W dhl.es

MRW
Avda. Santiago Puig, s/n,
Local 1, 38660 Arona
(Playa Americas).
Tel 922 750 010.

C/ Doctor Juan de Padilla,
12, 35002 Las Palmas de
Gran Canaria.
Tel 928 380 506.
W mrw.es

TRAVEL INFORMATION

Air links with most of Europe and the Canary Islands are extremely efficient. Each island has an airport. Tenerife, Gran Canaria and Lanzarote take in most of the international flights as well as those from mainland Spain, while the other smaller airports are principally for hopping from island to island. Most of the air transport to and from the islands is by charter flights. Air links between the islands are provided mainly by Binter Canarias Airlines. You can also travel to the Canary Islands by ship. Most boats sail from harbours on mainland Spain or the West African coast. Ferries and fast catamarans provide regular links between the islands.

Attended car park at Gran Canaria airport

Getting There

There are scheduled flights to the islands from all major Spanish cities. Flights from Madrid to Gran Canaria run almost every hour. These routes are served by several airlines: **Iberia**, Ryanair, Norwegian Air and Air Europa. Iberia planes fly to all the islands of the archipelago, while the other airlines fly only to Tenerife, Gran Canaria and Lanzarote. Vueling offers flights from Barcelona to most of the islands.

The Canary Islands also have scheduled flights to and from many European cities. Air links with Africa are provided by three airlines – Air Maroc, **Binter Canarias** and Air Atlantic. These connect the islands with the cities of Morocco and the former Spanish Sahara.

Apart from scheduled flights, all airports operate hundreds of charter flights. These are used mostly by German and British tourists, although holiday-makers come from all over Europe. Charter flight tickets were once only bought as part of a package tour. Now visitors can travel independently, making a ticket-only purchase and booking their accommodation separately.

When buying an air ticket you should always enquire about current offers. Occasionally, some airlines offer very good bargains. Bargains are also to be had if you book your ticket on the Internet. However, it is difficult to find a bargain during the high seasons, such as the school summer holidays, Christmas or during the carnivals, which take place in February and March. Information can be found on the Internet or obtained from travel agents.

You can also travel to the islands by ship. This is the only option if taking a motorbike or car.

There are weekly departures from Cádiz to Tenerife, Gran Canaria and La Palma. The voyage takes one-and-a-half to two days, depending on the destination. The ships are comfortable and offer quite a few amenities.

Flights Between the Islands

All the islands of the archipelago now have their own airports. Nevertheless, not all of them offer flights to all the other islands. For example, La Gomera only has flights to Tenerife and Gran Canaria. Most routes are served by Binter Canarias Airlines.

When hopping between the islands, it is a good idea to find out which airline provides the service. It is not a cheap option and some aircraft are very small, with a dozen or so seats. Often, the airline will not allow you to take large hand luggage. Travelling in a small, packed aircraft can be unpleasant.

Brochure for Binter Canarias

Flights between islands are short. Between La Palma and El Hierro takes just 20 minutes, while the longest – from La Palma to Lanzarote – takes 70 minutes.

Airports

Although each island has its own airport, not all are served by international flights. Tenerife has two

Gran Canaria airport, next to the sea

Fred. Olsen ferry

airports – Los Rodeos/Tenerife Norte in the north and Reina Sofía/Tenerife Sur in the southern part of the island. Tenerife Norte, 11 km (7 miles) south of capital Santa Cruz, is mainly for domestic flights, with about half linking Tenerife to the rest of the Canary Islands. International and charter flights generally fly from the more modern Reina Sofía airport, located approximately 60 km (37 miles) south of Santa Cruz. Bus number 343 connects Tenerife Norte with Tenerife Sur, without stopping; the journey takes 50 minutes.

Fuerteventura airport is only 5 km (3 miles) south of Puerto del Rosario. The airport primarily serves international charter flights, mainly from the UK, Germany, Austria and The Netherlands.

Gran Canaria airport, located on the east of the island, between Las Palmas, and Maspalomas is served internationally. The international airport on Lanzarote is located 5 km (3 miles) south of Arrecife. It serves mainly flights from Germany and the UK.

La Palma Airport is 8 km (5 miles) south of its capital, Santa Cruz. It offer flights mainly to and from Spain and the other Canary Islands. La Gomera's airport is close to Playa de Santiago and 34 km (21 miles) from the island capital of San Sebastián de La Gomera. The runway is too short for international flights so air travellers mainly land in Tenerife and catch a connecting flight.

The small airport of El Hierro is located in the northeast, 12 km (7 miles) outside the island's capital, Valverde. Most planes arrive via Tenerife North and Gran Canaria.

At all airports you will find restaurants, cafés, ATMs, car-rental companies, a variety of shops and taxi stands. All airports, cities and holiday resorts are well connected by bus.

Ferries

Ferries provide an alternative form of inter-island transport, although crossings are not always direct and might require a change. Direct crossings to all the other islands, or crossings with a single change, run only from Tenerife, which is the hub of island-hopping by sea *(see inside back cover)*. The most popular tourist resorts provide several daily crossings, by ferry or large, fast catamarans. These carry cars, buses and lorries as well as foot passengers. They also have restaurants and cabins.

When planning a tour around the archipelago remember that travelling by ferry is cheaper than flying and can be a very pleasant option. It can be timely, however; the longest service from Gran Canaria takes two days to reach the furthest islands.

Ticket prices for crossings with two of the biggest companies serving inter-island routes – **Acciona Trasmediterránea** and **Fred. Olsen** – are broadly similar. Slightly cheaper ticket options and special deals are offered by **Naviera Armas** lines.

DIRECTORY

Airports

El Hierro (VDE)
Tel 922 550 878.

Fuerteventura (FUE)
Tel 928 860 500.

Gran Canaria (LPA)
Tel 928 579 000.
(for all airports)
w aena.es (for all airports)

La Gomera (GMZ)
Tel 922 873 000.

La Palma (SPC)
Tel 922 411 540.

Lanzarote (ACE)
Tel 928 846 000.

Tenerife North (TFN)
Tel 922 635 800.

Tenerife South (TFS)
Tel 922 759 200.

Airlines

Binter Canarias
Tel 902 391 392.
w bintercanarias.com

Iberia
Tel 901 111 500.
w iberia.com

Ferry Lines

**Acciona
Trasmediterránea**
Tel 902 454 645.
w transmediterranea.es

Fred. Olsen
Tel 902 100 107.
w fredolsen.es

Naviera Armas
Tel 902 456 500.
w navieraarmas.com

Ferry harbour in Las Palmas de Gran Canaria

Getting Around the Islands

Depending on your plans for visiting the islands, you can choose one of many forms of transport. The bigger islands, such as Tenerife, Gran Canaria and Lanzarote, have efficient buses; here you can travel by bus to almost any point on the island. Exploring some of the smaller islands means hiring a car, motorbike or bicycle. However, some places are best visited as part of an organised tour, with an experienced guide and driver.

Winding roads in the vicinity of Masca

Roads

Visitors touring the Canary Islands by car cannot but be impressed with the state of the roads. Many are newly built and smoothly surfaced. All major towns and villages can be reached by road, without any problem. Larger islands have their own motorways (auto-pistas), along their coastlines, which connect with the airports and major resorts.

Roads in the central, mountainous regions, on the other hand, are narrow and winding. They often lead through narrow tunnels. Problems can arise when two vehicles try to pass each other, particularly when one of them is a bus or a lorry. Sometimes a hidden oncoming vehicle signals its approach by blowing its horn.

Driving conditions may become dangerous in some areas when it is raining or foggy, as the roads can become slippery and the visibility limited.

Many scenic spots are accessible only by rough tracks or unmade roads, requiring a four-wheel-drive vehicle. The best way to visit them is to join an organised tour. A heavy rainfall can make these roads impassable.

The islands' roads are largely well signposted, with clear signs for towns, major tourist attractions and viewpoints. El Hierro is the exception, and you may have problems spotting the small, wooden signposts from a distance. In town, the well-signposted streets make historic sites easy to find.

Buses and Taxis

On larger islands, such as Gran Canaria and Tenerife, there are no problems travelling by bus. You should, however, bear in mind that buses to some smaller towns or villages may run only once or twice a day, and you might have problems finding a bus to get you back to your hotel or apartment.

Travelling from a small town to a major nightlife centre later in the evening may also be something of a problem. Large towns have their own bus networks. These serve the town and its immediate environs.

Smaller islands have infrequent bus services, which means this is not the easiest method of exploring their sights.

In towns and major tourist resorts it is easy to get a taxi. They are a much more convenient, although more expensive, form of transport than buses. Taxi drivers are obliged to turn on the meter at the start of the journey, and the sum displayed is the one you pay. Only when travelling to and from an airport is there an additional airport fee as well as a small luggage charge.

Town Driving

If at all possible, you should avoid driving in the capital cities. Las Palmas and other cities often experience traffic jams during the rush hours, and at other times. Cars parked by the pavements make driving conditions more difficult. It is also very difficult to find a parking space, particularly in city centres. Most car parks charge hourly fees, ranging from around €2 to €3, and there are fines for non-payment.

Logo for CICAR –
a local car-hire company

Car Hire

On all the islands you can easily find a car-hire firm. Major companies, including **Avis** and **Hertz**, as well as the local ones, including **Cicar**, have their desks at the airports. Car hire is generally very reasonable, but

Tourist coach on La Gomera

An unorthodox form of transport on the islands

the price depends on many factors, including the time of year, the size of the car and the length of hire. Advance booking also affects the price. It is sensible to compare the prices quoted by various agencies and check exactly what the quote includes.

When hiring a car you should carefully inspect its condition, as you will have to return it in the same state or pay a fine.

The terms and conditions of hire vary according to individual companies. There are no established rules regarding insurance, mileage or petrol. Check carefully before signing any contract. For an ordinary car the terms will probably include a provision ensuring that you do not drive on unmade roads, or take the car by ferry to another island. Hire cars must be returned to where they were collected, or to another agreed place.

Firms offering motorbikes for hire are rare. Crash helmets are obligatory, and for anything over 50cc you'll need to produce a driving licence.

Buying Petrol

Petrol (gasoline) is cheaper on the islands than on mainland Spain. Petrol stations offer all types of fuel, but most cars use unleaded petrol.

Petrol station pumps are generally operated by the staff. Only a few are automatic and open 24 hours. When touring the small islands, such as

El Hierro, you should remember that there are very few petrol stations, and that a car uses more fuel on mountainous terrain than on a flat road. It is therefore worth filling the tank before setting off.

Rules of the Road

The traffic regulations on the islands are generally the same as those of other continental European countries. Vehicles drive on the right-hand side of the road, and there are few road signs specific to Spain or the islands. Speed limits, though not always obeyed by the Spaniards, are legally binding. On motorways the speed limit is 120 km/h (75 mph), on major roads, 90 km/h (56 mph) and in towns, 50 km/h (31 mph).

Road breakdown help point

The fines for exceeding the speed limit are high, just as they are for drunken driving. The highest permitted blood alcohol level is 0.05 per cent (random breath testing is carried out). Safety belts are obligatory for passengers as

well as drivers. Car seats or booster chairs are mandatory for children under 12 years of age.

Maps

When buying a map you should first check if it is up to date. This is important, in view of the continuing local road-development programme. You can get the island's map from each car-hire firm and street maps can be obtained from tourist offices.

DIRECTORY

Car Hire

Avis
Tel 902 135 531.
w avis.com

CICAR
Tel 928 822 900.
w cicar.com

Hertz
Tel 928 846 190.
w hertz.co.uk

Bus Stations

Gran Canaria
Tel 928 368 335.

Fuerteventura
Tel 928 855 726.

Lanzarote
Tel 928 811 522.

Tenerife
Tel 922 531 300.

La Gomera
Tel 922 141 101.

El Hierro
Tel 922 551 175.

La Palma
Tel 922 460 241.

Be aware of cyclists on winding streets

Travelling Between the Islands

The Canary Islands offer plenty of transport options, irrespective of the island you have chosen as a principal residence. Flight time between the islands is less than 90 minutes, and flights connect all the islands throughout the day. Modern ferries connect the Canary Islands by sea. High-speed ferries zip from Tenerife to Gran Canaria, La Gomera and La Palma; Gran Canaria to Fuerteventura; Lanzarote to Fuerteventura; and La Palma to La Gomera.

A Fred. Olsen express ferry at the Corralejo harbour, Fuerteventura

Flying between Islands

Although there are airports on every island, not all of them offer international connections. Hence, it is advisable to plan island-hopping prior to your trip. La Gomera, for example, is directly connected only to Tenerife North airport.

Most connections between the Canary Islands are run by the regional airline Binter Canarias (see pp200–201), which flies to all of the eight airports on the islands. The airline's headquarters is located in Telde, at Las Palmas airport. This airport is also the hub for Binter. Currently, the Binter fleet comprises 21 aircrafts, with turboprop engines for short-haul flights, and which can accommodate 70 passengers. A dozen more planes are to be gradually added, and by the end of 2018, the fleet will have 33 turboprops, plus two Bombardiers with seating for up to 78 passengers, for international flights.

It is also possible to go island-hopping by charter planes. However, visitors should note that this isn't cheap. These planes have just a few dozen places and are usually very small, with rows of seats rather tightly packed together. Due to the limited space, you cannot usually take much hand luggage. Inter-island flights don't take long: from La Palma to El Hierro, the flight takes just 20 minutes, and from La Palma to Lanzarote, 50 minutes.

If you plan to visit other islands by plane, it is best to book early, as many flights fill up well in advance.

Logo of the ferry company Naviera Armas

Ferries

Ferries are an important means of transport between the Canary Islands and can be a pleasant way of getting around. Not all the islands are directly connected, and you may have to change several times. Only from Tenerife do ferries go directly (or with just one change) to all the other islands. Tenerife is the focal point of all ferries to the Canary Islands (see inside back pages).

Popular resorts often have daily direct connections, with fast hydrofoils or car ferries that offer bars, restaurants and cabins. If the main destination is Tenerife, you can, for example, take the ferry to El Hierro, La Gomera or La Palma, tour the island during the day and in the evening travel back with the ferry. If you also want to visit the more remote islands of Gran Canaria, Fuerteventura and Lanzarote from Tenerife, you should, however, schedule two or three days for the trip in order to explore the islands leisurely. If you are on a tight schedule, flying would perhaps be a better option. The ferry service between the islands is run by the three companies Trasmediterránea, Fred. Olsen Express and Naviera Armas. All ferries that sail between the islands are car ferries, so you can also take your vehicle. However, if you are renting a car, it is advisable to check if your rental company will allow you to take the vehicle on the ferry. You may be required to pay an insurance surcharge for coverage on the second island. Visitors should note that travelling by ferry with a car is substantially more expensive than going as a foot passenger, so you may consider turning in your rental car before leaving, and either renting a new car at your destination, or using public transportation. Fred. Olsen Express also offers an express ferry.

A brightly painted Binter Canarias aircraft

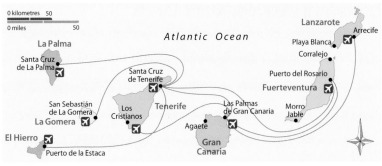

Flights between the Canary Islands

Ferry Ports

The harbour at Las Palmas is the most important in the Canaries, as ferries connect the port to all of the other islands. The port of Puerto de las Nieves at Agaete is the departure point for ferries to Tenerife, since this is the shortest distance between the islands.

The main port of Fuerteventura is in Puerto del Rosario. From Corralejo, ferries sail to Playa Blanca in Lanzarote and to the small island of Los Lobos. From the port of Morro Jable, ferries take the shortest route to Las Palmas.

The starting point on Lanzarote for ferries to the other islands is the port of Arrecife, Los Mármoles. From here, boats depart to La Graciosa, run by Líneas Marítimas Romero (www. lineasromero.com). The main port of Tenerife is in Santa Cruz de Tenerife. From here, the ferry lines connect Tenerife to Gran Canaria. From the port of Los Cristianos, ferries run to the ports of San Sebastián on La Gomera, La Estaca on El Hierro and Santa Cruz de La Palma. In addition, many boat trips to the cliffs of Los Gigantes (see p119) or for observing whales and dolphins (see p182) start here.

INTER-ISLAND FERRY ROUTES

Fred. Olsen Express
Tel 902 100 107. W fredolsen.es
Gran Canaria (Agaete)
– Tenerife (Santa Cruz)
Gran Canaria (Las Palmas)
– Fuerteventura (Morro Jable,
Puerto del Rosario)
Tenerife (Santa Cruz)
– Gran Canaria (Agaete)
Tenerife (Los Cristianos)
– La Gomera (San Sebastián)
– La Palma (Santa Cruz)
– El Hierro (Valverde)
Fuerteventura (Corralejo)
– Lanzarote (Playa Blanca)
Fuerteventura (Puerto del Rosario)
– Fuerteventura (Morro Jable)
– Gran Canaria (Las Palmas)
Fuerteventura (Morro Jable)
– Gran Canaria (Las Palmas)
Lanzarote (Playa Blanca)
– Fuerteventura (Corralejo)
La Palma (Santa Cruz)
– Tenerife (Los Cristianos)
– La Gomera (San Sebastián)
La Gomera (San Sebastián)
– Tenerife (Los Cristianos)
– La Palma (Santa Cruz)
– El Hierro (Valverde)

Naviera Armas
Tel 902 456 500.
W www.navieraarmas.com
Gran Canaria (Las Palmas)
– El Hierro (Valverde)

– Fuerteventura (Morro Jable,
Puerto del Rosario)
– La Gomera (San Sebastián)
– La Graciosa (Caleta de Sebo)
– Lanzarote (Arrecife)
– La Palma (Santa Cruz)
– Tenerife (Los Cristianos, Santa Cruz)
Tenerife (Los Cristianos)
– El Hierro (Valverde)
– La Gomera (San Sebastián)
– Fuerteventura (Santa Cruz)
Tenerife (Santa Cruz)
– Fuerteventura (Morro Jable,
Puerto del Rosario)
– Gran Canaria (Las Palmas)
– La Graciosa (Caleta de Sebo)
– Lanzarote (Arrecife)
Fuerteventura (Corralejo)
– Lanzarote (Playa Blanca)
Fuerteventura (Morro Jable)
– Gran Canaria (Las Palmas)
– Tenerife (Santa Cruz)
Fuerteventura (Puerto del Rosario)
– Gran Canaria (Las Palmas)
– Tenerife (Santa Cruz)
Lanzarote (Arrecife)
– Gran Canaria (Las Palmas)
– Tenerife (Santa Cruz)
Lanzarote (Playa Blanca)
– Fuerteventura (Corralejo)
La Palma (Santa Cruz)
– Gran Canaria (Las Palmas)
– La Gomera (San Sebastián)
– Tenerife (Los Cristianos)

La Gomera (San Sebastián)
– El Hierro (Valverde)
– Gran Canaria (Las Palmas)
– La Palma (Santa Cruz)
– Tenerife (Los Cristianos)
El Hierro (Valverde)
– La Gomera (San Sebastián)
– Tenerife (Los Cristianos)

Trasmediterránea
Tel 902 454 645.
W trasmediterranea.es
Lanzarote (Arrecife)
– Gran Canaria (Las Palmas)
– La Palma (Santa Cruz)
– Tenerife (Santa Cruz)
Gran Canaria (Las Palmas)
– Lanzarote (Arrecife)
– Fuerteventura (Puerto
del Rosario)
– La Palma (Santa Cruz)
– Tenerife (Santa Cruz)
La Palma (Santa Cruz)
– Lanzarote (Arrecife)
– Gran Canaria (Las Palmas)
– Fuerteventura (Puerto
del Rosario)
– Tenerife (Santa Cruz)
Tenerife (Santa Cruz)
– Lanzarote (Arrecife)
– Gran Canaria (Las Palmas)
– Fuerteventura (Puerto
del Rosario)
– La Palma (Santa Cruz)

General Index

Acknowledgements

Dorling Kindersley would like to thank the following people for their contributions to this guide: Jürgen Bingel, Magdalena Borzęcka, Zbigniew Dybowski, Joanna Egert-Romanowska, Daniel Poch, Javier Lopez Silvosa, Damian Sosa.

For Dorling Kindersley
Publisher Douglas Amrine
Publishing Manager Helen Townsend
Managing Art Editors Kate Poole, Ian Midson
Senior Editor Jacky Jackson
Revisions Team Emma Anacootee, Parnika Bagla, Claire Baranowski, Hilary Bird, Jill Benjamin, Marian Broderick, Jo Cowen, Conrad van Dyk, Marisa Renzullo, Jude Ledger, Carly Madden, Bhavika Mathur, Lynnette McCurdy Bastida, Kate Molan, Clare Peel, Helen Peters, Lucy Richards, Sands Publishing Solutions, Lucinda Smith, Stewart Wild.
Additional Picture Research Rachel Barber, Susie Peachey, Ellen Root, Lucy Sienkowska
DTP Vinod Harish, Azeem Siddiqui, Vincent-Kurien
Cartography Uma Bhattacharya, Mohammed Hassan, Jasneet Kaur.
Translator Andrew Brown in association with First Edition Translations Ltd, Cambridge, UK

Additional Photogrpahy Max Alexander, Philip Gatward, Matthew Hancock, Sven Larsson, David King, Neil Lukas, Ian O'Leary, Neil Mersh, David Murray, Brian Pitkin, William Reavell, Rough Guides/Neville Walker, Tony Russell, Kim Sayer, Tony Souter, Linda Whitwam.

The publisher would like to thank the following for their kind permission to reproduce their photogrpahs:

Casa de Colón, Las Palmas (Elena Acosta Guerrero, Ramon Gil); Casino Las Palmas, Las Palmas de Gran Canaria (Victoria Rivero); CORBIS (Małgorzata Gajdzińska); Fundación César Manrique (Bianca Visser); Hotel Rural Finca de Salinas, Yaiza; Hotel Santa Catalina, Las Palmas (Kati von Poroszlay); Loro Parque (Grettel Pérez Darias); Museo Arqueológico de Tenerife, Santa Cruz de Tenerife (Néstor Yanes); Museo de Cerámica, Casa Tafuriaste, La Orotava (Antonio Cid Menchén); Museo de Historia de Tenerife, La Laguna (Ana Moreno, Jorge Gorrin Morales); Museo Etnográfico Tanit, San Bartolomé (Remy de Quintana); Museo Municipal de Bellas Artes (María del Carmen Duque Hernández); Museo Néstor, Las Palmas (Pedro Luis Rosales-Pedrero); Patronato de Turismo de Fuerteventura; Patronato De Turismo de Gran Canaria (Alfonso Falcón); Sociedad de Promoción de Las Palmas (Candelaria Delgado); ZEFA (Ewa Kozłowska); ZOOM s.c.

Picture Credits
a-above; b-below/bottom; c-centre; f-far; l-left; r-right; t-top

The following artworks have been reproduced with the permission of the copyright holder: sculpture *Monumento al Campesino* in Mozaga 92c; *Logo* (sculpture) of the National Parks Timanfaya 94tr; *Cactus* sculpture in the Jardín de Cactus in Guatiza 88tl; *Mirador del Río* sculpture 90c; rooms in the house of the artist, Tahiche 87tr mosaics, Tahiche 84clb; all the work of César Manrique © DACS, London 2011.

123RF.com: Alexandr Chernyshov 116bl; Antonio Balaguer Soler 49bl. **4Corners:** SIME/Olimpio Fantuz 42, /Reinhard Schmid 11tr, 46br.
Alamy Stock Photo: Phil Crean A 29ca; Alan Dawson Photography 28cla, 55tl, 83b, 186crb; Bildarchiv Monheim GmbH/

Peter Eberts 12bl; FAN TravelStock / Katja Kreder 10bl; Peter Forsberg 198br; Eddie Gerald 47br; imageBROKER/Martin Moxter 56bl; Islandstock 13bl, 178br; LOOK The picture agency photographer GmbH/Juergen Richter 11bl, 46cla; Juan Moyano 68; Mehul Patel 54br; Nicholas Pitt 10cra; David Robertson 11cr; Alex Segre 167tr; Peter Titmuss 176cla, 182ml; Colin Underhill 72tl; Atman Victor 179tl; Jan Włodarczyk 2-3, 98. **AWL Images:** Carlos Sanchez Pereyra 82. **Buenavista Golf:** 186cla.
Carnaval Las Palmas: www.laspalmascarnaval.com 47tc.
Casa Brígida: 172tr. **Casa Santa María:** 171tr. **Corbis:** 73tr; Bettmann 30;Jack Fields 113bc; Robert Krist 27cl; José F. Poblete 195bl; Roger Ressmeyer 150b; Nik Wheeler 26br, 27br, 139tr; Zefa/Karl Kinne 14tr.
Disfruta! La Palma: Uwe S. Meschede 163c. **Dreamstime.com:** Alexirius 169ca; Bogdan 52-3; Canaryluc 25cl, 179br; Charles03 38-9, 124; Eska2005 37clb; Eyewave 5t; Fotoentusiasta 43b; Ifeelstock 196cl; Joseasreyes 188-9; Meinzahn 37tr; Musat 108tl; Nito100 184-5; Raulg2 13tr; Rosshelen 142; Silverfish81 178cla; Silvershadows 204cla; Slava296 116tr; Sveinotto 204br; Tamara_k 72br; Underworld 121tc.
European Central Bank: 197 all.
Finca Arminda: Carmen Capote 157tr. **Fundación César Manrique:** 87br.
Gran Hotel Bahia del Duque Resort: 156cla, 160br. **Getty Images:** Atlantide Phototravel 101crb; Stuart Franklin 186bl; Radius Images/F. Lukasseck 134; Andreas Weibel 94bl; Westend61 89b.
H10 Hotels: 154-5; Roger Mández 159tr. **Hacienda del Buen Suceso:** 156br, 158bc. **José Miquel Hernández Hernández:** 102br. **Hotel Jardín Tecina & Tecina Golf:** Baradel Enzo 174tl.
Hotel San Roque: 157bc.
Andrzej Lisowski: 122bl, 125b. **Loro Parque:** 116cla, 117 all.
The Massey Partnership Ltd: The Ritz-Carlton, Abama's El Mirador: Roger Méndez 162bc. **Carlos Minguel:** 20tr, 20cla, 20cl, 20clb, 21cr, 21bl, 21br. **Museo Arqueológico de Tenerife – Santa Cruz de Tenerife:** 32clb, 33br. **Museo Néstor - Las Palmas:** 48bl.
NASA: Novillo -Precoz: 170bc.
Oronoz: 32-3.
Robert G. Pasieczny: 18bl, 18bc, 19cr, 19cb, 33tl, 34c, 48cra, 54tl, 66br, 67br, 70cra, 71tr, 73tl, 74cr, 76tl, 77c, 78br, 79br, 80tc, 80crb, 84tcra, 96cb, 97bl, 102c, 119tr, 121bl, 139br, 140cr,180c, 180cr, 182tc. **Piotr Paszkiewicz:** 56tr. **El Patio de Lajares:** 163tl. **Ángel Gómez Pinchetti:** 50ca, 50clb, 50bc, 51tl, 51br. **Magdalena Polak:** 132tl, 151cla, 151cl, 151cr.
María Ángeles Sanchez: 24cra, 25br, 29bl, 130br, 151tr.
Sociedad de Promoción de Las Palmas de Gran Canaria: 4b, 24tr, 24br, 25tr. **SuperStock:** age fotostock/Ian Murray 15cla.
Tecina Golf: 187tr.
Venture Group Restaurants: 173br.
Wiki Commons: NASA LANDSAT7 14br; Bob Tubbs 145tr, 152cl.

Front Endpaper: 4Corners: SIME /Olimpio Fantuz Rbl; **Alamy Stock Photo:** Juan Moyano Rbr; Jan Wlodarczyk Lcra; **AWL Images** Carlos Sanchez Pereyra Rtl; **Dreamstime.com:** Charles03 Cbr; Rosshelen Ltl; **Getty Images:** Radius Images/F. Lukasseck Lbc;

Cover
Frontand spine: 4Corners.Reinhard Schmid. Front bl: **Dreamstime.com:** Ihar Balaikin.

All other images © Dorling Kindersley.
For more information visit www.dkimages.com

Phrase Book

In an Emergency

Help!	**Socorro**	soh-**koh**-roh
Stop!	**¡Pare!**	**pah**-reh
Call a doctor!	**¡Llame a un médico!**	**yah**-meh ah oon **meh**-dee-koh
Call an ambulance!	**¡Llame a una ambulancia!**	**yah**-meh ah **oonah** ahm-boo-**lahn**-thee-ah
Call the police!	**¡Llame a la policía!**	**yah**-meh ah lah poh-lee-**thee**-ah
Call the fire brigade!	**¡Llame a los bomberos!**	**yah**-meh ah lohs bohm-**beh**-rohs
Where is the nearest telephone?	**¿Dónde está el teléfono más próximo?**	**dohn**-deh ehs-**tah** ehl teh-**leh**-foh-noh mahs prohx-ee-moh
Where is the nearest hospital?	**¿Dónde está el hospital más próximo?**	**dohn**-deh ehs-**tah** ehl ohs-pee-**tahl** mahs prohx-ee-moh

Communication Essentials

Yes	**Sí**	see
No	**No**	noh
Please	**Por favor**	pohr fah-**vohr**
Thank you	**Gracias**	**grah**-thee-ahs
Excuse me	**Perdone**	pehr-**doh**-neh
Hello	**Hola**	**oh**-lah
Goodbye	**Adiós**	ah-dee-**ohs**
Goodnight	**Buenas noches**	**bweh**-nahs **noh** chehs
Morning	**La mañana**	lah mah-**nyah**-nah
Afternoon	**La tarde**	lah **tahr**-deh
Evening	**La tarde**	lah **tahr**-deh
Yesterday	**Ayer**	ah-**yehr**
Today	**Hoy**	oy
Tomorrow	**Mañana**	mah-**nyah**-nah
Here	**Aquí**	ah-**kee**
There	**Allí**	ah-**yee**
What?	**¿Qué?**	keh
When?	**¿Cuándo?**	**kwahn**-doh
Why?	**¿Por qué?**	pohr-**keh**
Where?	**¿Dónde?**	**dohn**-deh

Useful Phrases

How are you?	**¿Cómo está usted?**	**koh**-moh ehs-**tah** oos-**tehd**
Very well, thank you.	**Muy bien, gracias.**	mwee bee-**ehn grah**-thee-ahs
Pleased to meet you.	**Encantado de conocerle.**	ehn-kahn-**tah**-doh deh koh-noh-**thehr**-leh
See you soon.	**Hasta pronto.**	ahs-tah **prohn**-toh
That's fine.	**Está bien.**	ehs-**tah** bee-**ehn**
Where is/are …?	**¿Dónde está/están …?**	**dohn**-deh ehs-**tah**/ehs-**tahn**
How far is it to …?	**Cuántos metros/ kilómetros hay de aquí a …?**	**kwahn**-tohs **meh**-trohs/kee-**loh**-meh-trohs **eye** deh ah-**kee** ah
Which way to …?	**¿Por dónde se va a …?**	pohr **dohn**-deh seh **bah** ah
Do you speak English?	**¿Habla inglés?**	**ah**-blah een-**glehs**
I don't understand	**No comprendo.**	noh kohm-**prehn**-doh
Could you speak more slowly, please?	**¿Puede hablar más despacio, por favor?**	**pweh**-deh ah-**blahr** mahs dehs-pah-thee-oh pohr fah-**vohr**
I'm sorry.	**Lo siento.**	loh see-**ehn**-toh

Useful Words

big	**grande**	**grahn**-deh
small	**pequeño**	peh-**keh**-nyoh
hot	**caliente**	kah-lee-**ehn**-teh
cold	**frío**	**free**-oh
good	**bueno**	**bweh**-noh
bad	**malo**	**mah**-loh
enough	**bastante**	bahs-**tahn**-the
well	**bien**	bee-**ehn**
open	**abierto**	ah-bee-**ehr**-toh
closed	**cerrado**	thehr-**rah**-doh
left	**izquierda**	eeth-key-**ehr**-dah
right	**derecha**	deh-**reh**-chah
straight on	**todo recto**	toh-doh **rehk**-toh
near	**cerca**	**thehr**-kah
far	**lejos**	**leh**-hohs
up	**arriba**	ah-**ree**-bah
down	**abajo**	ah-**bah**-hoh
early	**temprano**	tehm-**prah**-noh
late	**tarde**	**tahr**-deh
entrance	**entrada**	ehn-**trah**-dah
exit	**salida**	sah-**lee**-dah
toilet	**lavabos, servicios**	lah-**vah**-bohs sehr-**bee**-thee-ohs
more	**más**	mahs
less	**menos**	**meh**-nohs

Shopping

How much does this cost?	**¿Cuánto cuesta esto?**	**kwahn**-toh **kwehs**-tah ehs-toh
I would like …	**Me gustaría …**	meh goos-ta-**ree**-ah
Do you have…?	**¿Tienen...?**	tee-**yeh**-nehn
I'm just looking, thank you.	**Sólo estoy mirando, gracias.**	**soh**-loh ehs-**toy** mee-**rahn**-doh **grah**-thee-ahs
Do you take credit cards?	**¿Aceptan tarjetas de crédito?**	ah-**thehp**-tahn tahr-**heh**-tahs deh **kreh**-dee-toh
What time do you open?	**¿A qué hora abren?**	ah keh oh-rah **ah**-brehn
What time do you close?	**¿A qué hora cierran?**	ah keh oh-rah thee-**ehr**-rahn
This one.	**Éste.**	**ehs**-the
That one.	**Ése.**	**eh**-she
expensive	**caro**	**kahr**-oh
cheap	**barato**	bah-**rah**-toh
size, clothes	**talla**	**tah**-yah
size, shoes	**número**	**noo**-mehr-oh
white	**blanco**	**blahn**-koh
black	**negro**	**neh**-groh
red	**rojo**	**roh**-hoh
yellow	**amarillo**	ah-mah-**ree**-yoh
green	**verde**	**behr**-deh
blue	**azul**	ah-**thool**
antiques shop	**la tienda de antigüedades**	lah tee-**ehn**-dah deh ahn-tee-gweh-**dah**-dehs
bakery	**la panadería**	lah pah-nah-deh-**ree**-ah
bank	**el banco**	ehl **bahn**-koh
book shop	**la librería**	lah lee-breh-**ree**-ah
butcher's	**la carnicería**	lah kahr-nee-theh-**ree**-ah
cake shop	**la pastelería**	lah pahs-teh-leh-**ree**-ah
chemist's	**la farmacia**	lah fahr-**mah**-thee-ah
fishmonger's	**la pescadería**	lah pehs-kah-deh-**ree**-ah
greengrocer's	**la frutería**	lah froo-teh-**ree**-ah
grocer's	**la tienda de comestibles**	lah tee-**yehn**-dah deh koh-mehs-**tee**-blehs
hairdresser's	**la peluquería**	lah peh-loo-keh-**ree**-ah
market	**el mercado**	ehl mehr-**kah**-doh
newsagent's	**el kiosko de prensa**	ehl kee-**ohs**-koh deh **prehn**-sah
post office	**la oficina de correos**	lah oh-fee-**thee**-nah deh kohr-**reh**-ohs
shoe shop	**la zapatería**	lah thah-pah-teh-**ree**-ah
supermarket	**el supermercado**	ehl soo-pehr-mehr-**kah**-doh
tobacconist	**el estanco**	ehl ehs-**tahn**-koh
travel agency	**la agencia de viajes**	lah ah-**hehn**-thee-ah deh bee-**ah**-hehs

Sightseeing

art gallery	**el museo de arte**	ehl moo-**seh**-oh deh **ahr**-the
cathedral	**la catedral**	lah kah-teh-**drahl**
church	**la iglesia**	lah ee-**gleh**-see-ah
	la basílica	lah bah-**see**-lee-kah
garden	**el jardín**	ehl hahr-**deen**
library	**la biblioteca**	lah bee-blee-oh-**teh**-kah
museum	**el museo**	ehl moo-**seh**-oh
tourist information office	**la oficina de turismo**	lah oh-fee-**thee**-nah deh too-**rees**-moh
town hall	**el ayuntamiento**	ehl ah-yoon-tah-mee-**ehn**-toh
closed for holiday	**cerrado por vacaciones**	thehr-**rah**-doh pohr bah-kah-thee-**oh**-nehs
bus station	**la estación de autobuses**	lah ehs-tah-thee-**ohn** deh owtoh-**boo**-sehs
railway station	**la estación de trenes**	lah ehs-tah-thee-**ohn** deh **treh**-nehs

Staying in a Hotel

Do you have a vacant room?	¿Tienen una habitación libre?	tee-**eh**-nehn oo-nah ah-bee-tah-thee-**ohn** lee-breh
double room	habitación doble	ah-bee-tah-thee-**ohn** doh-bleh
with double bed	con cama de matrimonio	kohn **kah**-mah deh mah-tree-**moh**-nee-oh
twin room	habitación con dos camas	ah-bee-tah-thee-**ohn** kohn dohs **kah**-mahs
single room	habitación individual	ah-bee-tah-thee-**ohn** een-dee-vee-doo-**ahl**
room with a bath	habitación con baño	ah-bee-tah-thee-**ohn** kohn bah-nyoh
shower	ducha	**doo**-chah
porter	el botones	ehl boh-**toh**-nehs
key	la llave	lah **yah**-veh
I have a reservation.	Tengo una habitación reservada.	tehn-goh **oo**-na ah-bee-tah-thee-**ohn** reh-sehr-**bah**-dah

Eating Out

Have you got a table for …?	¿Tienen mesa para …?	tee-**eh**-nehn meh-sah pah-**rah**
I want to reserve a table.	Quiero reservar una mesa.	kee-eh-roh reh-sehr-**bahr** oo-nah **meh**-sah
The bill, please.	La cuenta, por favor.	lah **kwehn**-tah pohr fah-**vohr**
I am a vegetarian	Soy vegetariano/a	soy beh-heh-tah-ree-**ah**-no/na
waitress/ waiter	camarera/ camarero	kah-mah-**reh**-rah/ kah-mah-**reh**-roh
menu	la carta	lah **kahr**-tah
fixed-price menu	menú del día	meh-**noo** dehl **dee**-ah
wine list	la carta de vinos	lah **kahr**-tah deh **bee**-nohs
glass	un vaso	oon **bah**-soh
bottle	una botella	oo-nah boh-**teh**-yah
knife	un cuchillo	oon koo-**chee**-yoh
fork	un tenedor	oon teh-neh-**dohr**
spoon	una cuchara	oo-nah koo-**chah**-rah
breakfast	el desayuno	ehl deh-sah-**yoo**-noh
lunch	la comida/ el almuerzo	lah koh-**mee**-dah/ ehl ahl-**mwehr**-thoh
dinner	la cena	lah **theh**-nah
main course	el segundo plato	ehl pree-**mehr plah**-toh
starters	los primeros	lohs ehn-treh **meh**-sehs
dish of the day	el plato del día	ehl **plah**-toh dehl **dee**-ah
coffee	el café	ehl kah-**feh**
rare	poco hecho	**poh**-koh **eh**-choh
medium	medio hecho	**meh**-dee-oh **eh**-choh
well done	muy hecho	mwee **eh**-choh

Menu Decoder

asado	ah-**sah**-doh	roast
el aceite	ah-**thee-eh**-teh	oil
las aceitunas	ah-theh-**toon**-ahs	olives
el agua mineral	**ah**-gwa mee-neh-**rahl**	mineral water
sin gas/con gas	seen gas/kohn gas	still/sparkling
el ajo	**ah**-hoh	garlic
el arroz	ahr-**rohth**	rice
el azúcar	ah-**thoo**-kahr	sugar
la carne	**kahr**-neh	meat
la cebolla	theh-**boh**-yah	onion
la cerveza	thehr-**beh**-thah	beer
el cerdo	**therh**-doh	pork
el chocolate	choh-koh-**lah**-teh	chocolate
el chorizo	choh-**ree**-thoh	red sausage
el cordero	kohr-**deh**-roh	lamb
el fiambre	fee-**ahm**-breh	cold meat
frito	**free**-toh	fried
la fruta	**froo**-tah	fruit
los frutos secos	froo-tohs **seh**-kohs	nuts
las gambas	**gahm**-bahs	prawns
el helado	eh-**lah**-doh	ice cream
al horno	ahl **ohr**-noh	baked
el huevo	oo-**eh**-voh	egg
el jamón serrano	hah-**mohn** sehr-**rah**-noh	cured ham
el jerez	heh-**rehz**	sherry

la langosta	lahn-**gohs**-tah	lobster
la leche	**leh**-cheh	milk
el limón	lee-**mohn**	lemon
la limonada	lee-moh-**nah**-dah	lemonade
la mantequilla	mahn-teh-**kee**-yah	butter
la manzana	mahn-**thah**-nah	apple
los mariscos	mah-**rees**-kohs	seafood
la menestra	meh-**nehs**-trah	vegetable stew
la naranja	nah-**rahn**-hah	orange
el pan	pahn	bread
el pastel	pahs-**tehl**	cake
las patatas	pah-**tah**-tahs	potatoes
el pescado	pehs-**kah**-doh	fish
la pimienta	pee-mee-**yehn**-tah	pepper
el plátano	**plah**-tah-noh	banana
el pollo	**poh**-yoh	chicken
el postre	**pohs**-treh	dessert
el queso	**keh**-soh	cheese
la sal	sahl	salt
las salchichas	sahl-**chee**-chahs	sausages
la salsa	**sahl**-sah	sauce
seco	**seh**-koh	dry
el solomillo	soh-loh-**mee**-yoh	sirloin
la sopa	**soh**-pah	soup
la tarta	**tahr**-tah	pie/cake
el té	teh	tea
la ternera	tehr-**neh**-rah	beef
las tostadas	tohs-**tah**-dahs	toast
el vinagre	bee-**nah**-greh	vinegar
el vino blanco	**bee**-noh **blahn**-koh	white wine
el vino rosado	**bee**-noh roh-**sah**-doh	rosé wine
el vino tinto	**bee**-noh **teen**-toh	red wine

Numbers

0	cero	**theh**-roh
1	uno	**oo**-noh
2	dos	dohs
3	tres	trehs
4	cuatro	**kwa**-troh
5	cinco	**theen**-koh
6	seis	says
7	siete	see-**eh**-the
8	ocho	**oh**-choh
9	nueve	**nweh**-veh
10	diez	dee-**ehth**
11	once	**ohn**-theh
12	doce	**doh**-theh
13	trece	**treh**-theh
14	catorce	kah-**tohr**-theh
15	quince	**keen**-theh
16	dieciséis	dee-eh-thee-**seh-ees**
17	diecisiete	dee-eh-thee-see-**eh**-the
18	dieciocho	dee-eh-thee-**oh**-choh
19	diecinueve	dee-eh-thee-**nweh**-veh
20	veinte	**beh**-een-the
21	veintiuno	beh-een-tee-**oo**-noh
22	veintidós	beh-een-tee-**dohs**
30	treinta	**treh**-een-tah
31	treinta y uno	treh-een-tah ee **oo**-noh
40	cuarenta	kwah-**rehn**-tah
50	cincuenta	theen-**kwehn**-tah
60	sesenta	seh-**sehn**-tah
70	setenta	seh-**tehn**-tah
80	ochenta	oh-**chehn**-tah
90	noventa	noh-**vehn**-tah
100	cien	thee-**ehn**
101	ciento uno	thee-**ehn**-toh oo-noh
102	ciento dos	thee-**ehn**-toh **dohs**
200	doscientos	dohs-thee-**ehn**-tohs
500	quinientos	khee-nee-**ehn**-tohs
700	setecientos	seh-teh-thee-**ehn**-tohs
900	novecientos	noh-veh-thee-**ehn**-tohs
1,000	mil	meel
1,001	mil uno	meel **oo**-noh

Time

one minute	un minuto	**oon** mee-**noo**-toh
one hour	una hora	**oo**-na oh-rah
half an hour	media hora	**meh**-dee-a oh-rah
Monday	lunes	**loo**-nehs
Tuesday	martes	**mahr**-tehs
Wednesday	miércoles	mee-**ehr**-koh-lehs
Thursday	jueves	hoo-**weh**-vehs
Friday	viernes	bee-**ehr**-nehs
Saturday	sábado	**sah**-bah-doh
Sunday	domingo	doh-**meen**-goh

2/18

Canary Island Ferry Routes

LA PALMA

Santa Cruz
de La Palma

Santa Cruz
de Tenerife

LA GOMERA

San Sebastián
de La Gomera

TENERIFE

Los Cristianos

Puerto de
la Estaca

EL HIERRO

*Atlantic
Ocean*

Ferry Lines

Trasmediterránea
Tel 902 454 645.
W trasmediterranea.es

Líneas Fred. Olsen
Tel 902 100 107.
W fredolsen.es

Tenerife
Santa Cruz de Tenerife
Tel 922 628 200.

Los Cristianos
Tel 922 790 215.

La Gomera
San Sebastián de
La Gomera
Tel 922 871 007.

La Palma
Santa Cruz de La Palma
Tel 922 415 433.

Naviera Armas
Tel 902 456 500.
W navieraarmas.com

Gran Canaria
Las Palmas de Gran
Canaria
Tel 928 300 600.

Fuerteventura
Puerto del Rosario
Tel 928 851 542.
Morro Jable
Tel 928 542 113.
Corralejo
Tel 928 867 080.

Lanzarote
Arrecife
Tel 928 824 931.
Playa Blanca
Tel 928 517 912.

Tenerife
Santa Cruz de Tenerife
Tel 922 534 050.

El Hierro
Puerto de la Estaca
Tel 922 550 905.

La Palma
Santa Cruz de
La Palma
Tel 922 411 445.

**Líneas Marítimas
Romero**
W lineas-romero.com

La Graciosa
Tel 928 842 070.

Biosfera Express
Tel 928 842 585.
W biosferaexpress.com

Key

- - - Ferry route
—— Motorway/Highway
—— Major road
═══ Other road
▣ Major ferry port
✈ Airport